DRUMHELLAR

image
www.ShadowlineOnline.com

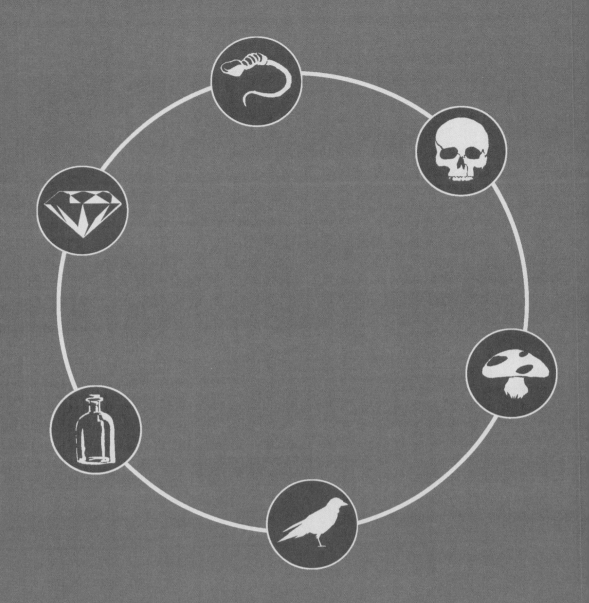

FIRST PRINTING: MAY, 2014

ISBN: 978-1-60706-954-

image® COMICS PRESENTS

RILEY ROSSMO
STORY, ART, COLORS

ALEX LINK
SCRIPT

KARL FAN
COLOR FLATS

KELLY TINDALL
LETTERER

LAURA TAVISHATI
EDITOR

MARC LOMBARDI
COMMUNICATIONS

JIM VALENTINO
PUBLISHER/BOOK DESIGN

A
Shadowline®
PRODUCTION

www.ShadowlineOnline.com

Follow SHADOWLINECOMICS on f FACEBOOK and t TWITTER

IMAGE COMICS, INC.
Robert Kirkman – Chief Operating Officer
Erik Larsen – Chief Financial Officer
Todd McFarlane – President
Marc Silvestri – Chief Executive Officer
Jim Valentino – Vice-President

Eric Stephenson – Publisher
Ron Richards – Director of Business Development
Jennifer de Guzman – Director of Trade Book Sales
Kat Salazar – Director of PR & Marketing
Jeremy Sullivan – Director of Digital Sales
Emilio Bautista – Sales Assistant
Branwyn Bigglestone – Senior Accounts Manager
Emily Miller – Accounts Manager
Jessica Ambriz – Administrative Assistant
Tyler Shainline – Events Coordinator
David Brothers – Content Manager
Jonathan Chan – Production Manager
Drew Gill – Art Director
Meredith Wallace – Print Manager
Monica Garcia – Senior Production Artist
Jenna Savage – Production Artist
Addison Duke – Production Artist
Tricia Ramos – Production Assistant
IMAGECOMICS.COM

image

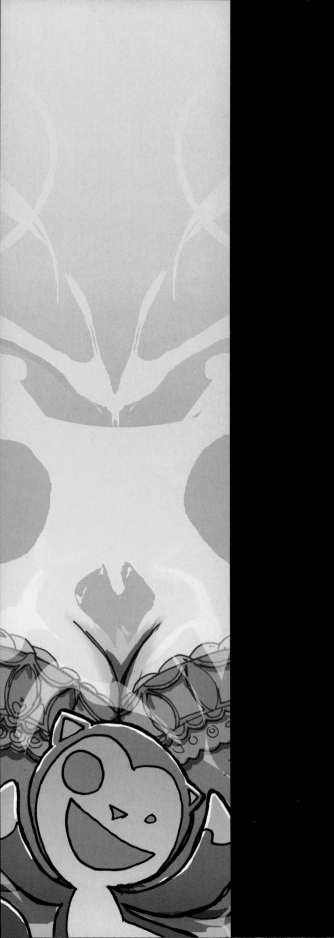

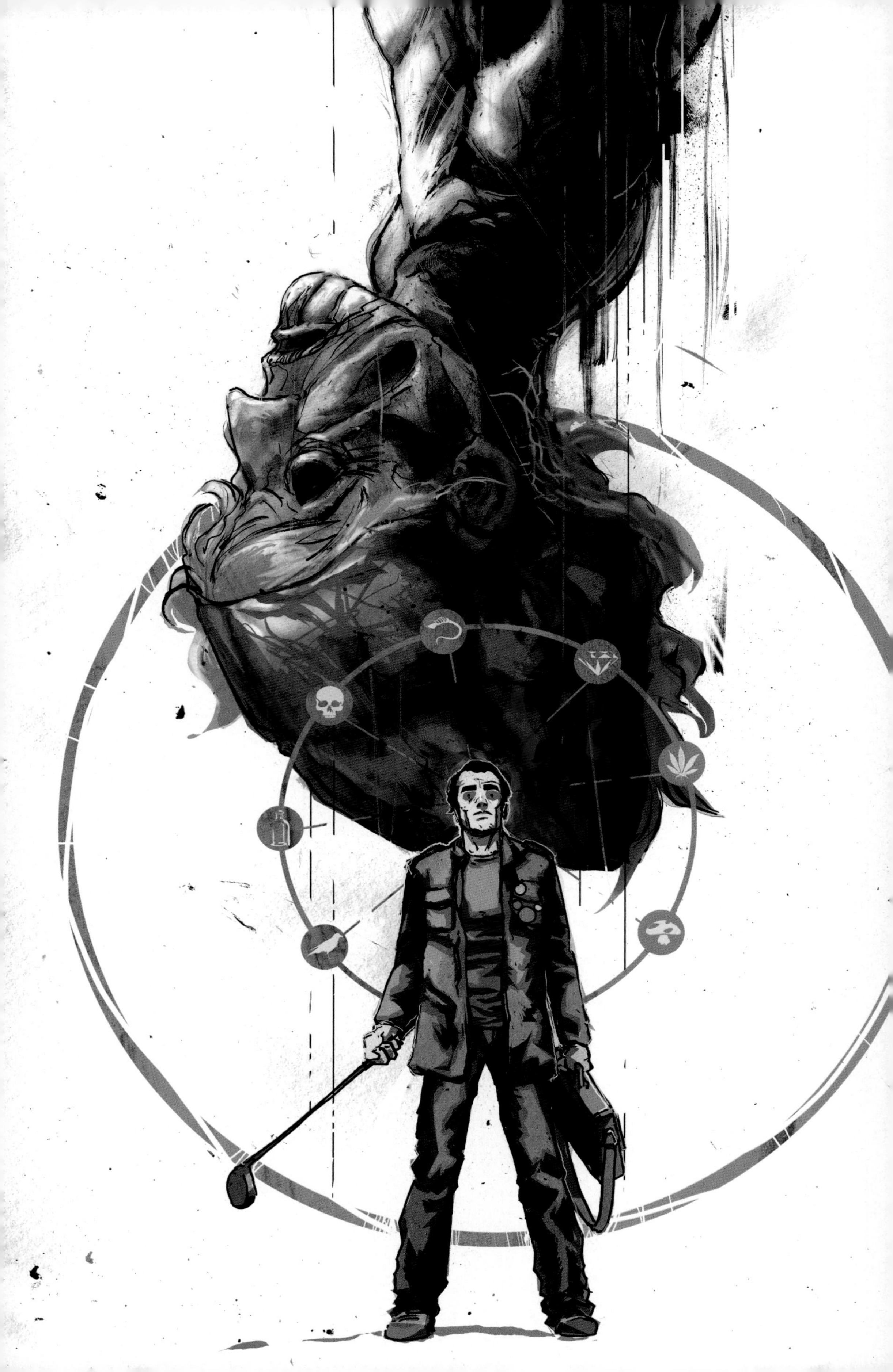

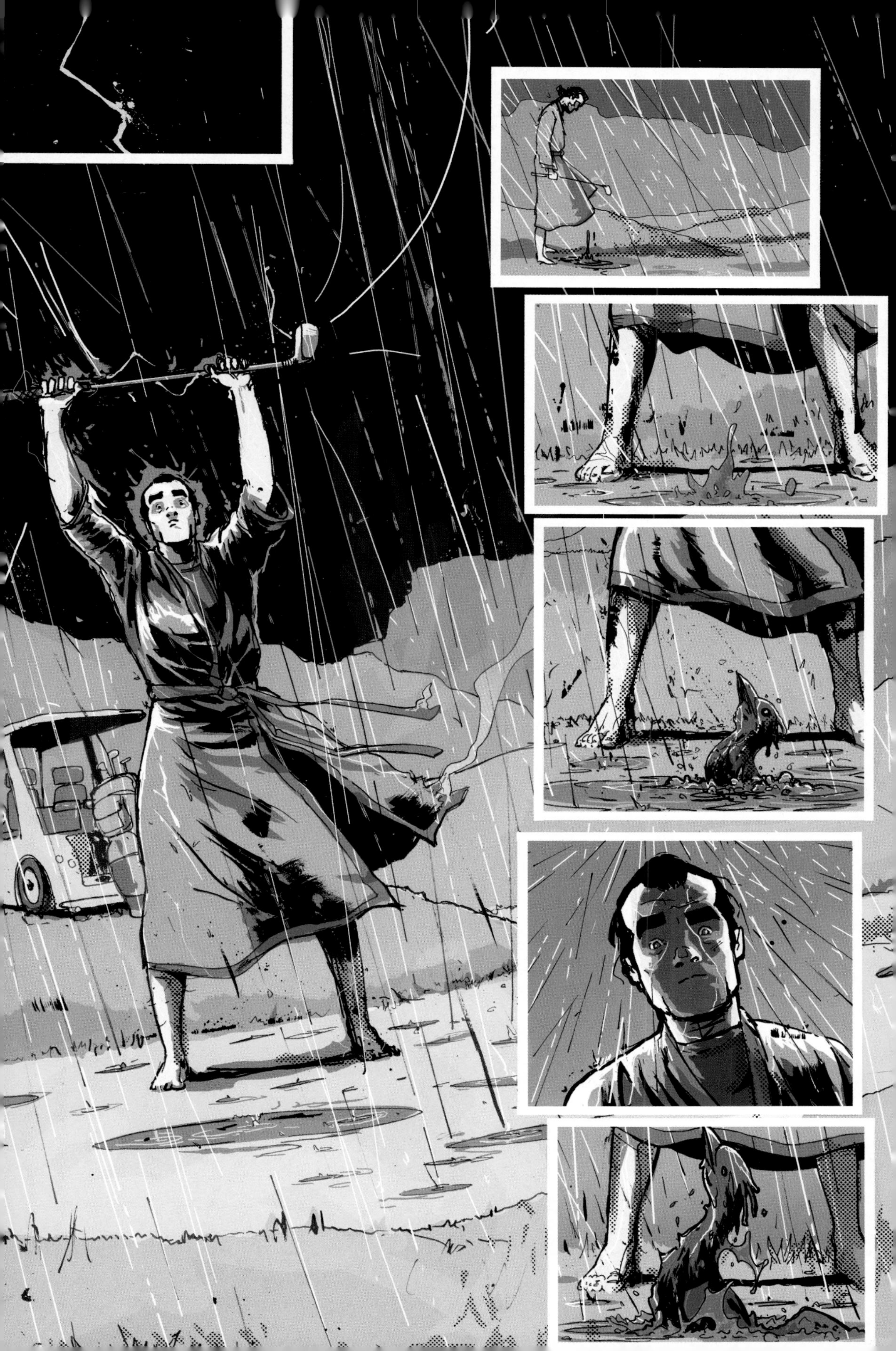

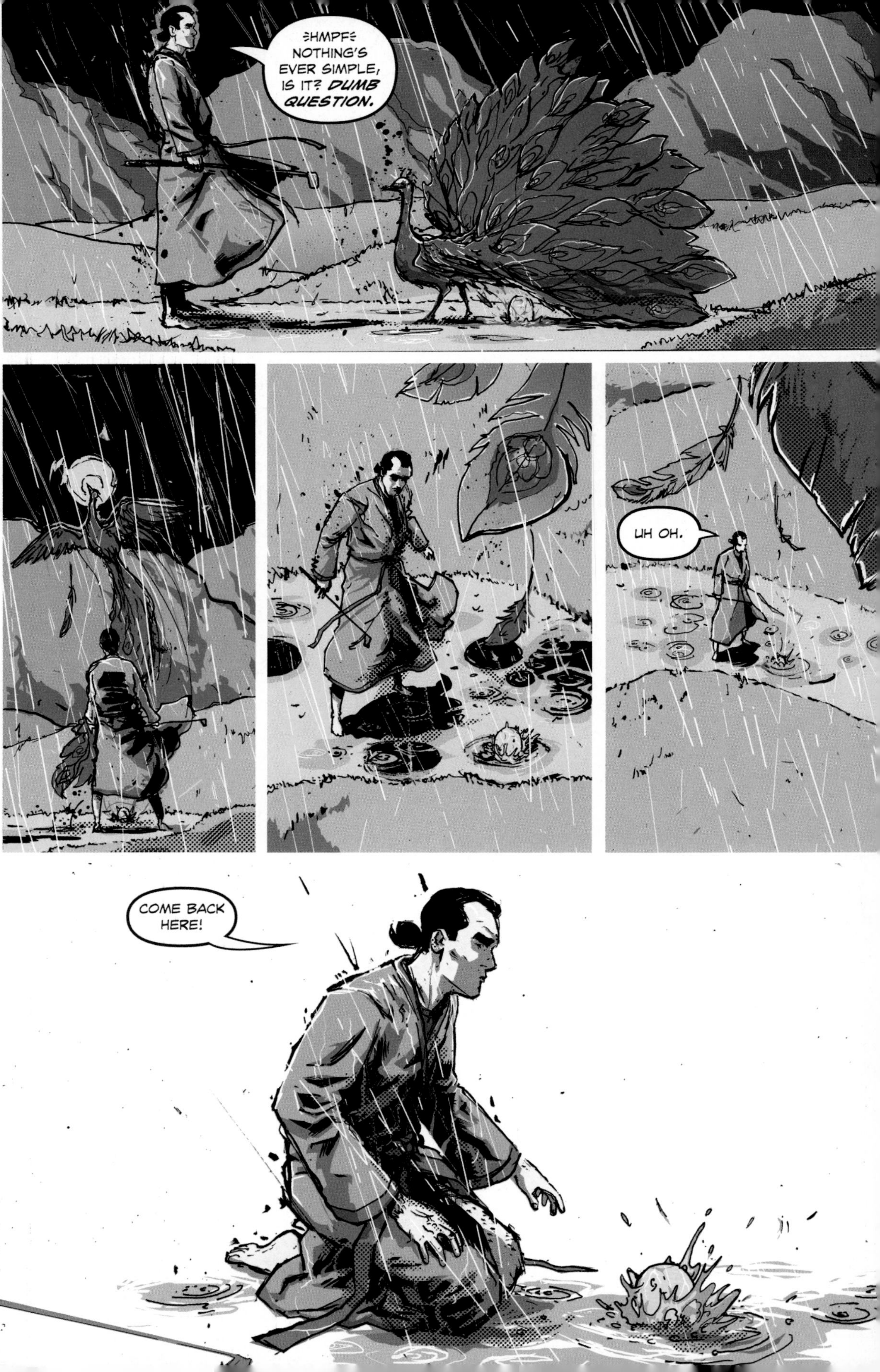

=HMPF= NOTHING'S EVER SIMPLE, IS IT? DUMB QUESTION.
UH OH.
COME BACK HERE!

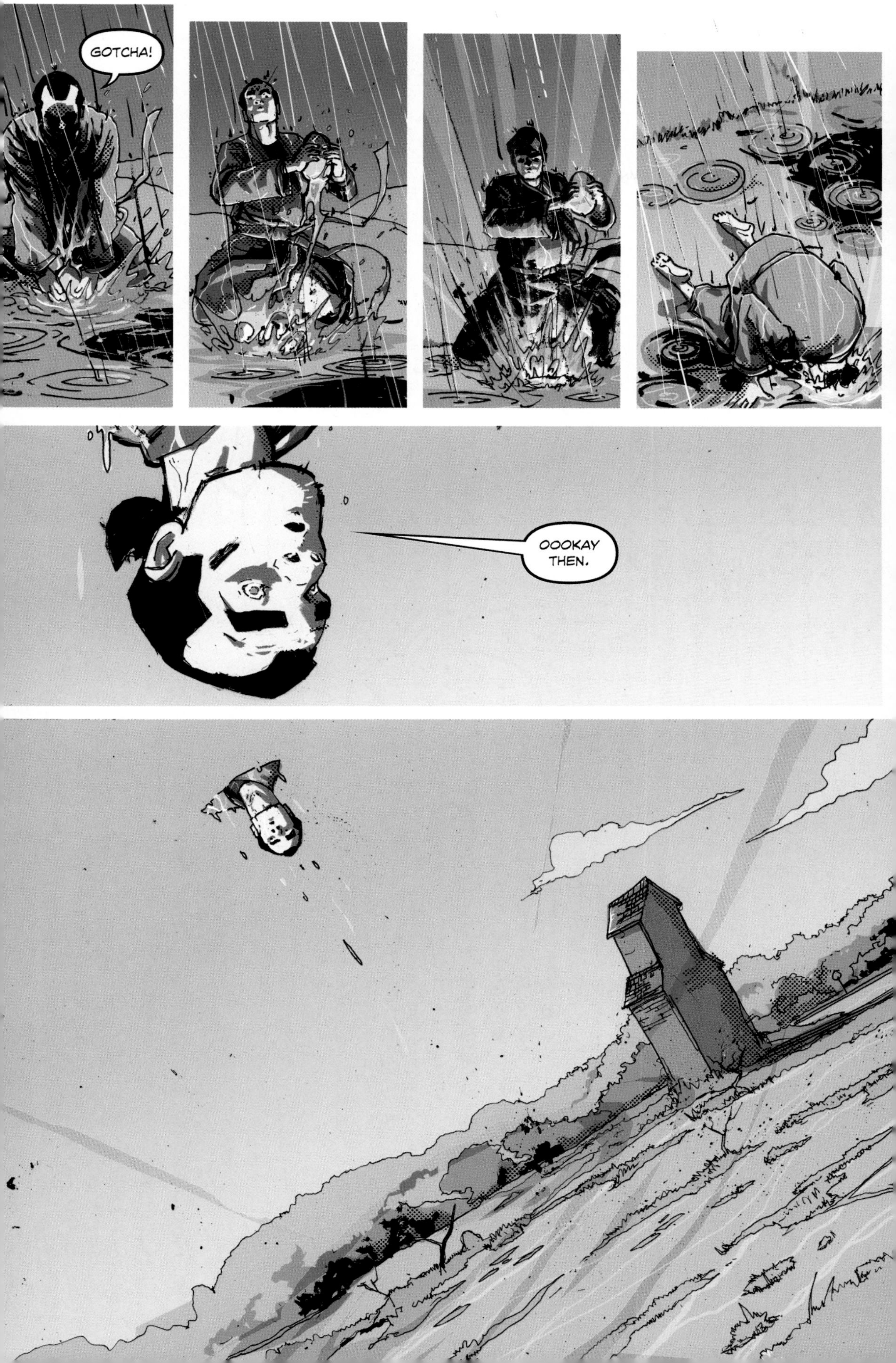
GOTCHA!
OOOKAY THEN.

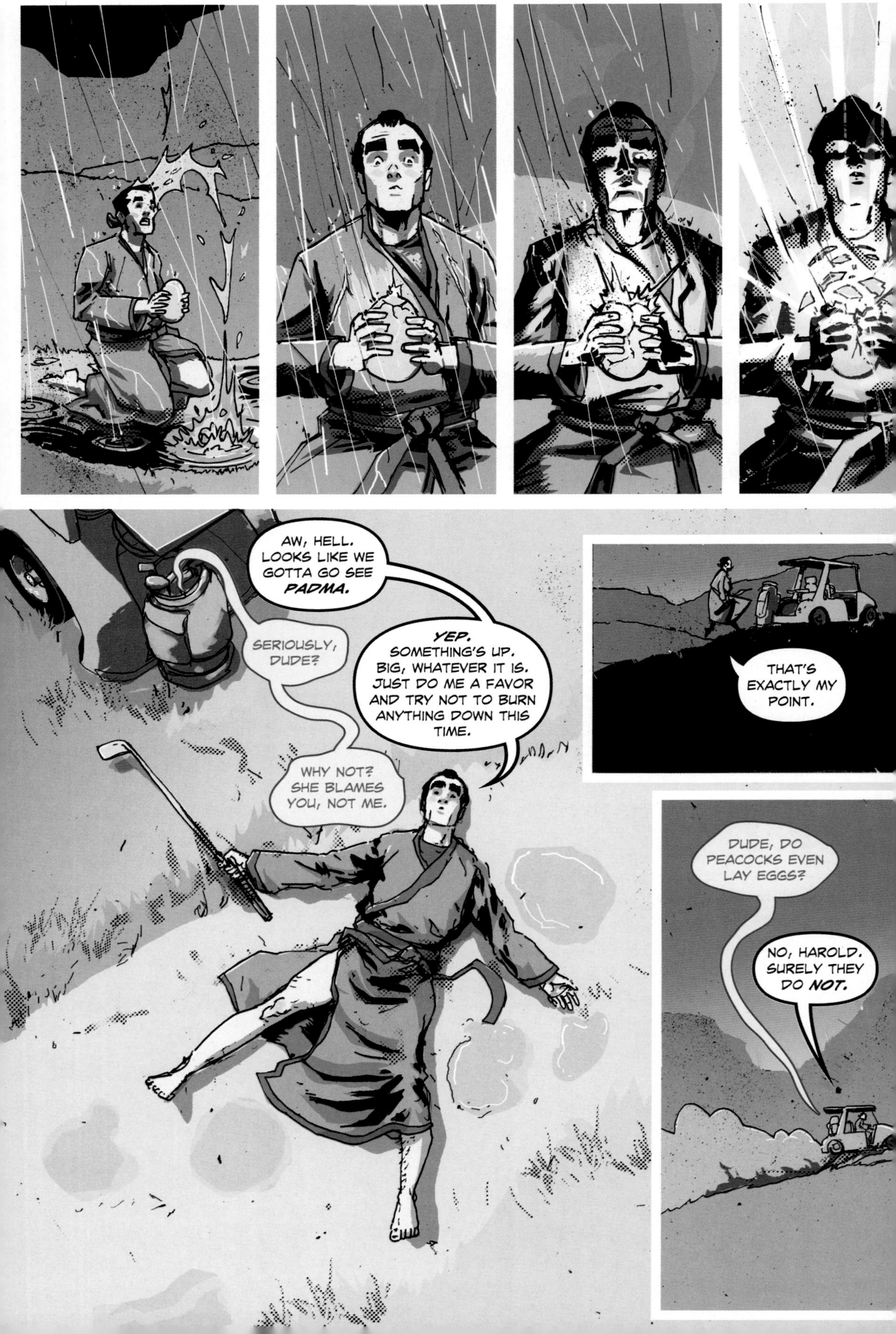
AW, HELL. LOOKS LIKE WE GOTTA GO SEE PADMA.
SERIOUSLY, DUDE?
YEP. SOMETHING'S UP. BIG, WHATEVER IT IS. JUST DO ME A FAVOR AND TRY NOT TO BURN ANYTHING DOWN THIS TIME.
WHY NOT? SHE BLAMES YOU, NOT ME.
THAT'S EXACTLY MY POINT.
DUDE, DO PEACOCKS EVEN LAY EGGS?
NO, HAROLD. SURELY THEY DO NOT.

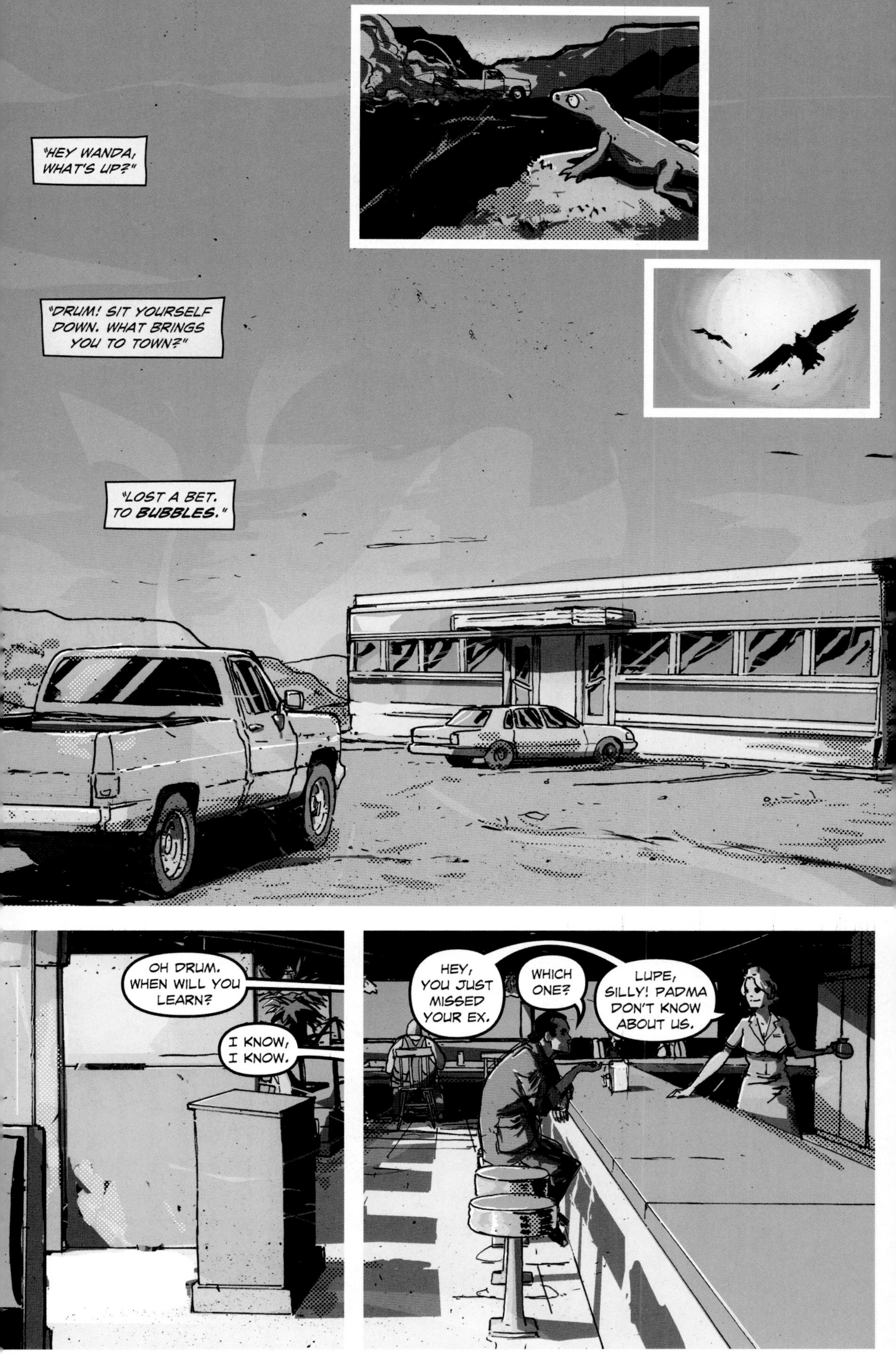
"HEY WANDA, WHAT'S UP?"
"DRUM! SIT YOURSELF DOWN. WHAT BRINGS YOU TO TOWN?"
"LOST A BET. TO BUBBLES."
OH DRUM. WHEN WILL YOU LEARN?
I KNOW, I KNOW.
HEY, YOU JUST MISSED YOUR EX.
WHICH ONE?
LUPE, SILLY! PADMA DON'T KNOW ABOUT US.

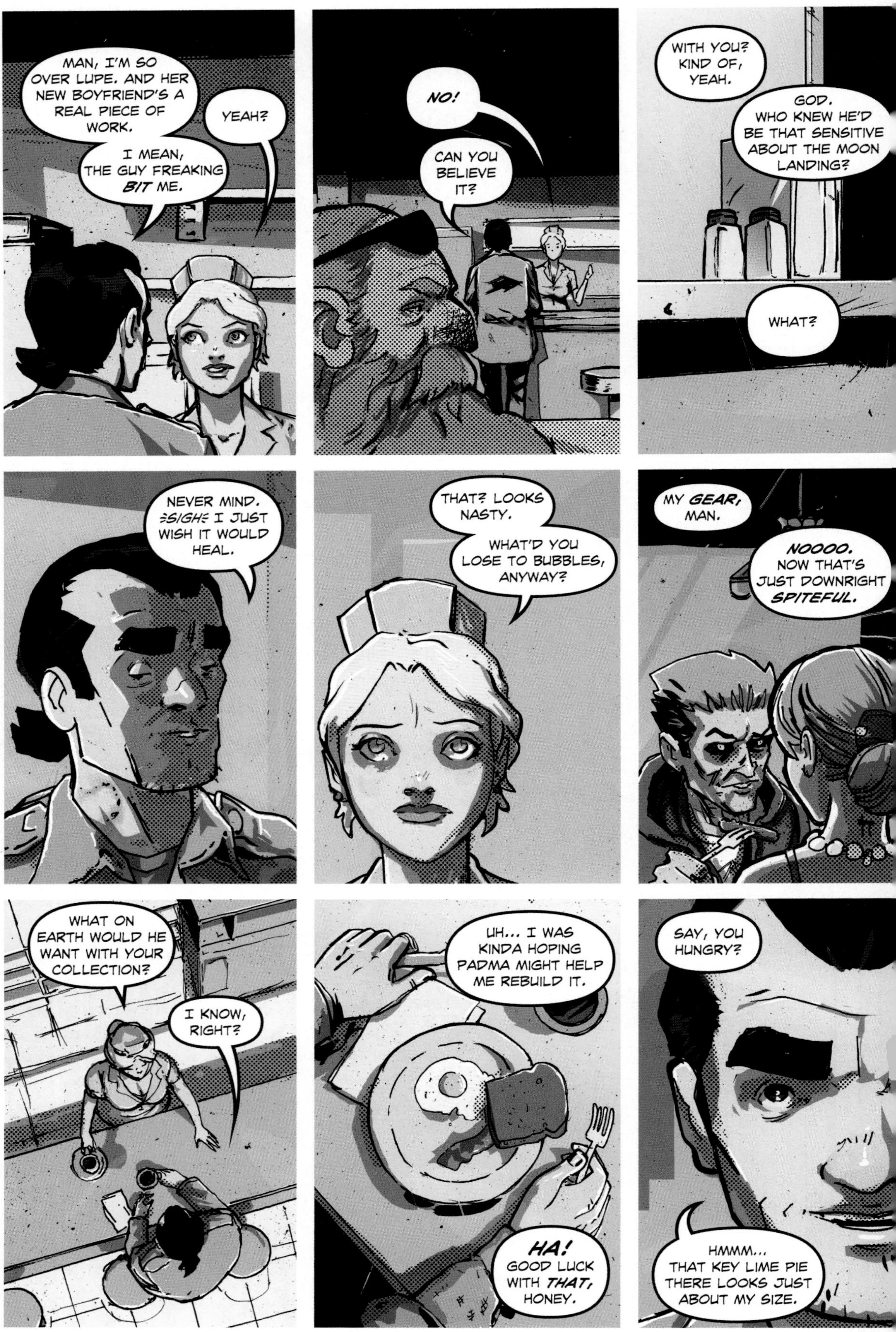
MAN, I'M SO OVER LUPE. AND HER NEW BOYFRIEND'S A REAL PIECE OF WORK.
I MEAN, THE GUY FREAKING *BIT* ME.
YEAH?
NO!
CAN YOU BELIEVE IT?
WITH YOU? KIND OF, YEAH.
GOD. WHO KNEW HE'D BE THAT SENSITIVE ABOUT THE MOON LANDING?
WHAT?
NEVER MIND. *SIGH* I JUST WISH IT WOULD HEAL.
THAT? LOOKS NASTY.
WHAT'D YOU LOSE TO BUBBLES, ANYWAY?
MY *GEAR*, MAN.
NOOOO. NOW THAT'S JUST DOWNRIGHT *SPITEFUL.*
WHAT ON EARTH WOULD HE WANT WITH YOUR COLLECTION?
I KNOW, RIGHT?
UH... I WAS KINDA HOPING PADMA MIGHT HELP ME REBUILD IT.
HA! GOOD LUCK WITH *THAT,* HONEY.
SAY, YOU HUNGRY?
HMMM... THAT KEY LIME PIE THERE LOOKS JUST ABOUT MY SIZE.

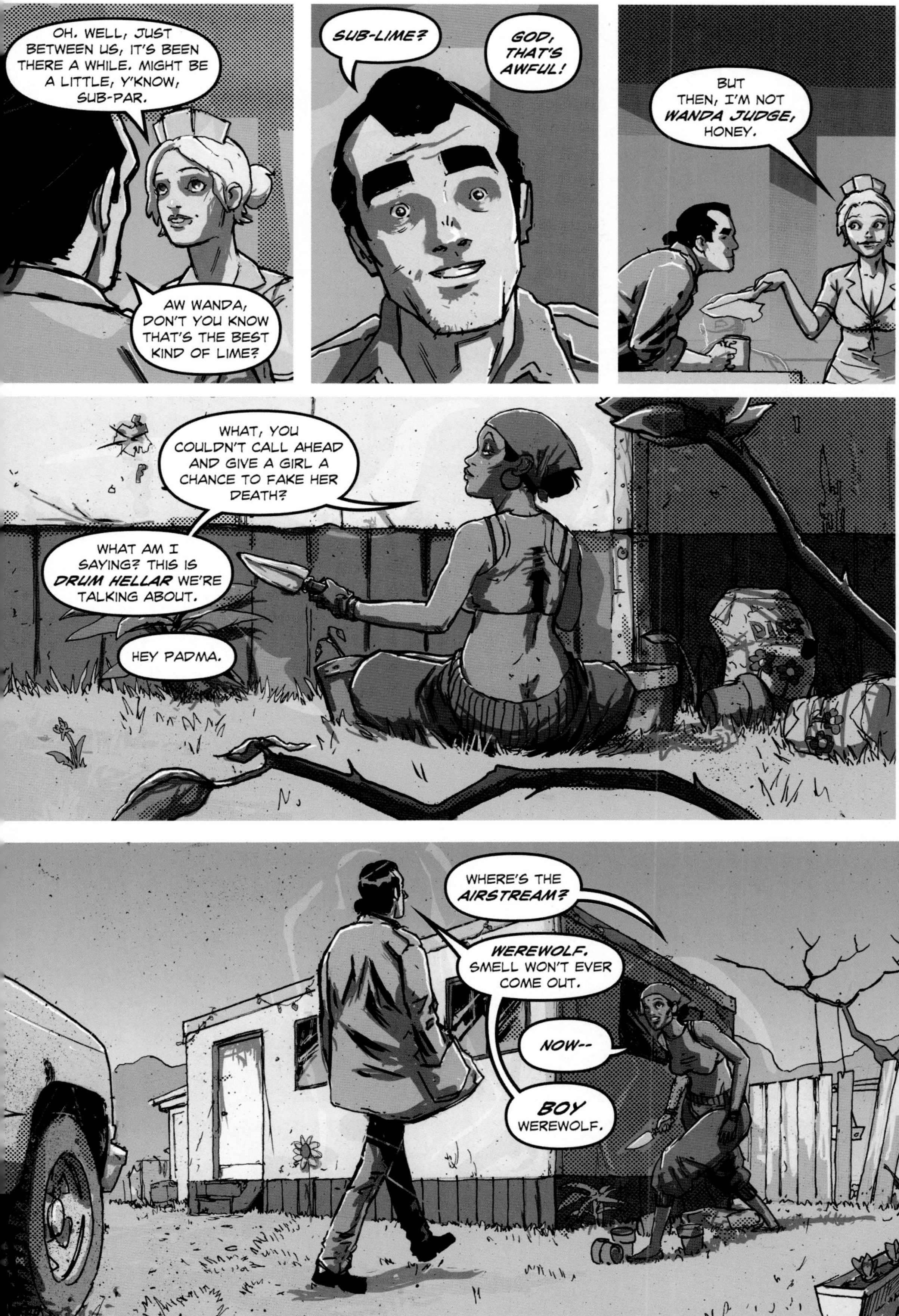
OH. WELL, JUST BETWEEN US, IT'S BEEN THERE A WHILE. MIGHT BE A LITTLE, Y'KNOW, SUB-PAR.
AW WANDA, DON'T YOU KNOW THAT'S THE BEST KIND OF LIME?
SUB-LIME?
GOD, THAT'S AWFUL!
BUT THEN, I'M NOT WANDA JUDGE, HONEY.
WHAT, YOU COULDN'T CALL AHEAD AND GIVE A GIRL A CHANCE TO FAKE HER DEATH?
WHAT AM I SAYING? THIS IS DRUM HELLAR WE'RE TALKING ABOUT.
HEY PADMA.
WHERE'S THE AIRSTREAM?
WEREWOLF. SMELL WON'T EVER COME OUT.
NOW--
BOY WEREWOLF.

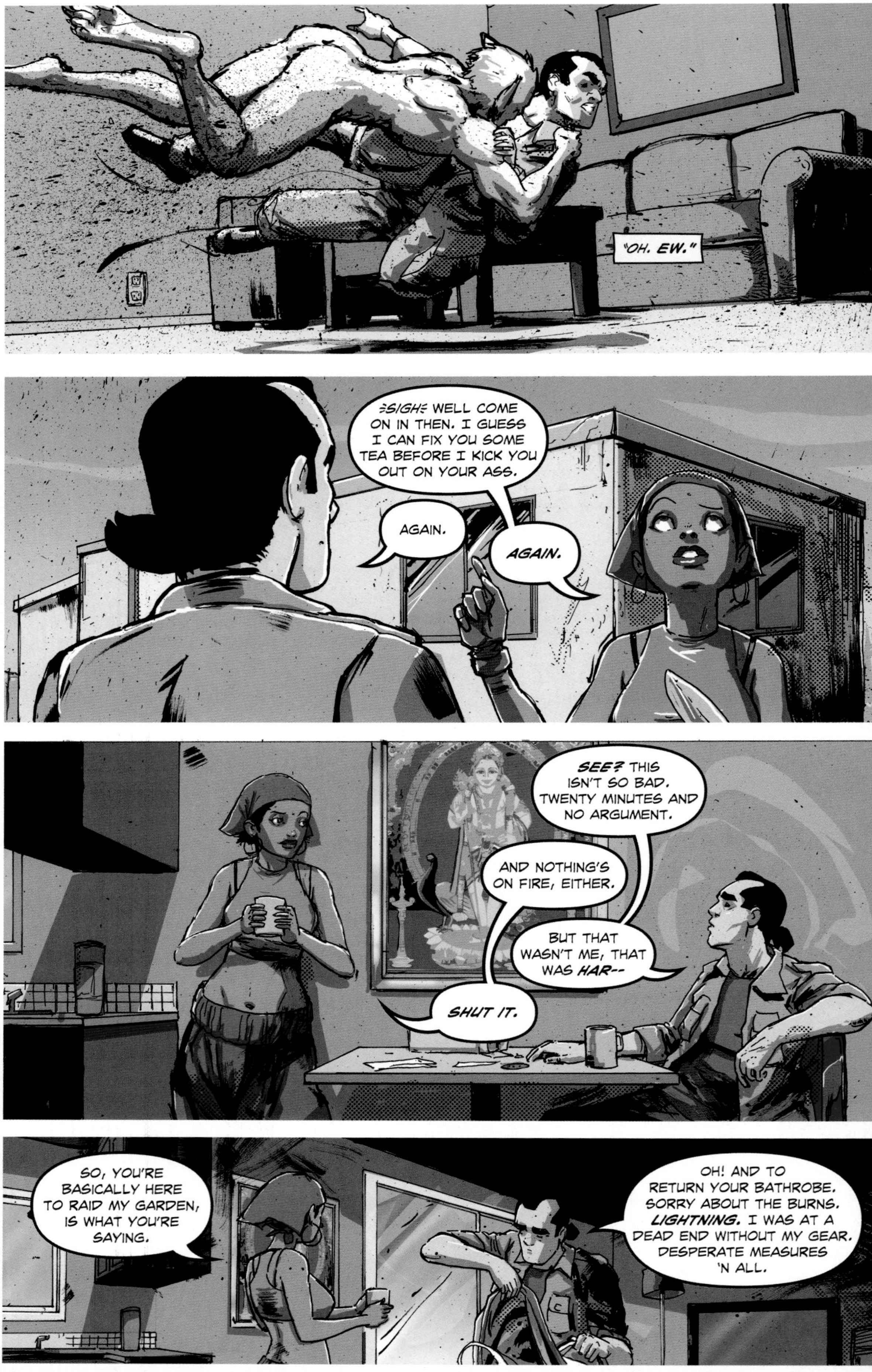
"OH. EW."
=SIGH= WELL COME ON IN THEN. I GUESS I CAN FIX YOU SOME TEA BEFORE I KICK YOU OUT ON YOUR ASS.
AGAIN.
AGAIN.
SEE? THIS ISN'T SO BAD. TWENTY MINUTES AND NO ARGUMENT.
AND NOTHING'S ON FIRE, EITHER.
BUT THAT WASN'T ME, THAT WAS HAR--
SHUT IT.
SO, YOU'RE BASICALLY HERE TO RAID MY GARDEN, IS WHAT YOU'RE SAYING.
OH! AND TO RETURN YOUR BATHROBE. SORRY ABOUT THE BURNS. LIGHTNING. I WAS AT A DEAD END WITHOUT MY GEAR. DESPERATE MEASURES 'N ALL.

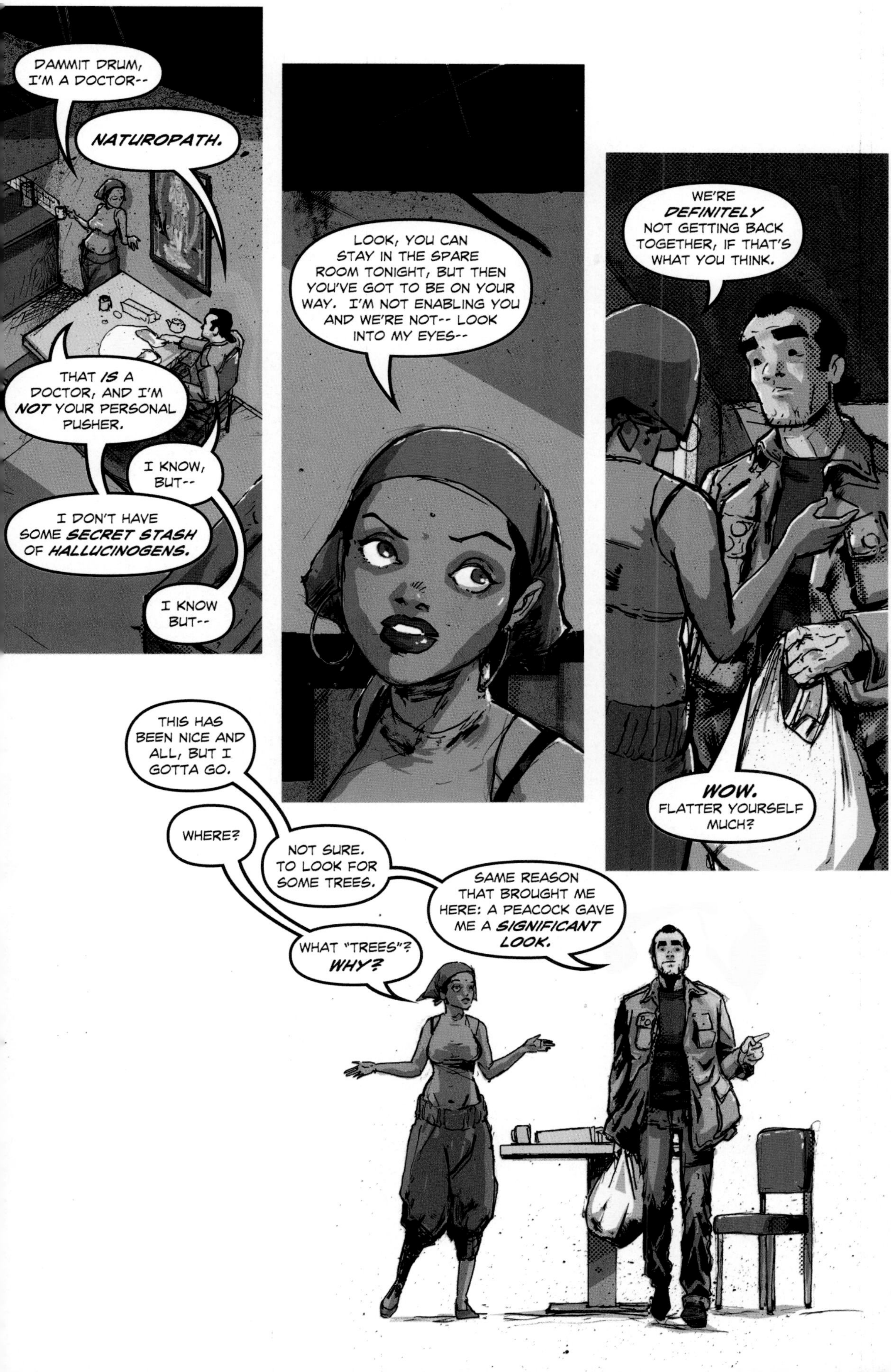
DAMMIT DRUM, I'M A DOCTOR--
NATUROPATH.
THAT IS A DOCTOR, AND I'M NOT YOUR PERSONAL PUSHER.
I KNOW, BUT--
I DON'T HAVE SOME SECRET STASH OF HALLUCINOGENS.
I KNOW BUT--
LOOK, YOU CAN STAY IN THE SPARE ROOM TONIGHT, BUT THEN YOU'VE GOT TO BE ON YOUR WAY. I'M NOT ENABLING YOU AND WE'RE NOT-- LOOK INTO MY EYES--
WE'RE DEFINITELY NOT GETTING BACK TOGETHER, IF THAT'S WHAT YOU THINK.
WOW. FLATTER YOURSELF MUCH?
THIS HAS BEEN NICE AND ALL, BUT I GOTTA GO.
WHERE?
NOT SURE. TO LOOK FOR SOME TREES.
WHAT "TREES"? WHY?
SAME REASON THAT BROUGHT ME HERE: A PEACOCK GAVE ME A SIGNIFICANT LOOK.

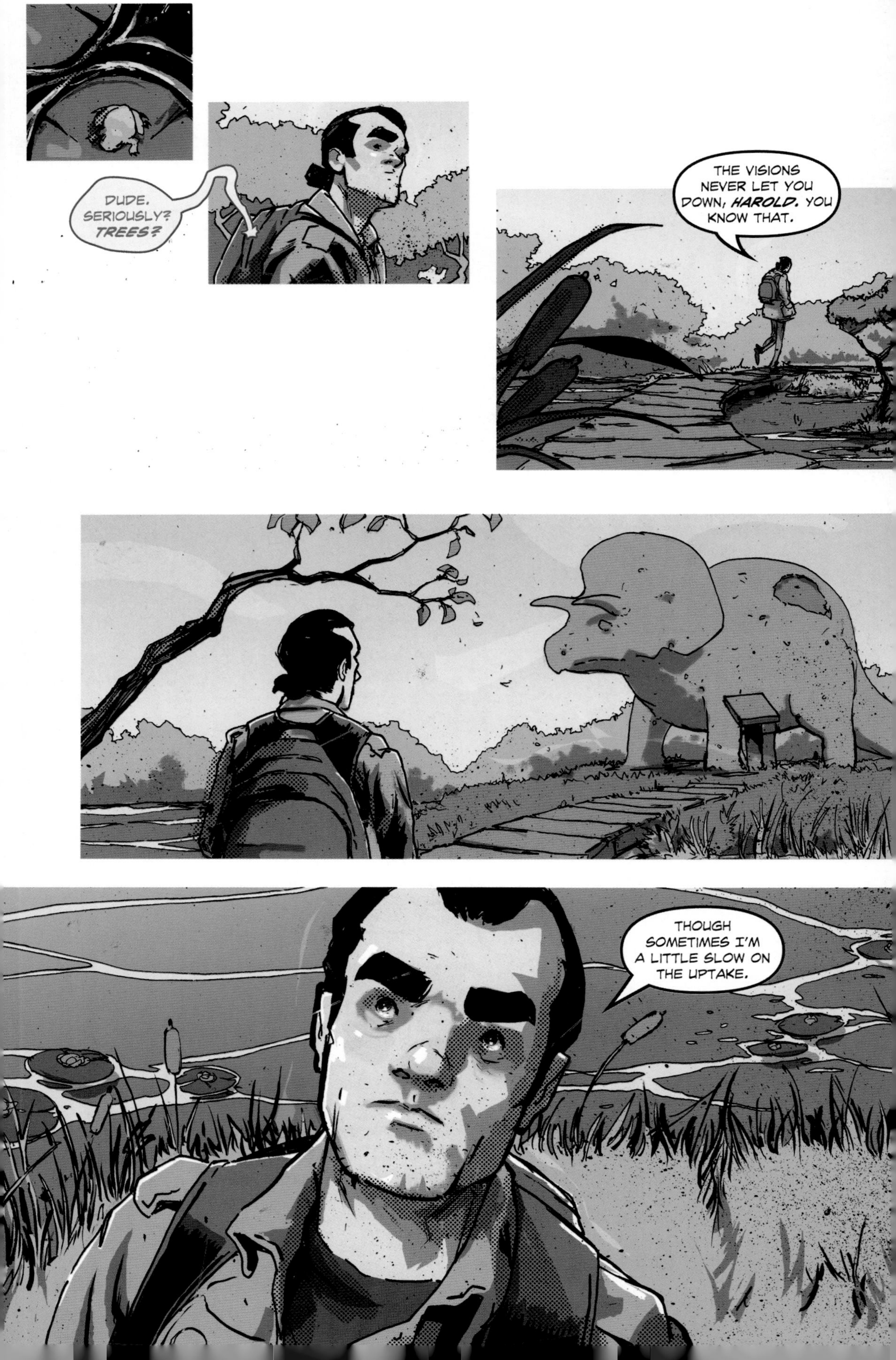
DUDE. SERIOUSLY? TREES?
THE VISIONS NEVER LET YOU DOWN, HAROLD. YOU KNOW THAT.
THOUGH SOMETIMES I'M A LITTLE SLOW ON THE UPTAKE.

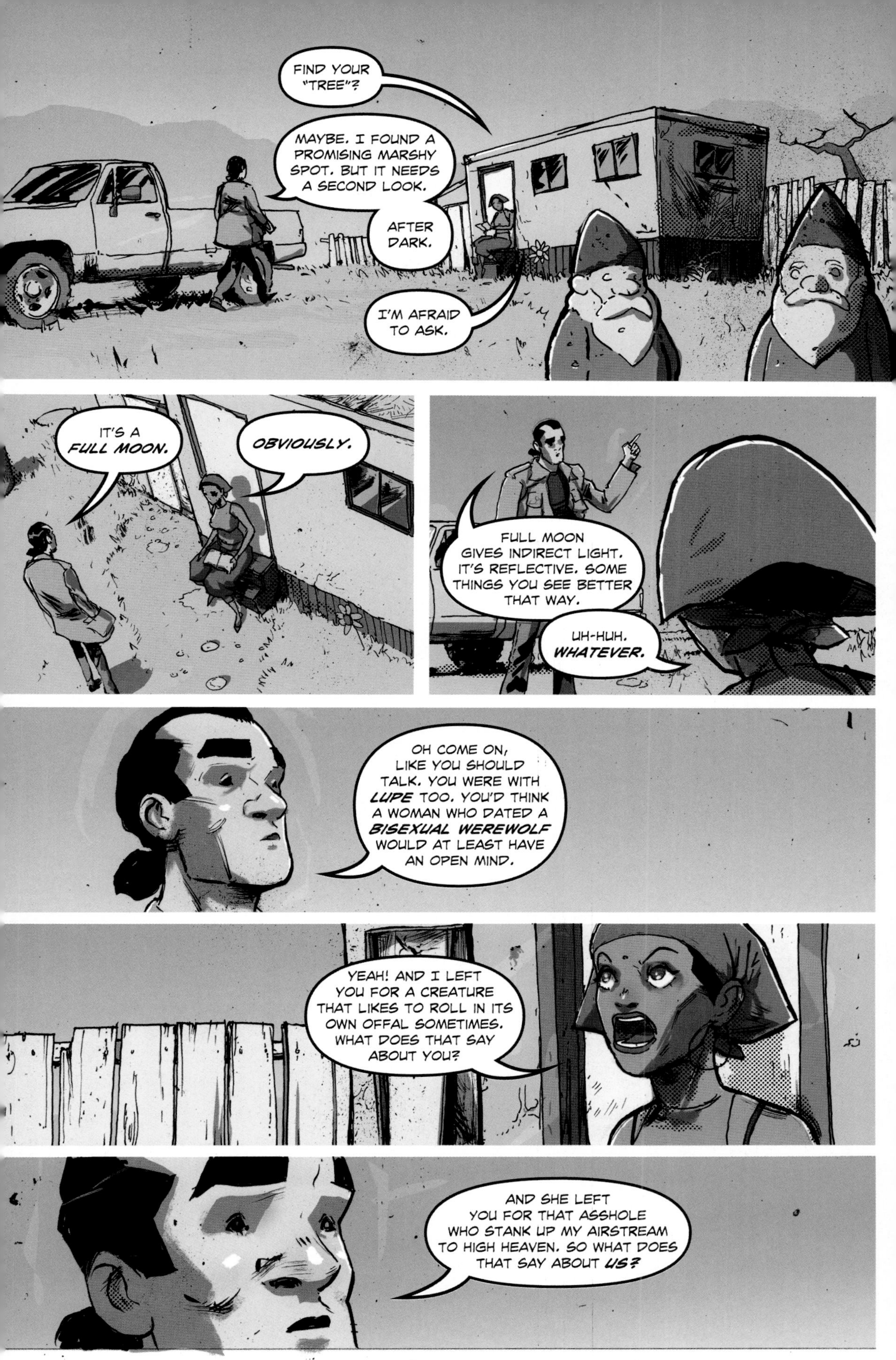

FIND YOUR "TREE"?
MAYBE. I FOUND A PROMISING MARSHY SPOT. BUT IT NEEDS A SECOND LOOK.
AFTER DARK.
I'M AFRAID TO ASK.
IT'S A FULL MOON.
OBVIOUSLY.
FULL MOON GIVES INDIRECT LIGHT. IT'S REFLECTIVE. SOME THINGS YOU SEE BETTER THAT WAY.
UH-HUH. WHATEVER.
OH COME ON, LIKE YOU SHOULD TALK. YOU WERE WITH LUPE TOO. YOU'D THINK A WOMAN WHO DATED A BISEXUAL WEREWOLF WOULD AT LEAST HAVE AN OPEN MIND.
YEAH! AND I LEFT YOU FOR A CREATURE THAT LIKES TO ROLL IN ITS OWN OFFAL SOMETIMES. WHAT DOES THAT SAY ABOUT YOU?
AND SHE LEFT YOU FOR THAT ASSHOLE WHO STANK UP MY AIRSTREAM TO HIGH HEAVEN. SO WHAT DOES THAT SAY ABOUT US?

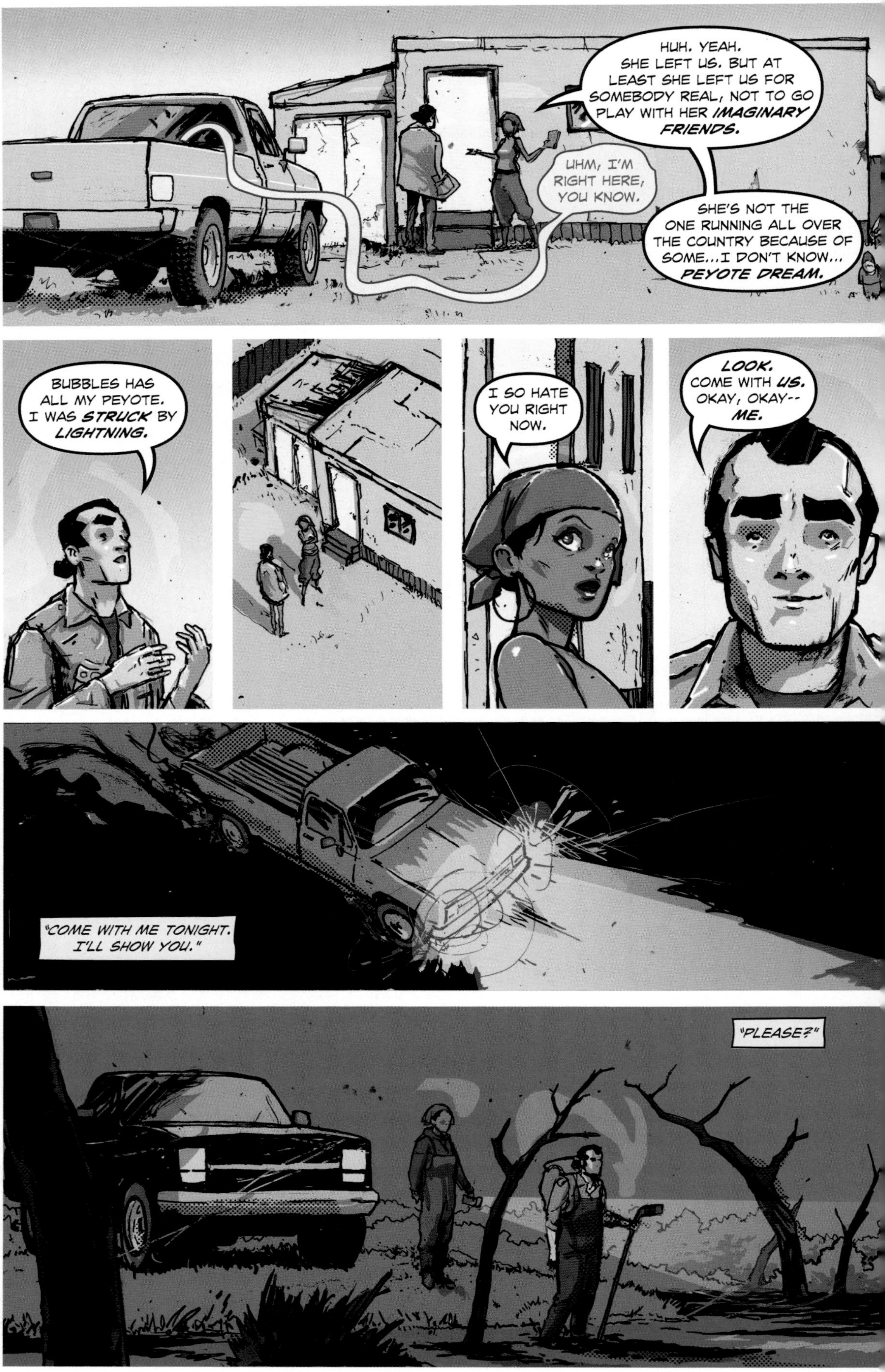
HUH. YEAH. SHE LEFT US. BUT AT LEAST SHE LEFT US FOR SOMEBODY REAL, NOT TO GO PLAY WITH HER IMAGINARY FRIENDS.
UHM, I'M RIGHT HERE, YOU KNOW.
SHE'S NOT THE ONE RUNNING ALL OVER THE COUNTRY BECAUSE OF SOME...I DON'T KNOW... PEYOTE DREAM.
BUBBLES HAS ALL MY PEYOTE. I WAS STRUCK BY LIGHTNING.
I SO HATE YOU RIGHT NOW.
LOOK. COME WITH US. OKAY, OKAY-- ME.
"COME WITH ME TONIGHT. I'LL SHOW YOU."
"PLEASE?"

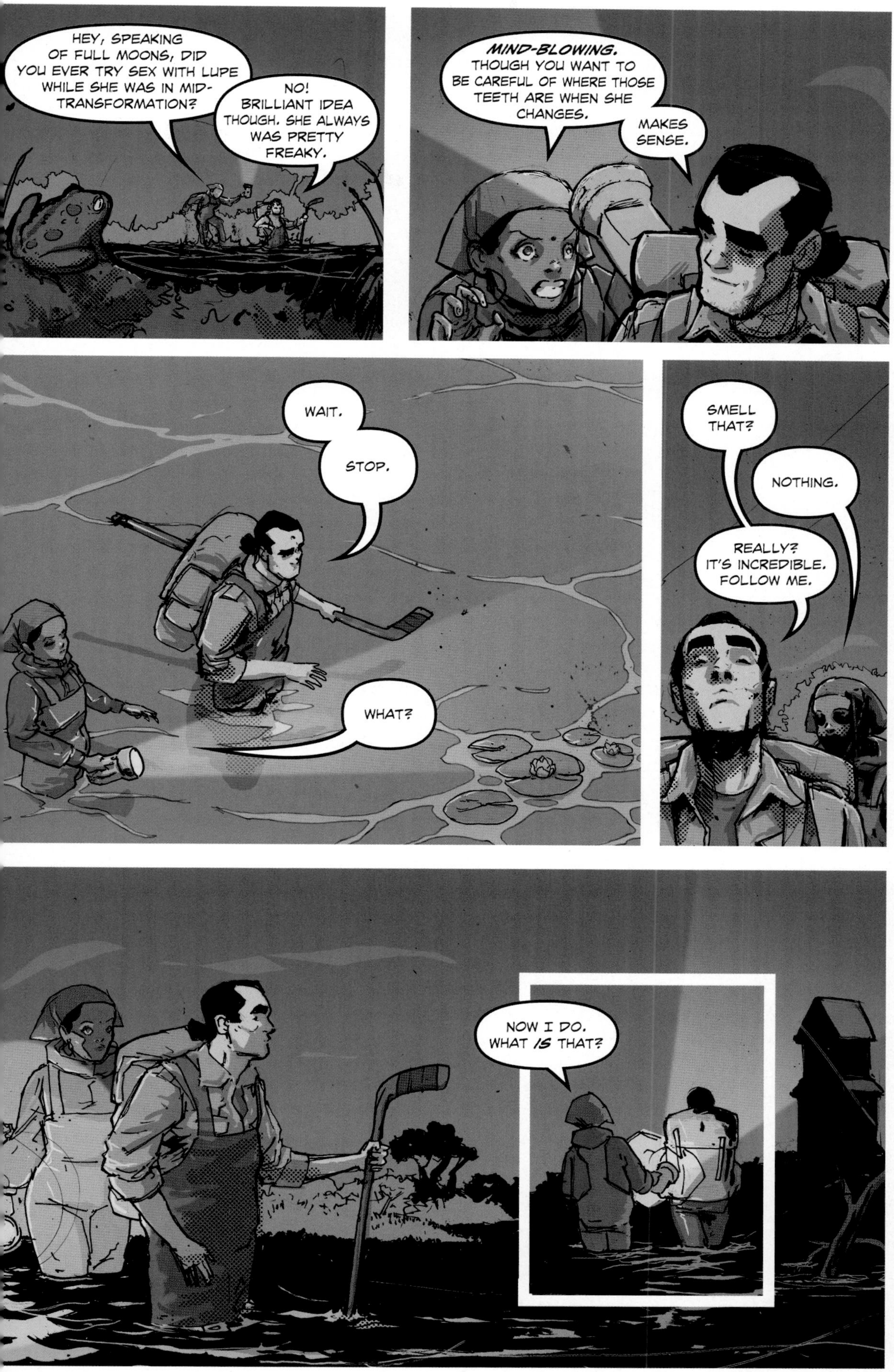
HEY, SPEAKING OF FULL MOONS, DID YOU EVER TRY SEX WITH LUPE WHILE SHE WAS IN MID-TRANSFORMATION?
NO! BRILLIANT IDEA THOUGH. SHE ALWAYS WAS PRETTY FREAKY.
MIND-BLOWING. THOUGH YOU WANT TO BE CAREFUL OF WHERE THOSE TEETH ARE WHEN SHE CHANGES.
MAKES SENSE.
WAIT.
STOP.
WHAT?
SMELL THAT?
NOTHING.
REALLY? IT'S INCREDIBLE. FOLLOW ME.
NOW I DO. WHAT *IS* THAT?

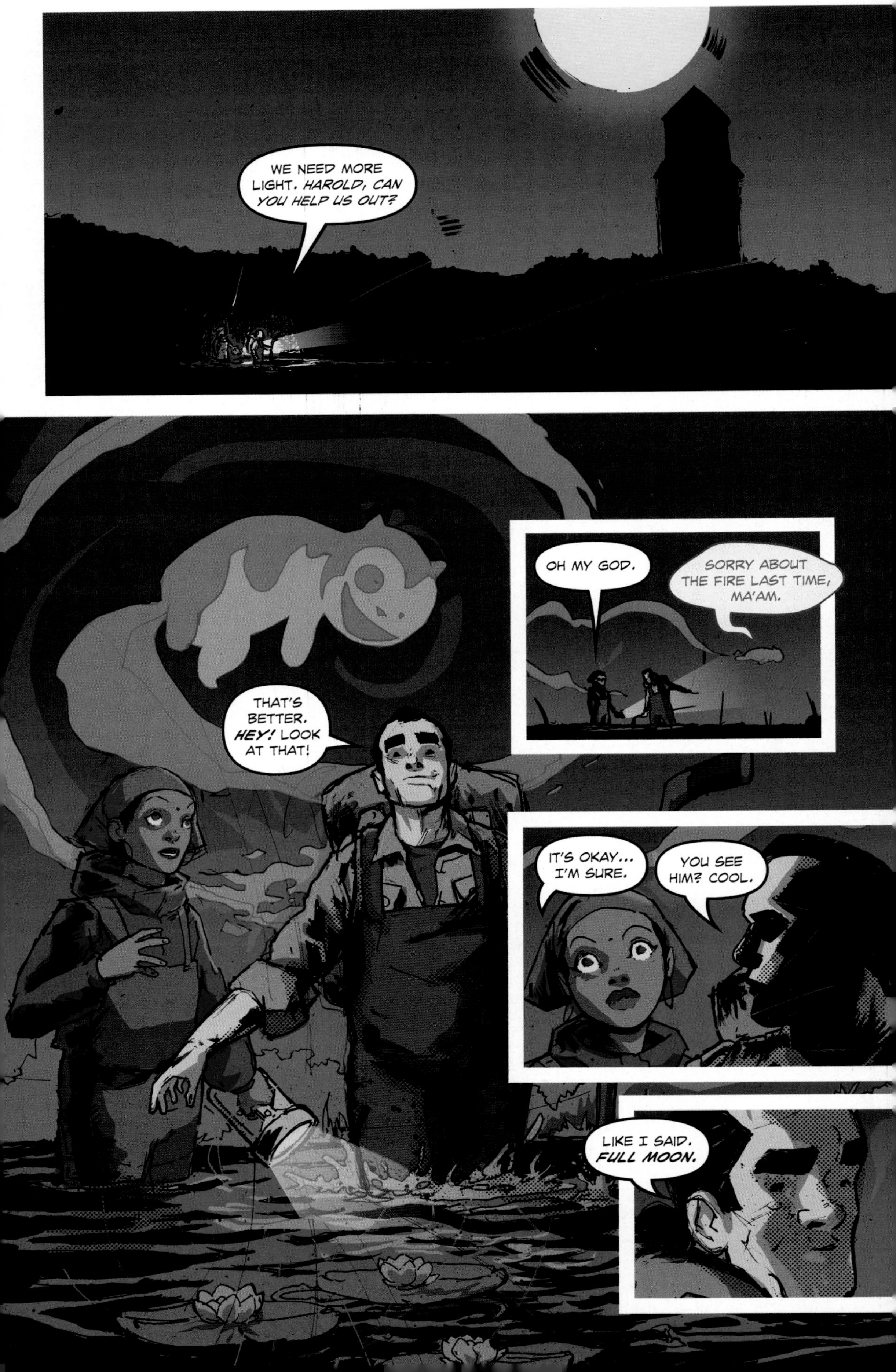
WE NEED MORE LIGHT. HARDOLD, CAN YOU HELP US OUT?
OH MY GOD.
SORRY ABOUT THE FIRE LAST TIME, MA'AM.
THAT'S BETTER. HEY! LOOK AT THAT!
IT'S OKAY... I'M SURE.
YOU SEE HIM? COOL.
LIKE I SAID. FULL MOON.

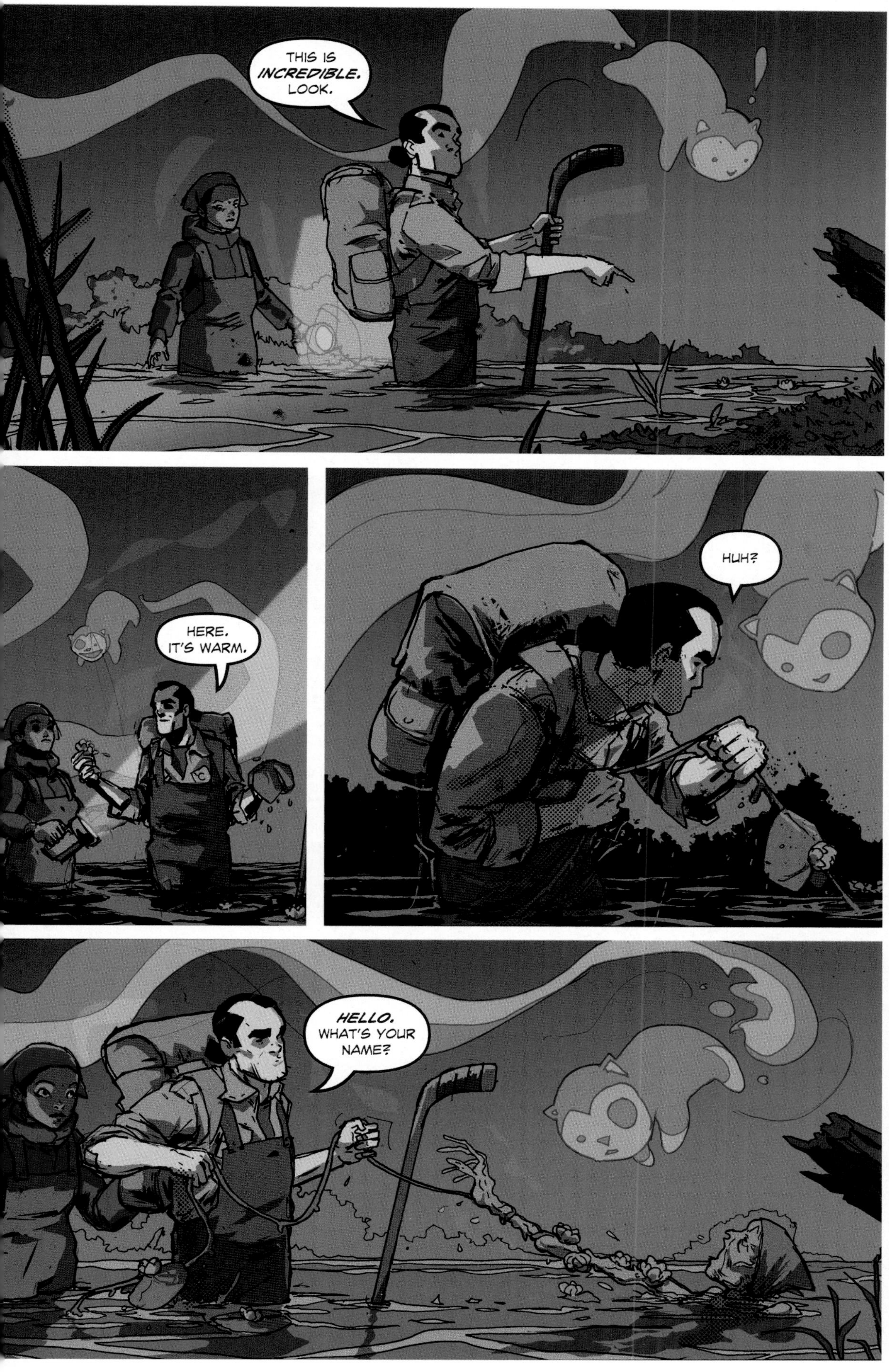
THIS IS *INCREDIBLE.* LOOK.
HERE. IT'S WARM.
HUH?
HELLO. WHAT'S YOUR NAME?

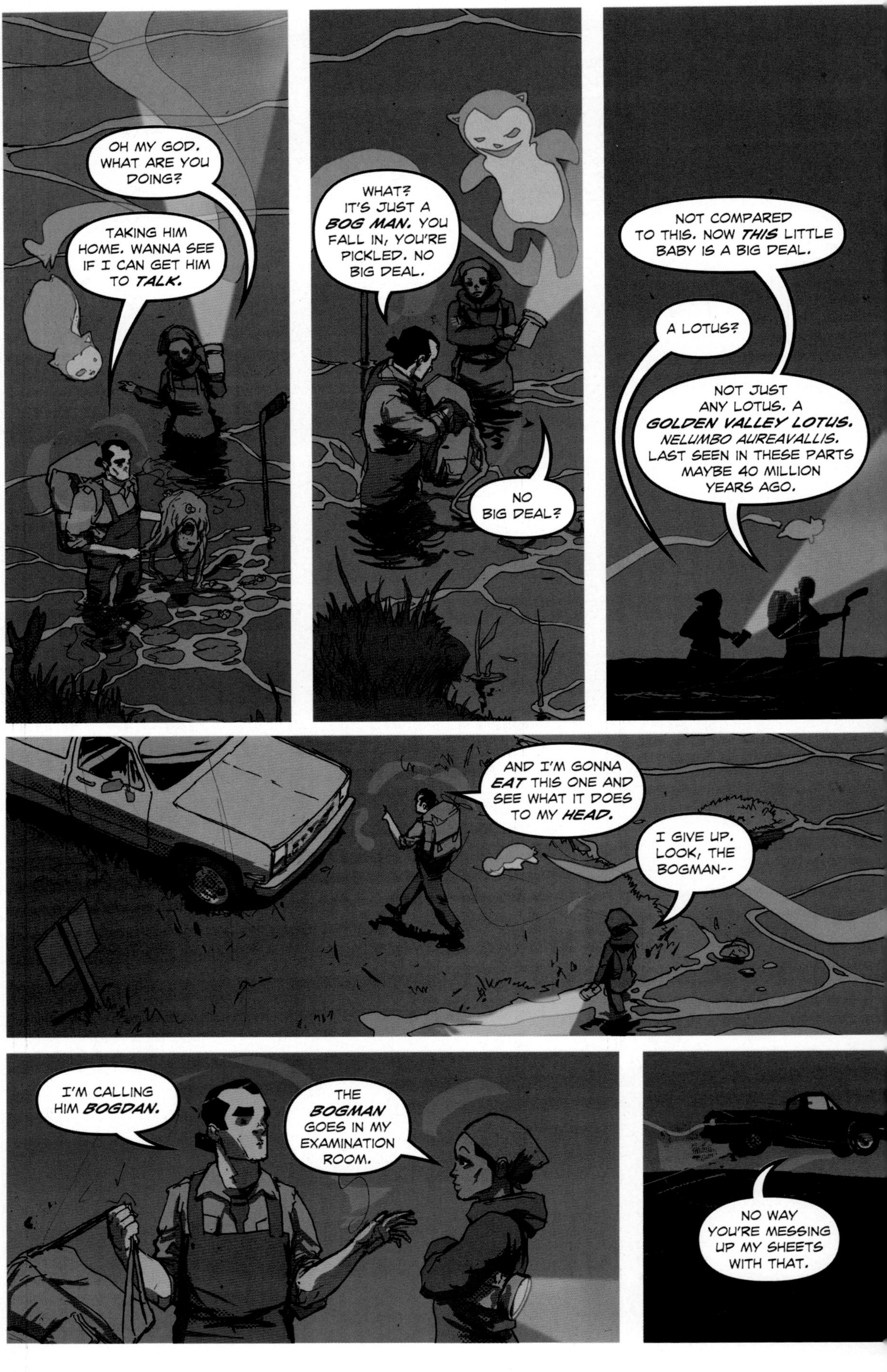
OH MY GOD. WHAT ARE YOU DOING?
TAKING HIM HOME. WANNA SEE IF I CAN GET HIM TO *TALK.*
WHAT? IT'S JUST A *BOG MAN.* YOU FALL IN, YOU'RE PICKLED. NO BIG DEAL.
NO BIG DEAL?
NOT COMPARED TO THIS. NOW *THIS* LITTLE BABY IS A BIG DEAL.
A LOTUS?
NOT JUST ANY LOTUS. A *GOLDEN VALLEY LOTUS.* *NELUMBO AUREAVALLIS.* LAST SEEN IN THESE PARTS MAYBE 40 MILLION YEARS AGO.
AND I'M GONNA *EAT* THIS ONE AND SEE WHAT IT DOES TO MY *HEAD.*
I GIVE UP. LOOK, THE BOGMAN--
I'M CALLING HIM *BOGDAN.*
THE *BOGMAN* GOES IN MY EXAMINATION ROOM.
NO WAY YOU'RE MESSING UP MY SHEETS WITH THAT.

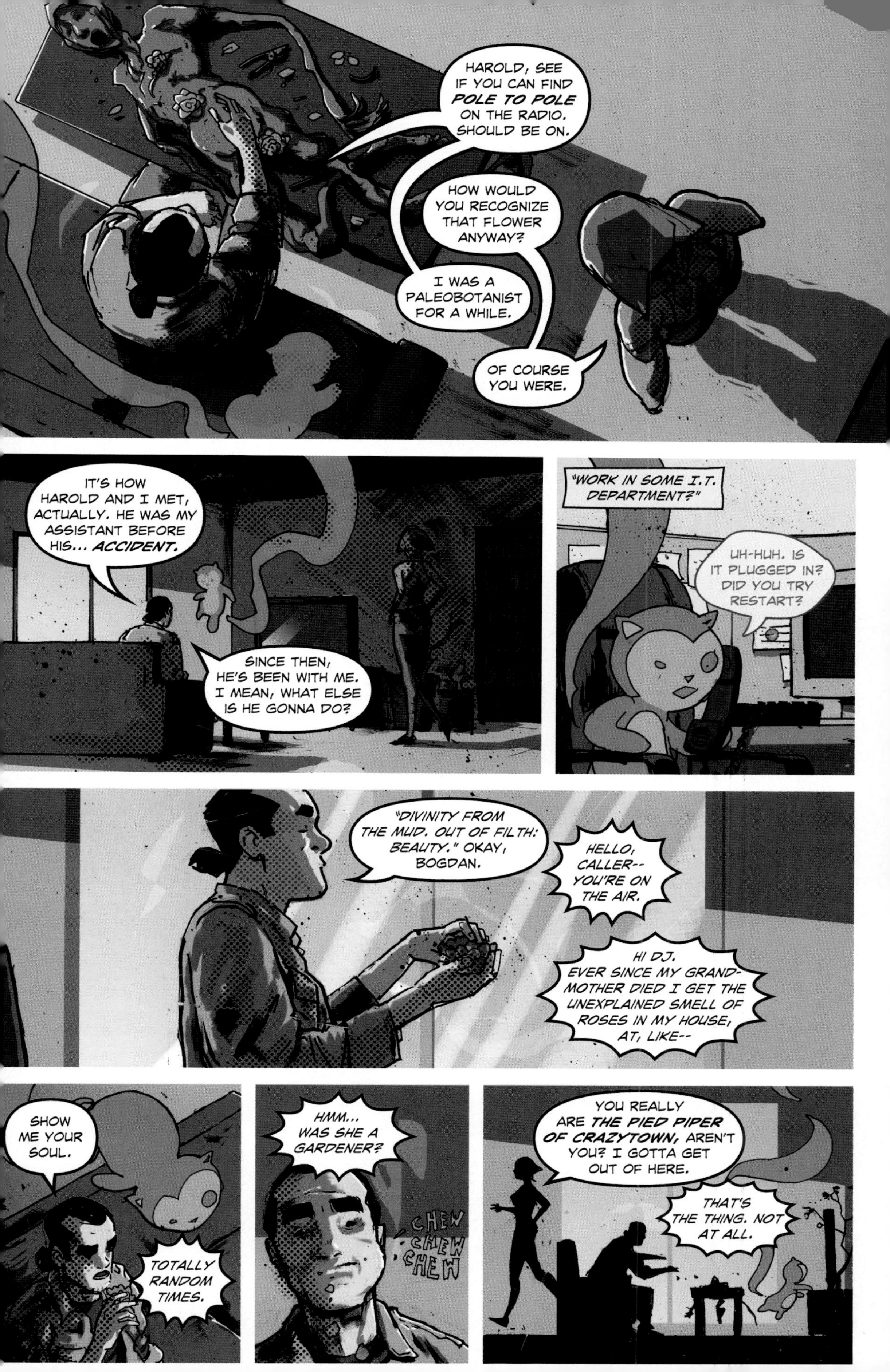
HAROLD, SEE IF YOU CAN FIND POLE TO POLE ON THE RADIO. SHOULD BE ON.
HOW WOULD YOU RECOGNIZE THAT FLOWER ANYWAY?
I WAS A PALEOBOTANIST FOR A WHILE.
OF COURSE YOU WERE.
IT'S HOW HAROLD AND I MET, ACTUALLY. HE WAS MY ASSISTANT BEFORE HIS... ACCIDENT.
SINCE THEN, HE'S BEEN WITH ME. I MEAN, WHAT ELSE IS HE GONNA DO?
"WORK IN SOME I.T. DEPARTMENT?"
UH-HUH. IS IT PLUGGED IN? DID YOU TRY RESTART?
"DIVINITY FROM THE MUD. OUT OF FILTH: BEAUTY." OKAY, BOGDAN.
HELLO, CALLER-- YOU'RE ON THE AIR.
HI DJ. EVER SINCE MY GRAND-MOTHER DIED I GET THE UNEXPLAINED SMELL OF ROSES IN MY HOUSE, AT, LIKE--
SHOW ME YOUR SOUL.
TOTALLY RANDOM TIMES.
HMM... WAS SHE A GARDENER?
CHEW CHEW CHEW
YOU REALLY ARE THE PIED PIPER OF CRAZYTOWN, AREN'T YOU? I GOTTA GET OUT OF HERE.
THAT'S THE THING. NOT AT ALL.

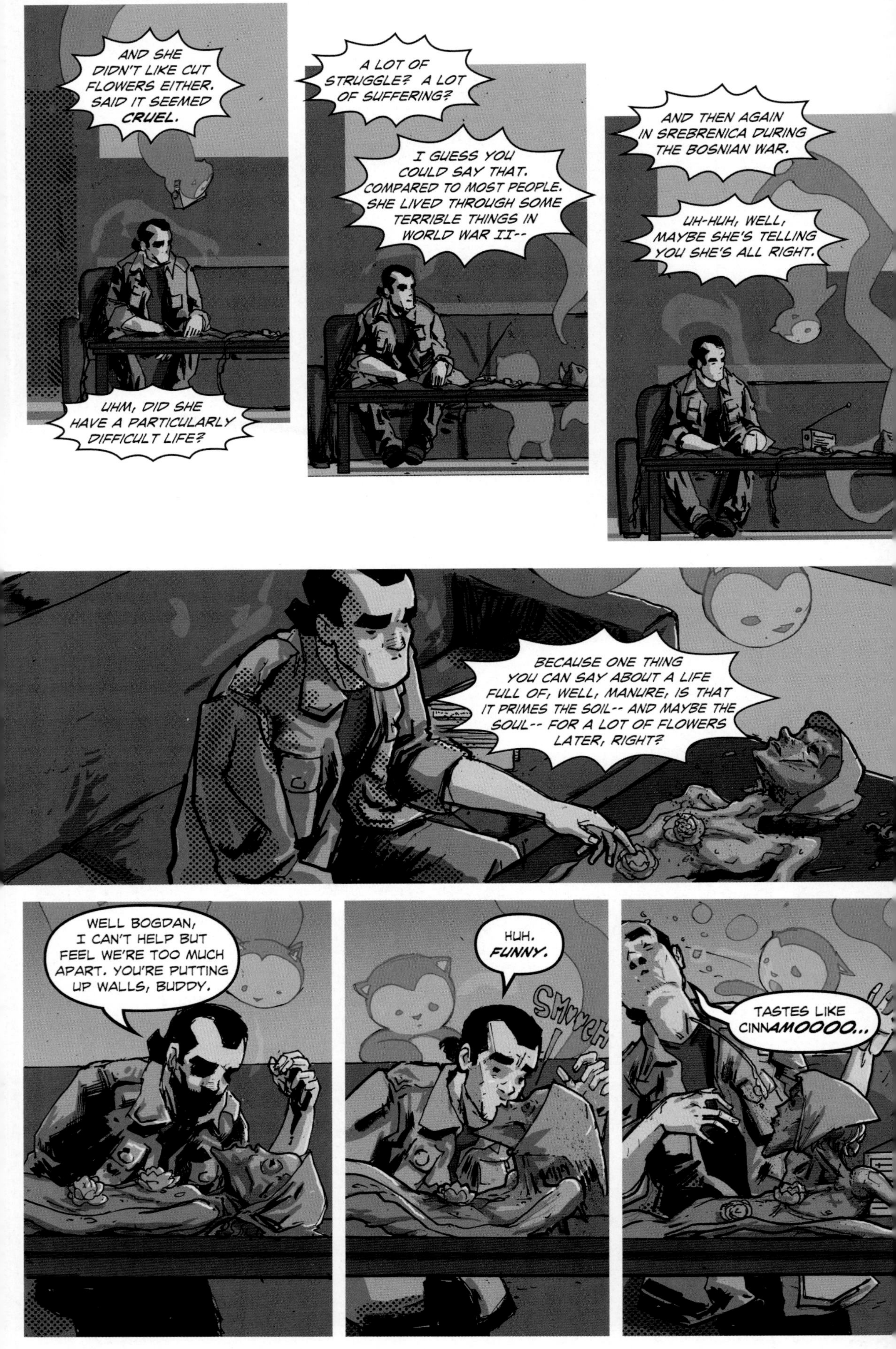
AND SHE DIDN'T LIKE CUT FLOWERS EITHER. SAID IT SEEMED CRUEL.
UHM, DID SHE HAVE A PARTICULARLY DIFFICULT LIFE?
A LOT OF STRUGGLE? A LOT OF SUFFERING?
I GUESS YOU COULD SAY THAT. COMPARED TO MOST PEOPLE. SHE LIVED THROUGH SOME TERRIBLE THINGS IN WORLD WAR II--
AND THEN AGAIN IN SREBRENICA DURING THE BOSNIAN WAR.
UH-HUH, WELL, MAYBE SHE'S TELLING YOU SHE'S ALL RIGHT.
BECAUSE ONE THING YOU CAN SAY ABOUT A LIFE FULL OF, WELL, MANURE, IS THAT IT PRIMES THE SOIL-- AND MAYBE THE SOUL-- FOR A LOT OF FLOWERS LATER, RIGHT?
WELL BOGDAN, I CAN'T HELP BUT FEEL WE'RE TOO MUCH APART. YOU'RE PUTTING UP WALLS, BUDDY.
HUH. FUNNY.
SMUUCH
TASTES LIKE CINNAMOOOO...

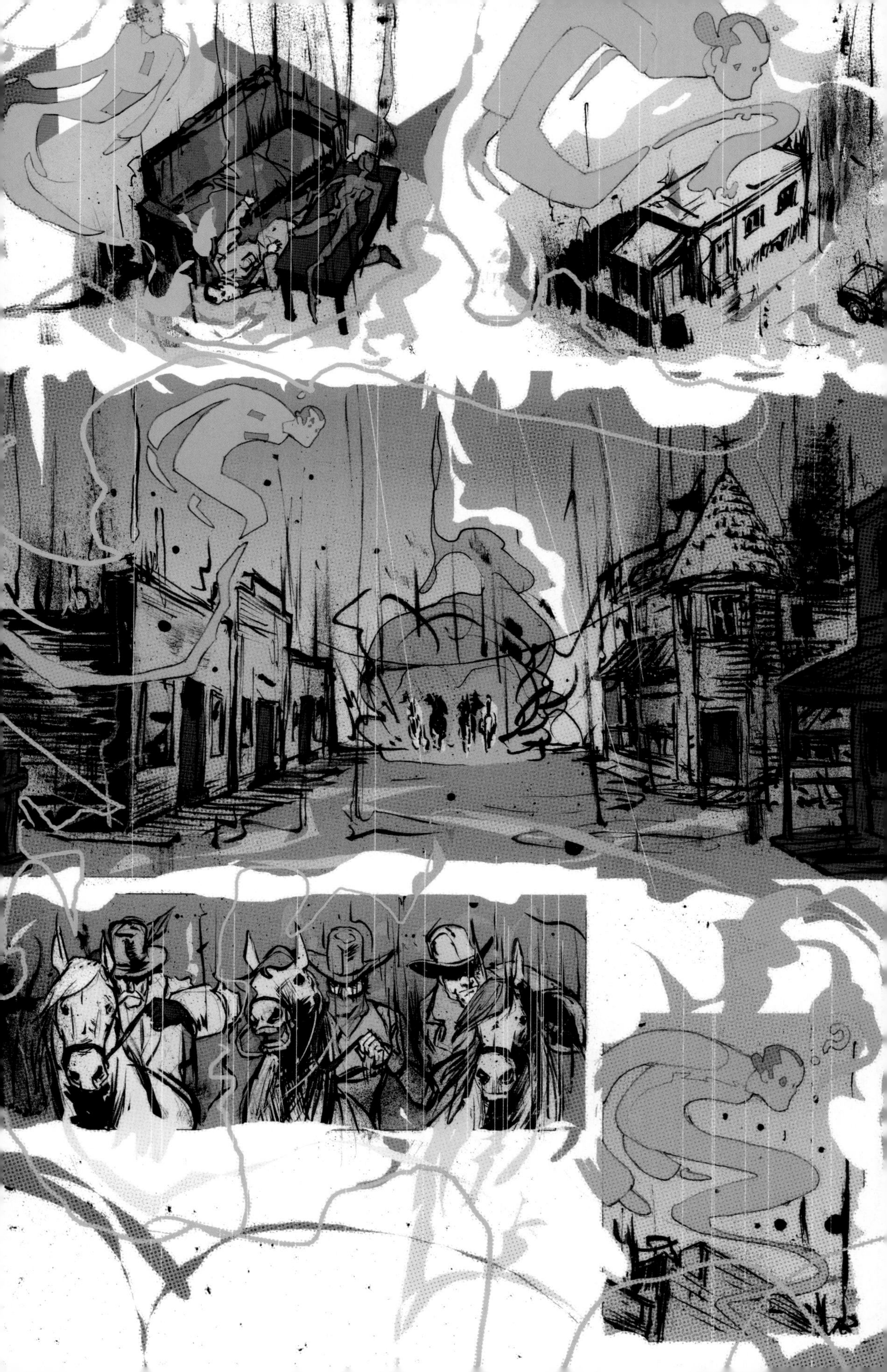

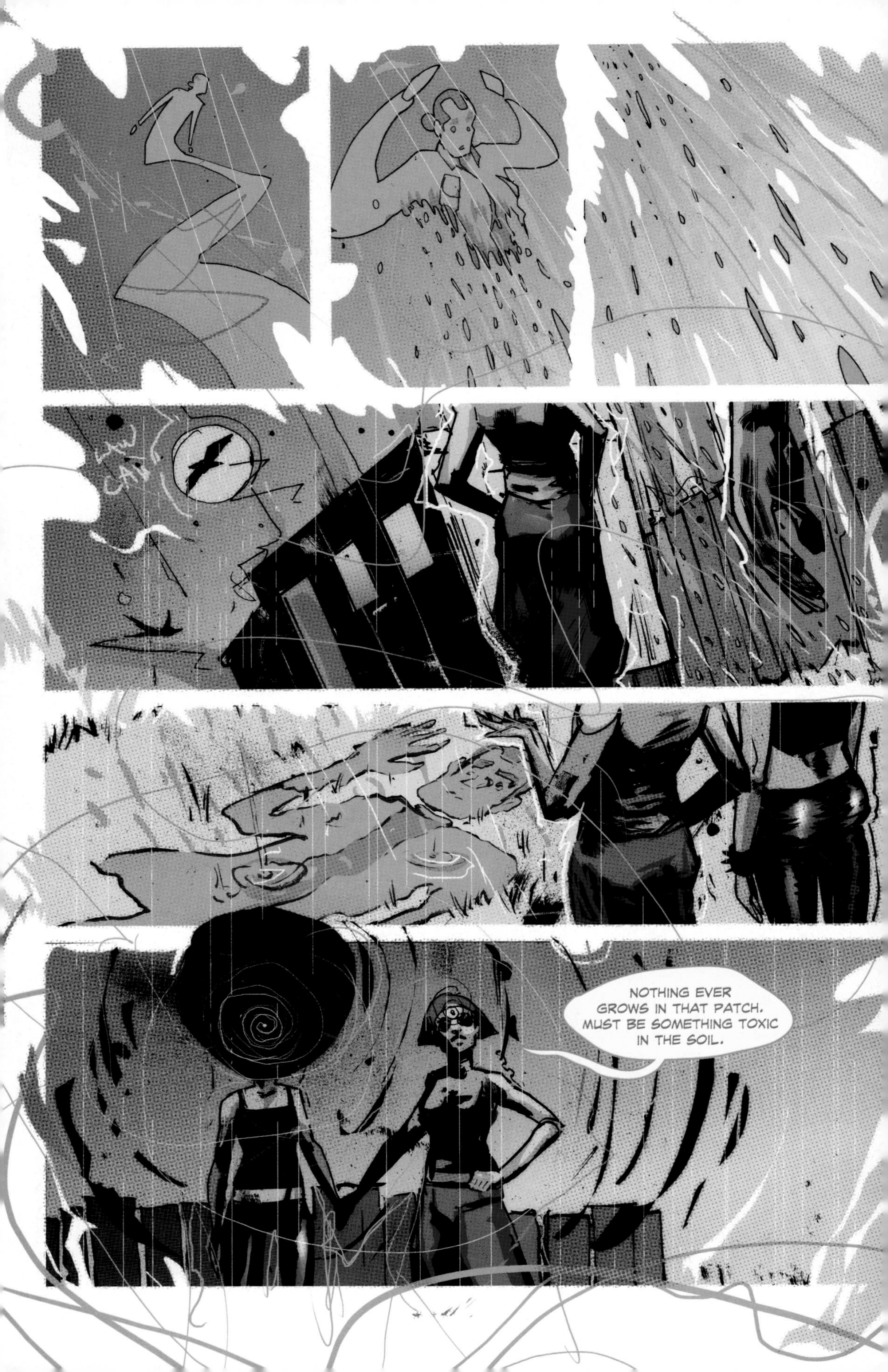
CAW
CAW
NOTHING EVER GROWS IN THAT PATCH. MUST BE SOMETHING TOXIC IN THE SOIL.

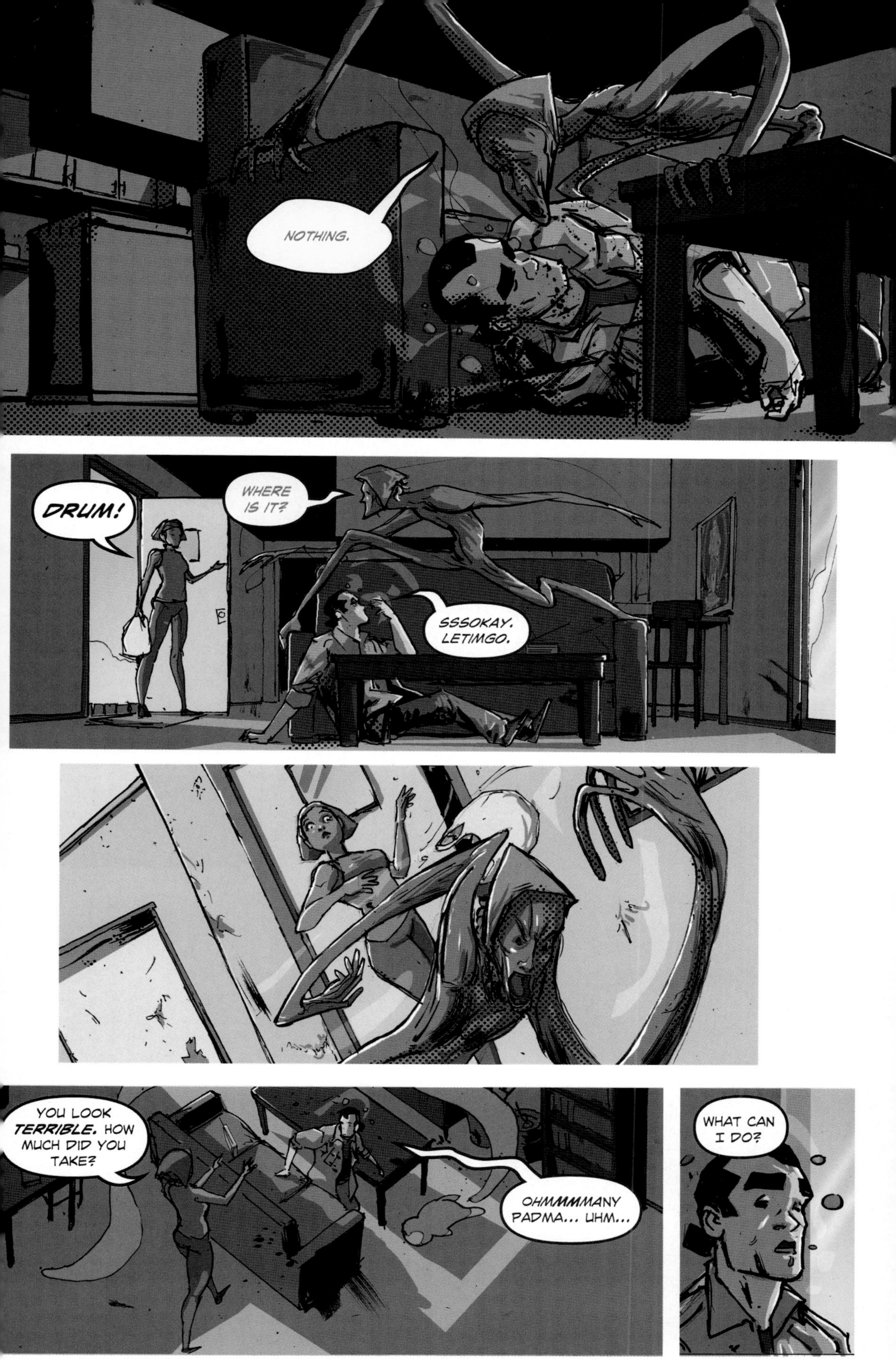
NOTHING.
DRUM!
WHERE IS IT?
SSSOKAY. LETIMGO.
YOU LOOK TERRIBLE. HOW MUCH DID YOU TAKE?
OHMMMMANY PADMA... UHM...
WHAT CAN I DO?

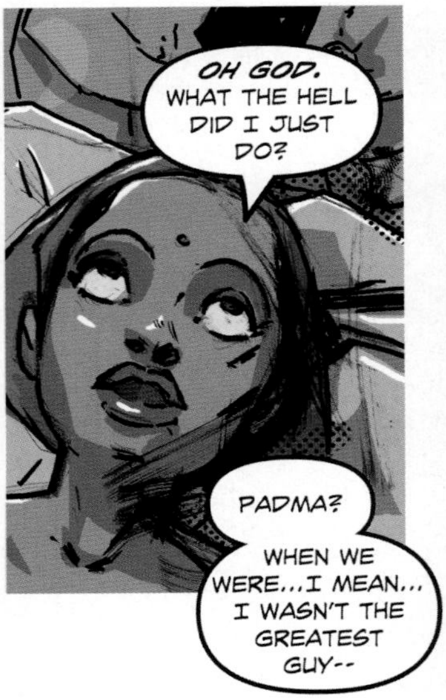
OH GOD. WHAT THE HELL DID I JUST DO?
PADMA?
WHEN WE WERE...I MEAN... I WASN'T THE GREATEST GUY--

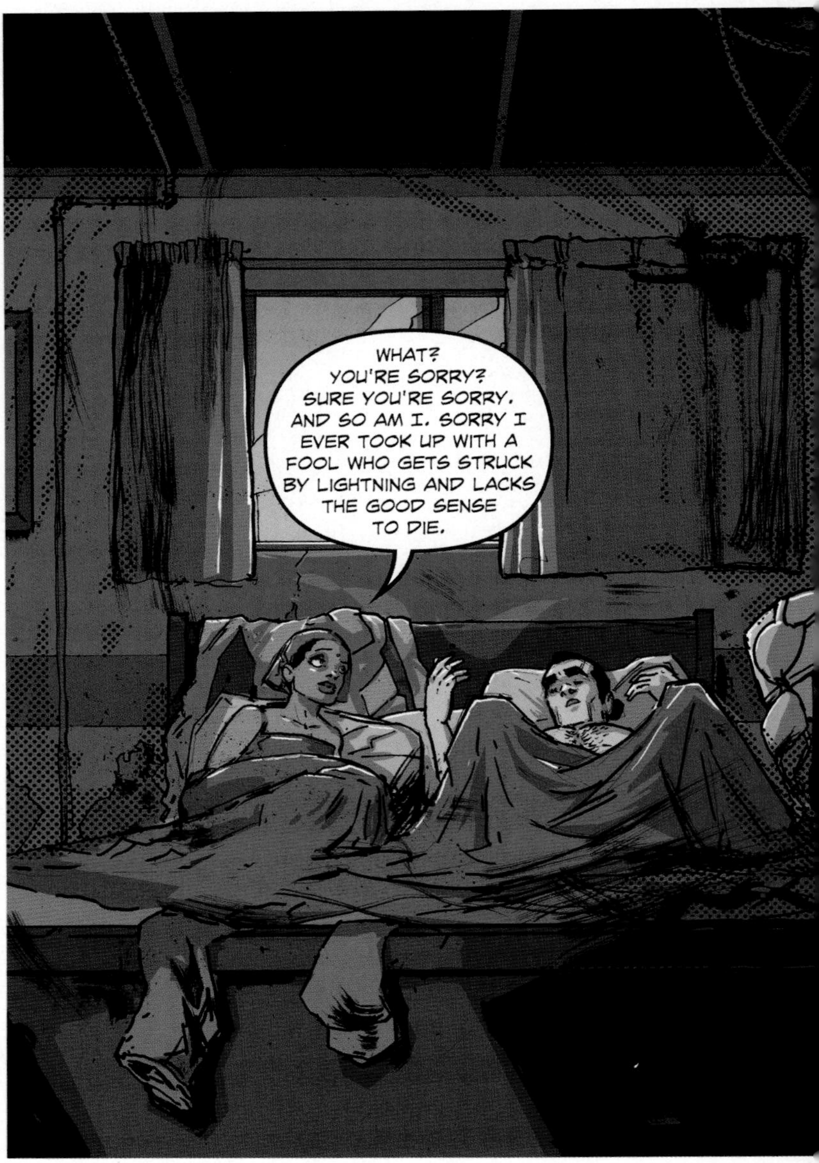
WHAT? YOU'RE SORRY? SURE YOU'RE SORRY. AND SO AM I. SORRY I EVER TOOK UP WITH A FOOL WHO GETS STRUCK BY LIGHTNING AND LACKS THE GOOD SENSE TO DIE.

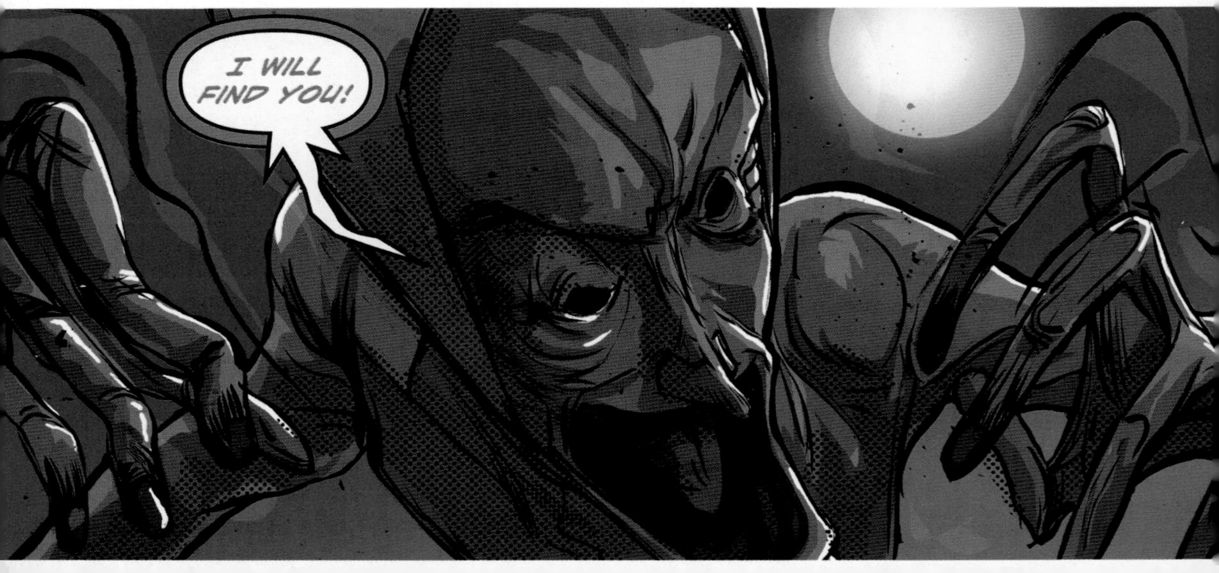
I WILL FIND YOU!

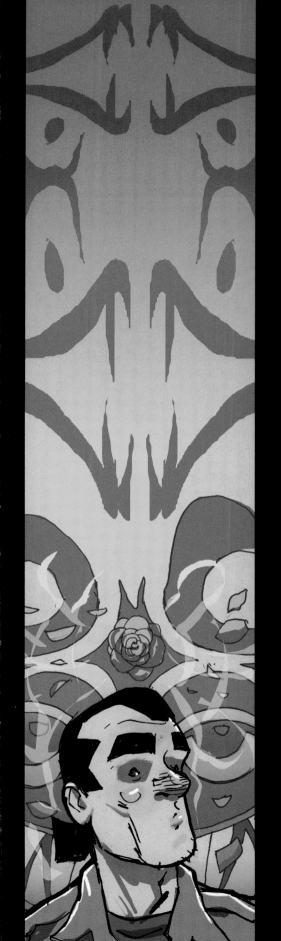

TWO

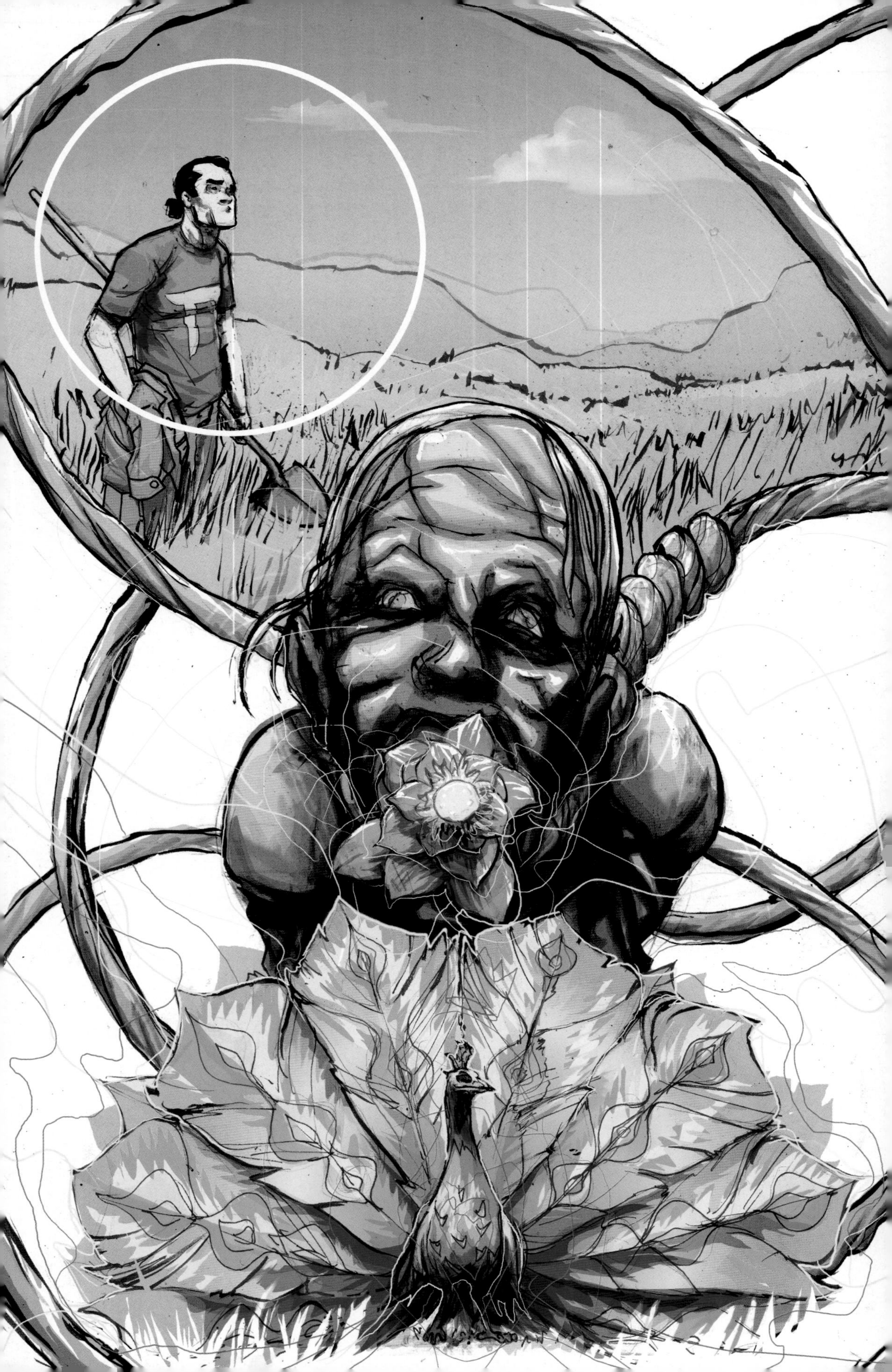

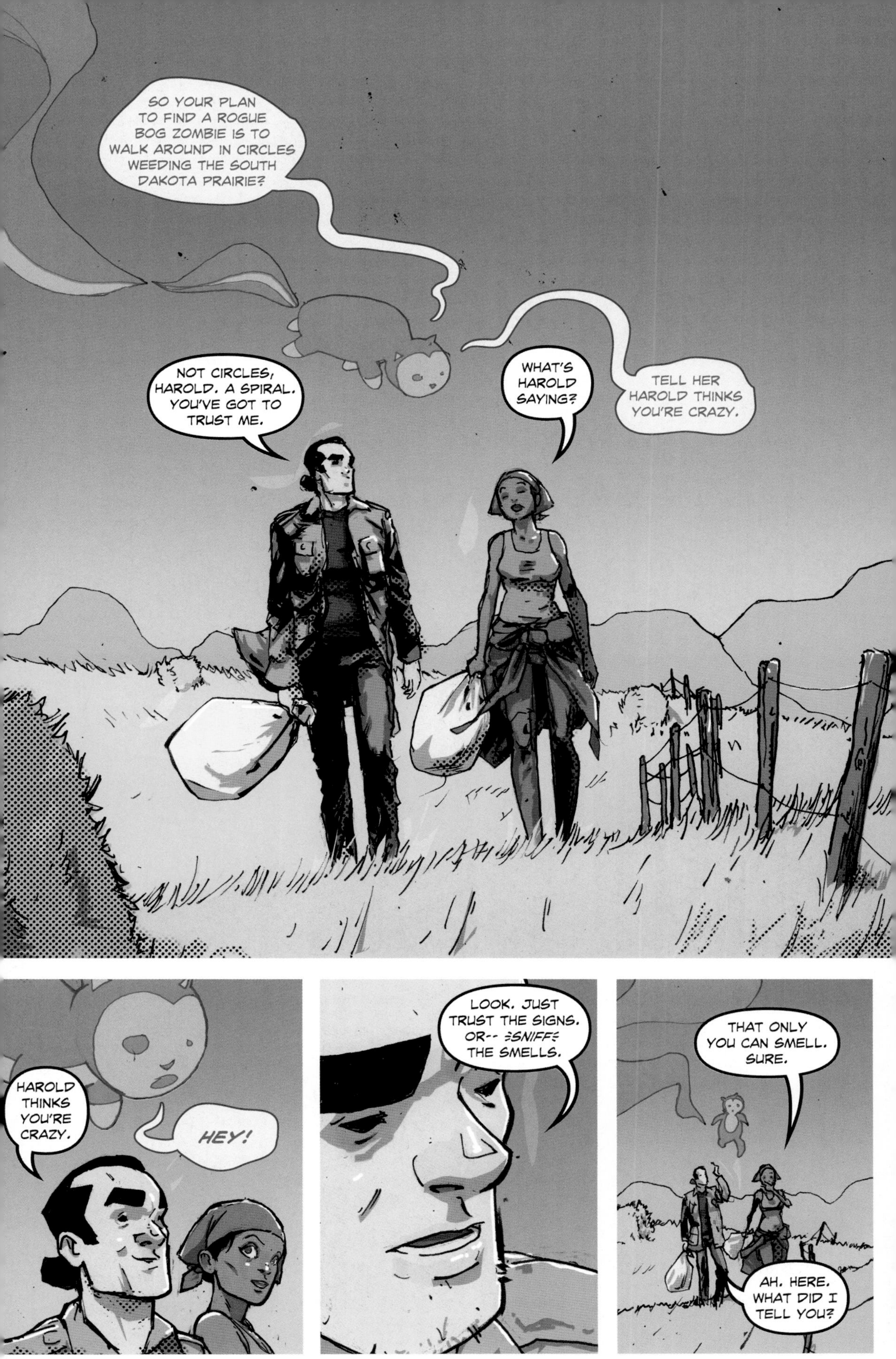
SO YOUR PLAN TO FIND A ROGUE BOG ZOMBIE IS TO WALK AROUND IN CIRCLES WEEDING THE SOUTH DAKOTA PRAIRIE?
NOT CIRCLES, HAROLD. A SPIRAL. YOU'VE GOT TO TRUST ME.
WHAT'S HAROLD SAYING?
TELL HER HAROLD THINKS YOU'RE CRAZY.
HAROLD THINKS YOU'RE CRAZY.
HEY!
LOOK. JUST TRUST THE SIGNS. OR-- =SNIFF= THE SMELLS.
THAT ONLY YOU CAN SMELL. SURE.
AH. HERE. WHAT DID I TELL YOU?

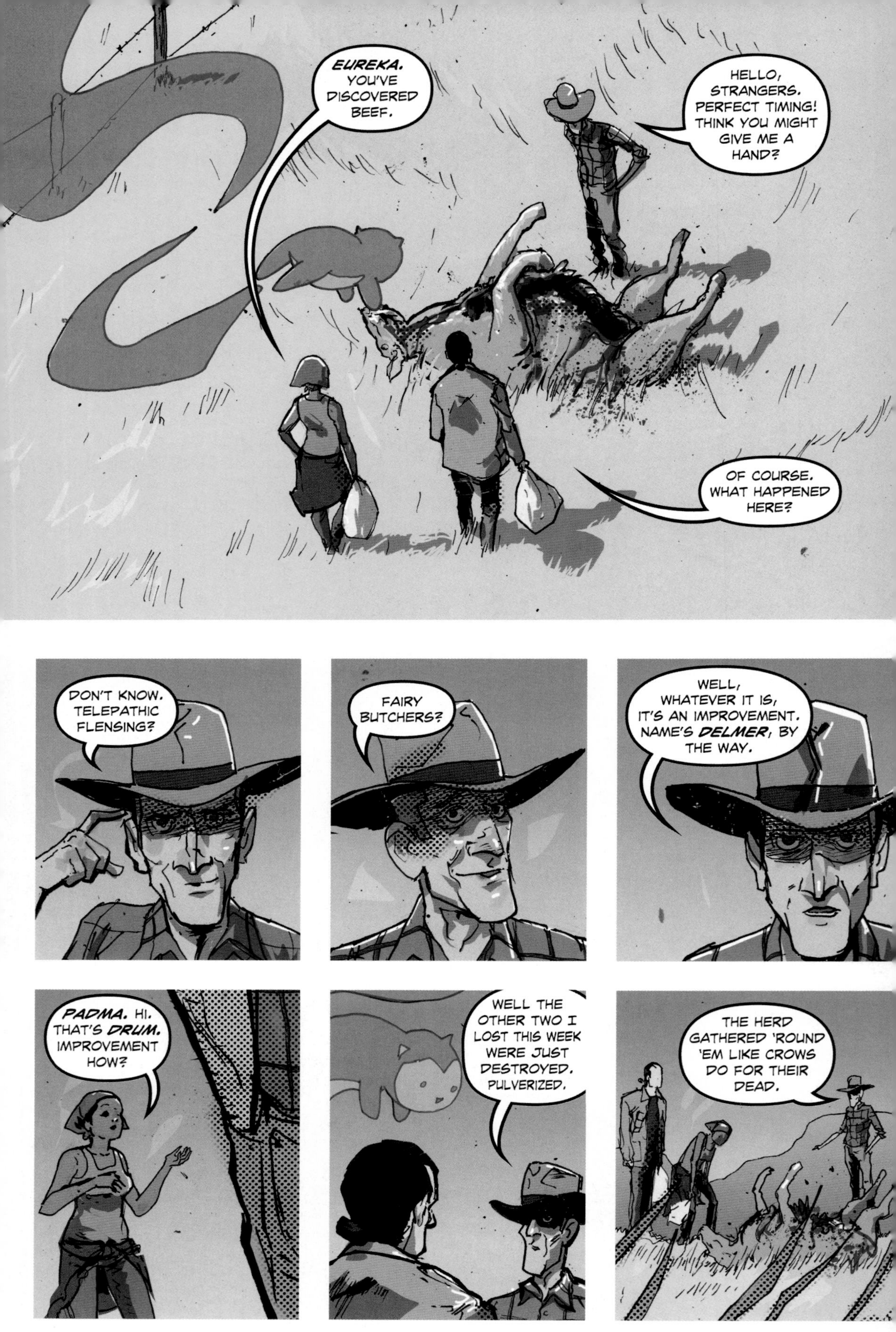

EUREKA. YOU'VE DISCOVERED BEEF.
HELLO, STRANGERS. PERFECT TIMING! THINK YOU MIGHT GIVE ME A HAND?
OF COURSE. WHAT HAPPENED HERE?
DON'T KNOW. TELEPATHIC FLENSING?
FAIRY BUTCHERS?
WELL, WHATEVER IT IS, IT'S AN IMPROVEMENT. NAME'S DELMER, BY THE WAY.
PADMA. HI. THAT'S DRUM. IMPROVEMENT HOW?
WELL THE OTHER TWO I LOST THIS WEEK WERE JUST DESTROYED. PULVERIZED.
THE HERD GATHERED 'ROUND 'EM LIKE CROWS DO FOR THEIR DEAD.

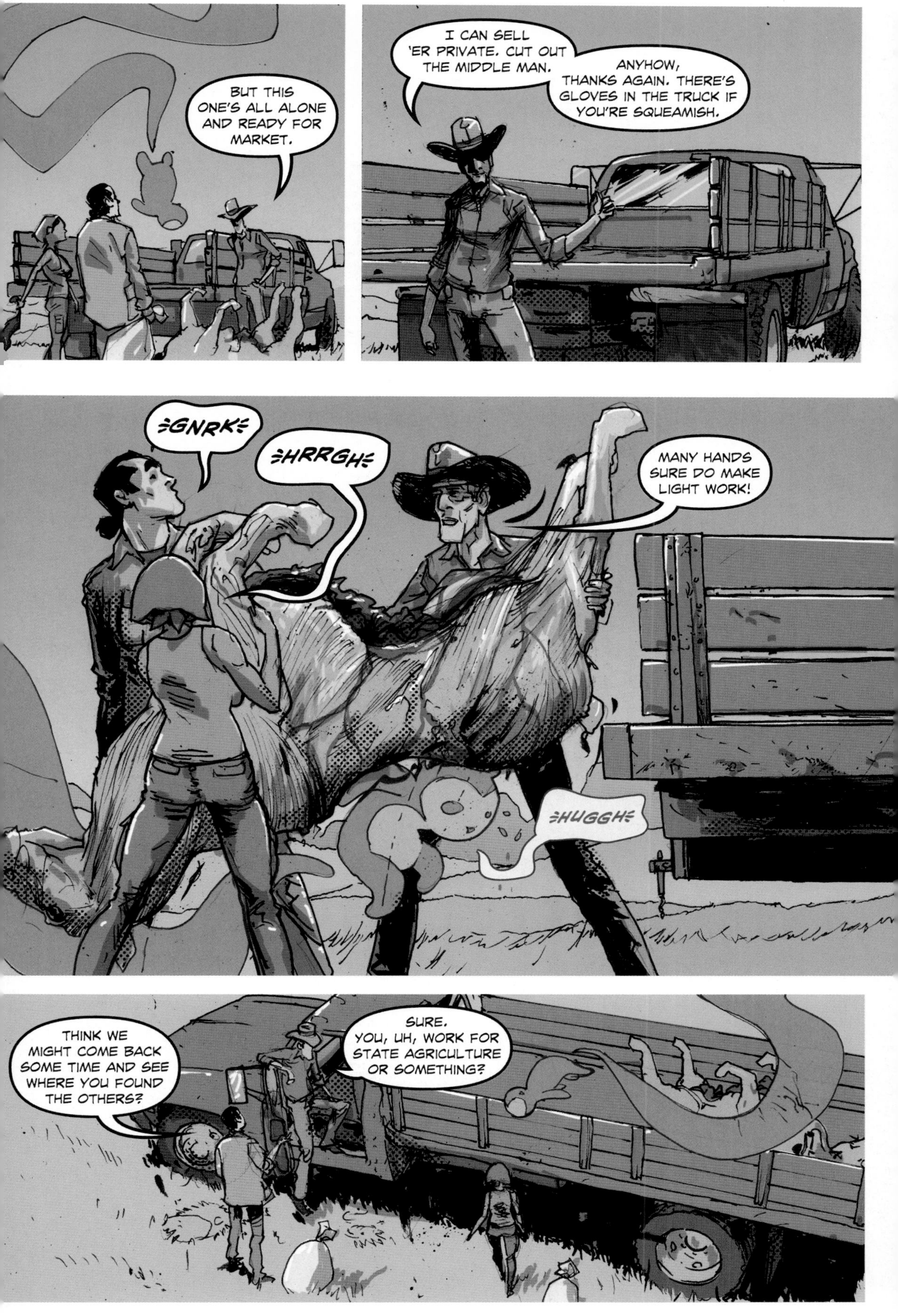
BUT THIS ONE'S ALL ALONE AND READY FOR MARKET.
I CAN SELL 'ER PRIVATE. CUT OUT THE MIDDLE MAN.
ANYHOW, THANKS AGAIN. THERE'S GLOVES IN THE TRUCK IF YOU'RE SQUEAMISH.
GNRK
HRRGH
MANY HANDS SURE DO MAKE LIGHT WORK!
HUGGH
THINK WE MIGHT COME BACK SOME TIME AND SEE WHERE YOU FOUND THE OTHERS?
SURE. YOU, UH, WORK FOR STATE AGRICULTURE OR SOMETHING?

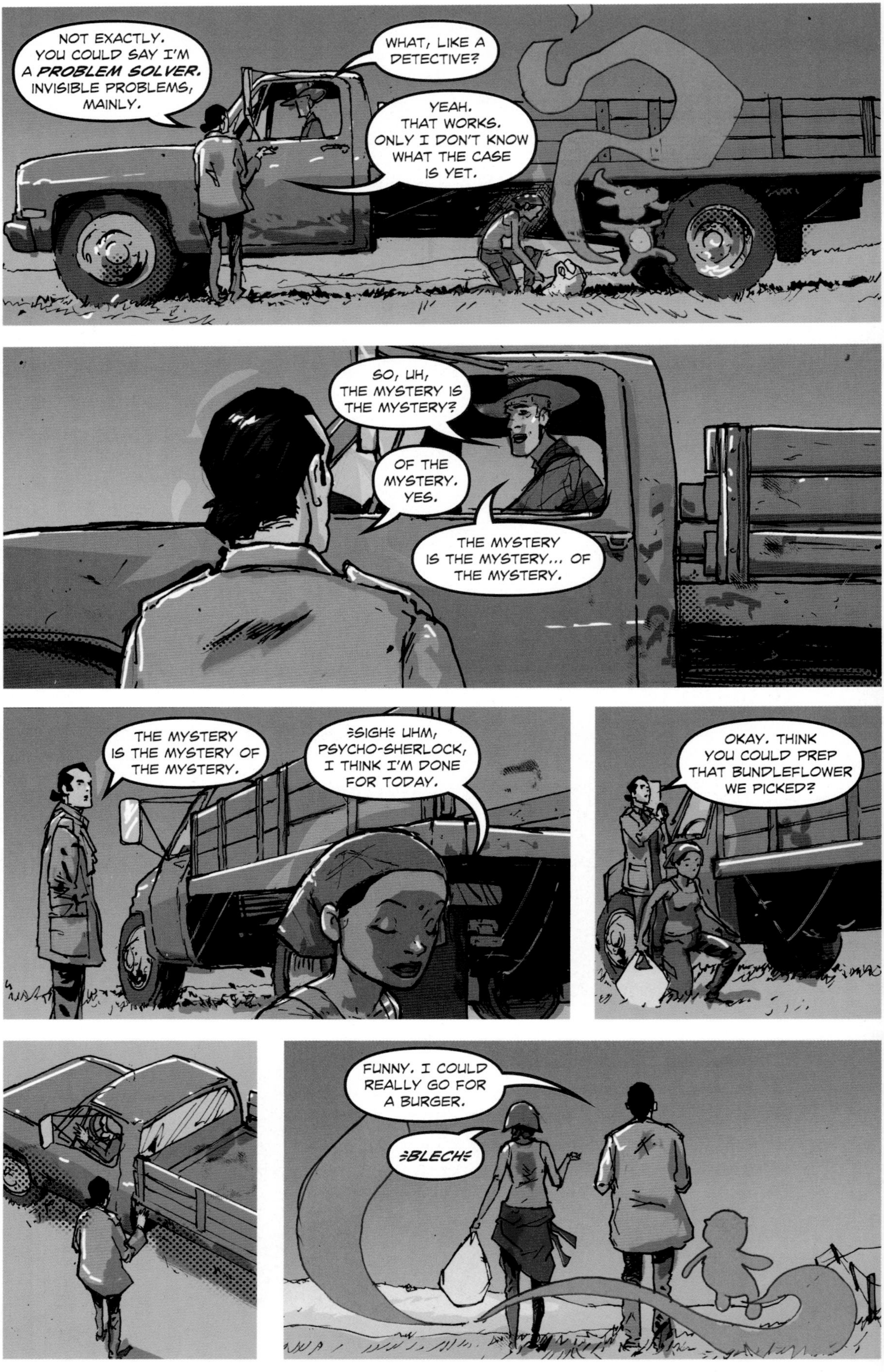
NOT EXACTLY. YOU COULD SAY I'M A **PROBLEM SOLVER.** INVISIBLE PROBLEMS, MAINLY.
WHAT, LIKE A DETECTIVE?
YEAH. THAT WORKS. ONLY I DON'T KNOW WHAT THE CASE IS YET.
SO, UH, THE MYSTERY IS THE MYSTERY?
OF THE MYSTERY. YES.
THE MYSTERY IS THE MYSTERY... OF THE MYSTERY.
THE MYSTERY IS THE MYSTERY OF THE MYSTERY.
=SIGH= UHM, PSYCHO-SHERLOCK, I THINK I'M DONE FOR TODAY.
OKAY. THINK YOU COULD PREP THAT BUNDLEFLOWER WE PICKED?
FUNNY. I COULD REALLY GO FOR A BURGER.
=BLECH=

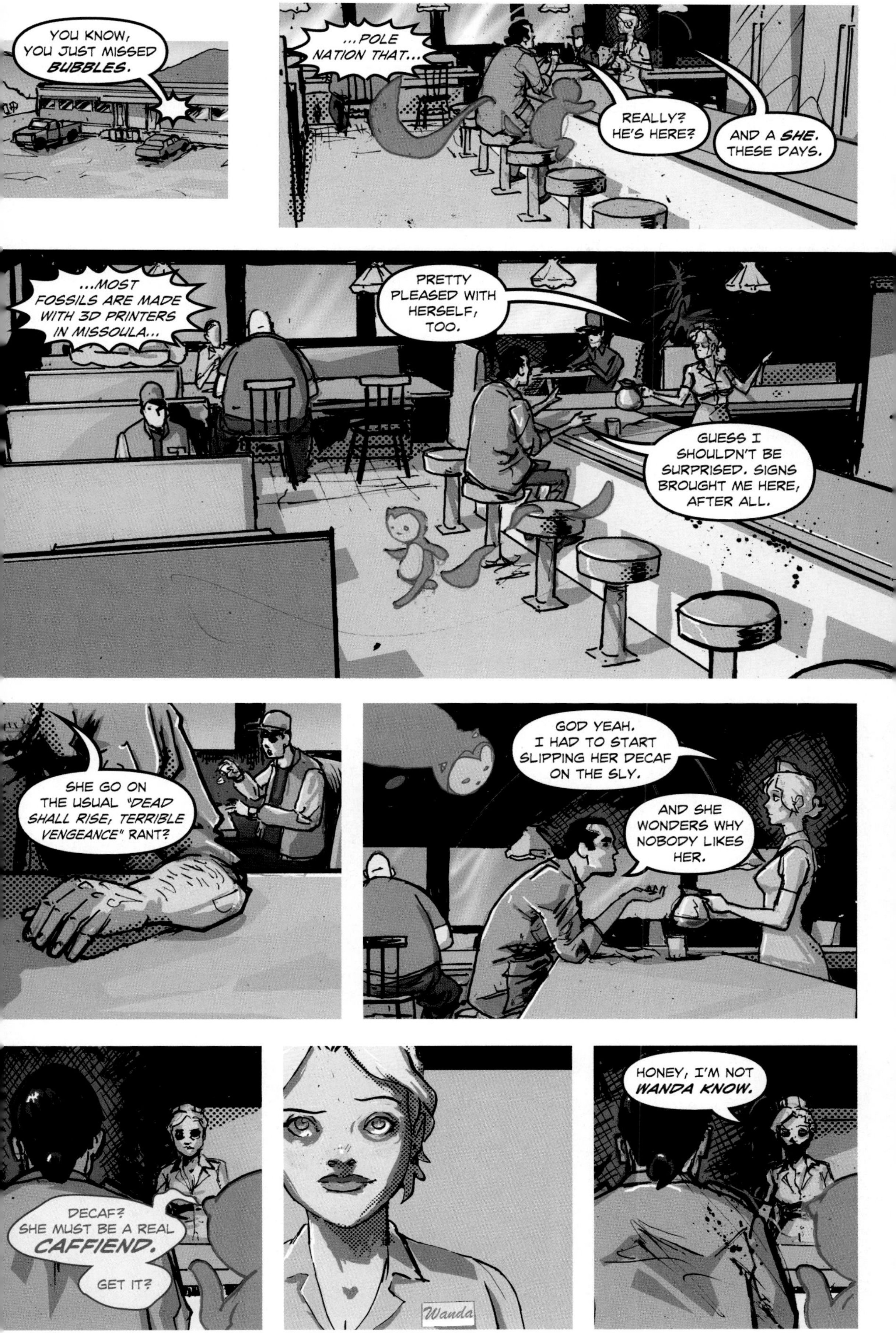
YOU KNOW, YOU JUST MISSED *BUBBLES.*
...POLE NATION THAT...
REALLY? HE'S HERE?
AND A *SHE.* THESE DAYS.
...MOST FOSSILS ARE MADE WITH 3D PRINTERS IN MISSOULA...
PRETTY PLEASED WITH HERSELF, TOO.
GUESS I SHOULDN'T BE SURPRISED. SIGNS BROUGHT ME HERE, AFTER ALL.
SHE GO ON THE USUAL "*DEAD SHALL RISE; TERRIBLE VENGEANCE*" RANT?
GOD YEAH. I HAD TO START SLIPPING HER DECAF ON THE SLY.
AND SHE WONDERS WHY NOBODY LIKES HER.
DECAF? SHE MUST BE A REAL *CAFFIEND.*
GET IT?
Wanda
HONEY, I'M NOT *WANDA KNOW.*

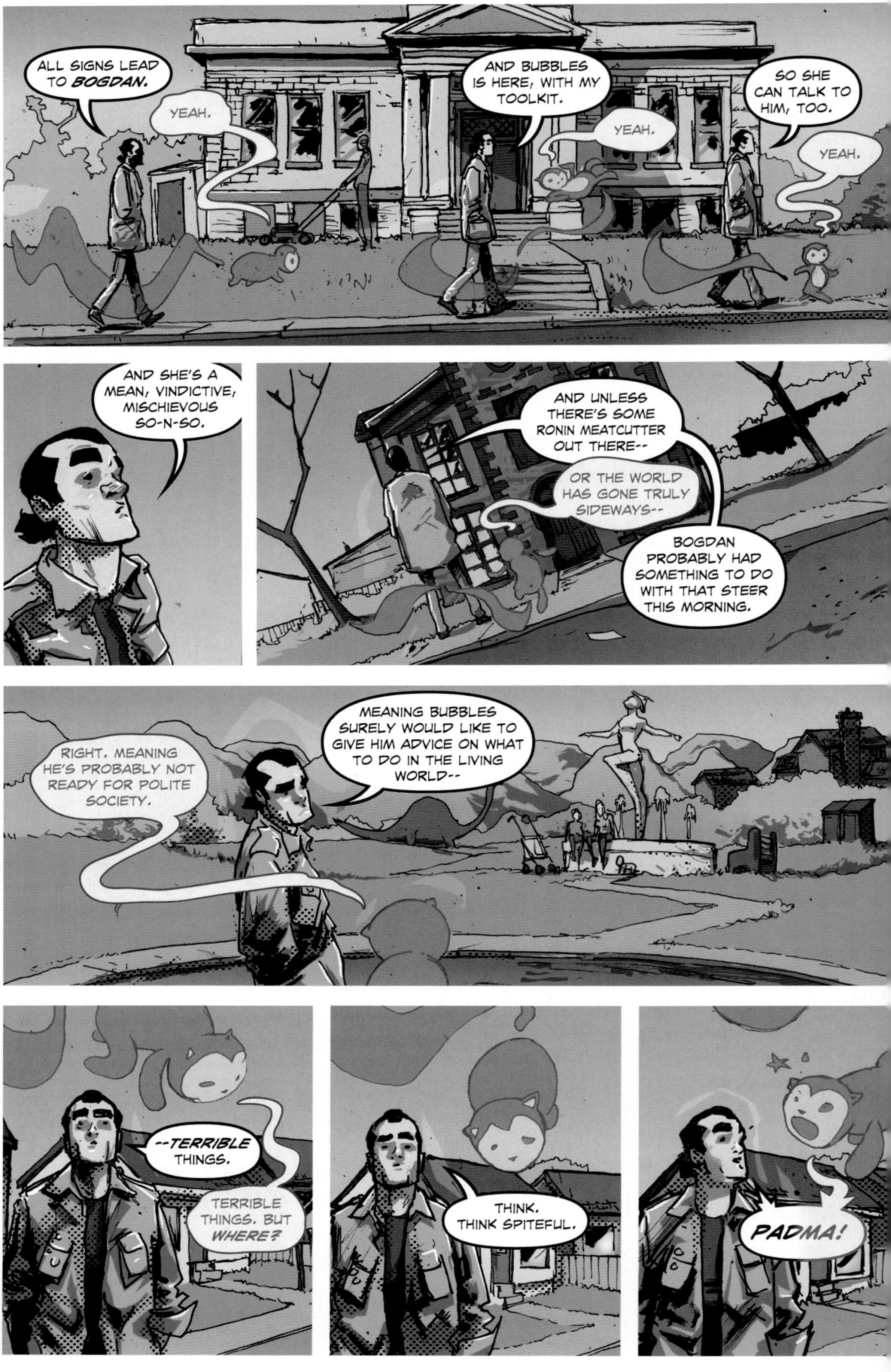
ALL SIGNS LEAD TO *BOGDAN.*
YEAH.
AND BUBBLES IS HERE, WITH MY TOOLKIT.
YEAH.
SO SHE CAN TALK TO HIM, TOO.
YEAH.
AND SHE'S A MEAN, VINDICTIVE, MISCHIEVOUS SO-N-SO.
AND UNLESS THERE'S SOME RONIN MEATCUTTER OUT THERE--
OR THE WORLD HAS GONE TRULY SIDEWAYS--
BOGDAN PROBABLY HAD SOMETHING TO DO WITH THAT STEER THIS MORNING.
RIGHT. MEANING HE'S PROBABLY NOT READY FOR POLITE SOCIETY.
MEANING BUBBLES SURELY WOULD LIKE TO GIVE HIM ADVICE ON WHAT TO DO IN THE LIVING WORLD--
--*TERRIBLE* THINGS.
TERRIBLE THINGS. BUT *WHERE?*
THINK. THINK SPITEFUL.
PADMA!

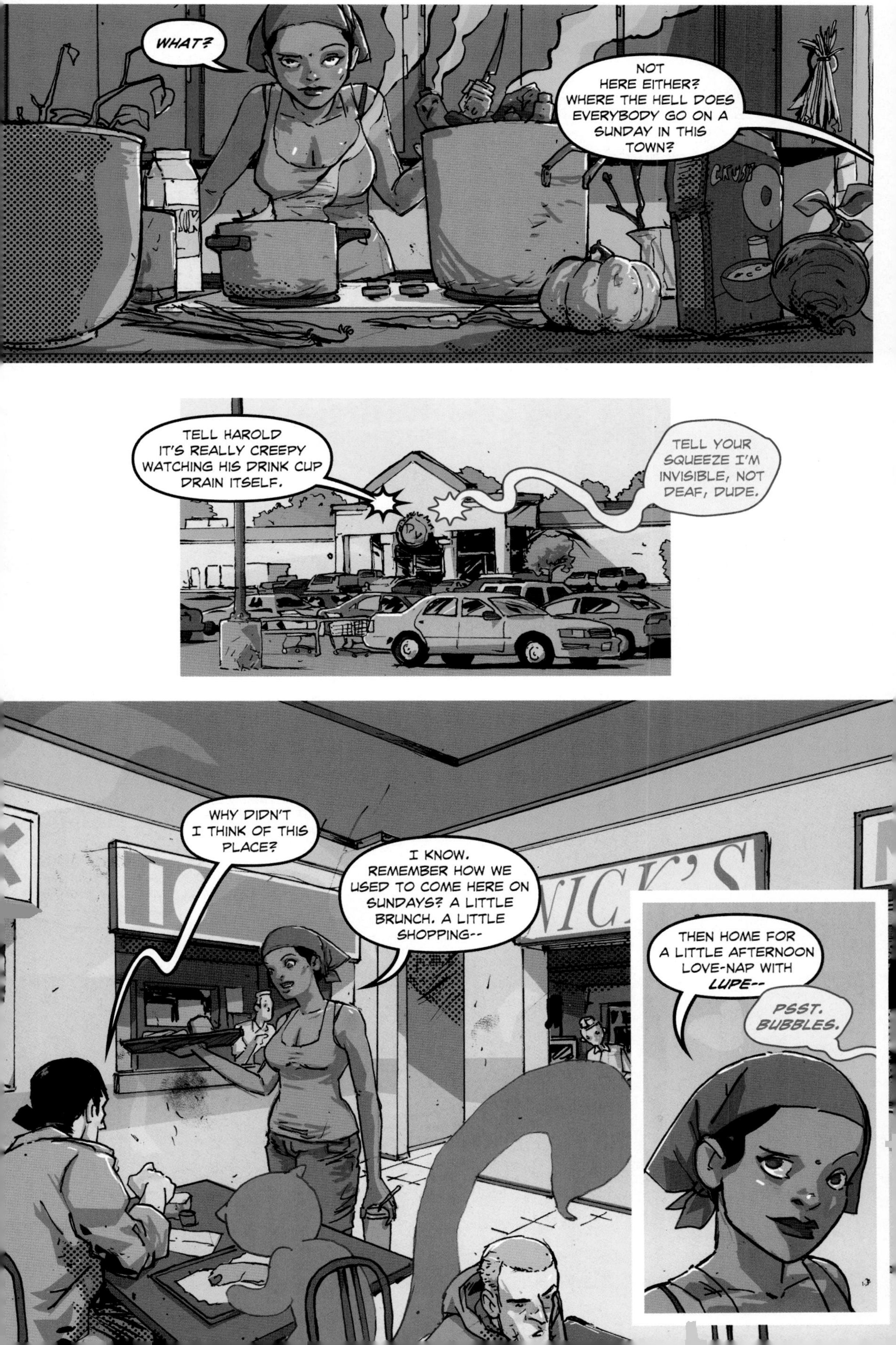
WHAT?
NOT HERE EITHER? WHERE THE HELL DOES EVERYBODY GO ON A SUNDAY IN THIS TOWN?
CRUSTY
TELL HAROLD IT'S REALLY CREEPY WATCHING HIS DRINK CUP DRAIN ITSELF.
TELL YOUR SQUEEZE I'M INVISIBLE, NOT DEAF, DUDE.
WHY DIDN'T I THINK OF THIS PLACE?
I KNOW. REMEMBER HOW WE USED TO COME HERE ON SUNDAYS? A LITTLE BRUNCH. A LITTLE SHOPPING--
NICK'S
THEN HOME FOR A LITTLE AFTERNOON LOVE-NAP WITH LUPE--
PSST. BUBBLES.

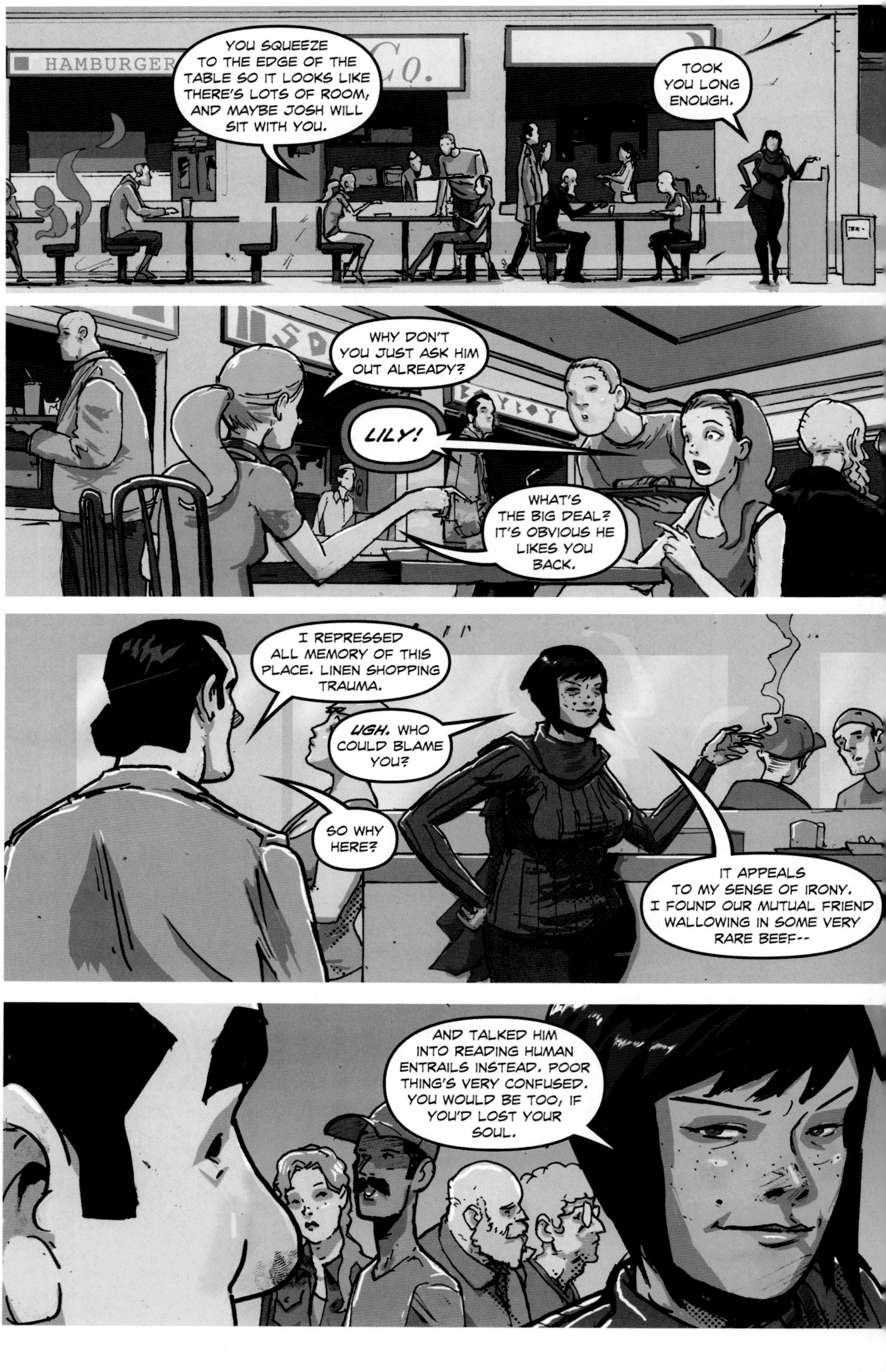
HAMBURGER
Co.
YOU SQUEEZE TO THE EDGE OF THE TABLE SO IT LOOKS LIKE THERE'S LOTS OF ROOM, AND MAYBE JOSH WILL SIT WITH YOU.
TOOK YOU LONG ENOUGH.
WHY DON'T YOU JUST ASK HIM OUT ALREADY?
LILY!
WHAT'S THE BIG DEAL? IT'S OBVIOUS HE LIKES YOU BACK.
I REPRESSED ALL MEMORY OF THIS PLACE. LINEN SHOPPING TRAUMA.
UGH. WHO COULD BLAME YOU?
SO WHY HERE?
IT APPEALS TO MY SENSE OF IRONY. I FOUND OUR MUTUAL FRIEND WALLOWING IN SOME VERY RARE BEEF--
AND TALKED HIM INTO READING HUMAN ENTRAILS INSTEAD. POOR THING'S VERY CONFUSED. YOU WOULD BE TOO, IF YOU'D LOST YOUR SOUL.

HE'S JUST GONE TO WAKE SOME FRIENDS. SHOULD BE ALONG SHORTLY.

I HAVE TO SAY, A CENTURY OF LIQUEFACTION HASN'T MADE HIM A STIMULATING CONVERSATIONALIST.

CURLY FRIES? THEY'RE SEASONED.

FINE, MOCK ME.

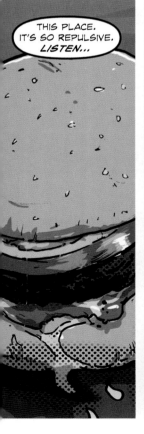

THIS PLACE. IT'S SO REPULSIVE. *LISTEN...*

THE REVOLTING SPLURTS OF *SPIT* AND *SNOT*--

THE MINDLESS MASTICATION. THE SLURPING, HORKING... IDIOT ANIMAL *FLESHINESS* OF IT ALL.

THERE'S NOTHING HERE FOR HIM TO FIND.

IS THAT REALLY ALL YOU SEE?

THAT'S ALL THERE IS. AND BELIEVE ME, I'VE LOOKED FOR A LONG, LONG TIME.

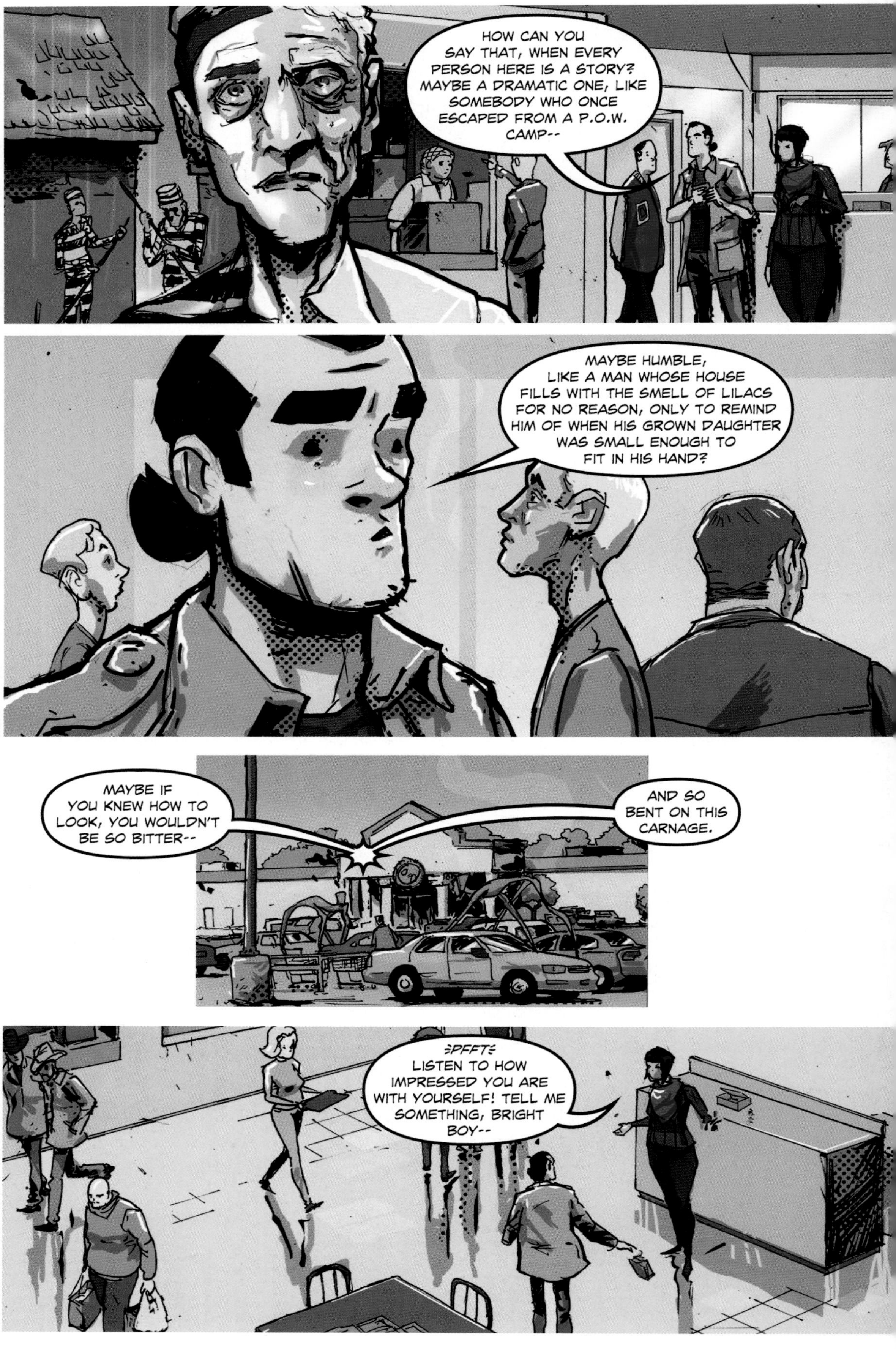
HOW CAN YOU SAY THAT, WHEN EVERY PERSON HERE IS A STORY? MAYBE A DRAMATIC ONE, LIKE SOMEBODY WHO ONCE ESCAPED FROM A P.O.W. CAMP--
MAYBE HUMBLE, LIKE A MAN WHOSE HOUSE FILLS WITH THE SMELL OF LILACS FOR NO REASON, ONLY TO REMIND HIM OF WHEN HIS GROWN DAUGHTER WAS SMALL ENOUGH TO FIT IN HIS HAND?
MAYBE IF YOU KNEW HOW TO LOOK, YOU WOULDN'T BE SO BITTER--
AND SO BENT ON THIS CARNAGE.
PFFT
LISTEN TO HOW IMPRESSED YOU ARE WITH YOURSELF! TELL ME SOMETHING, BRIGHT BOY--

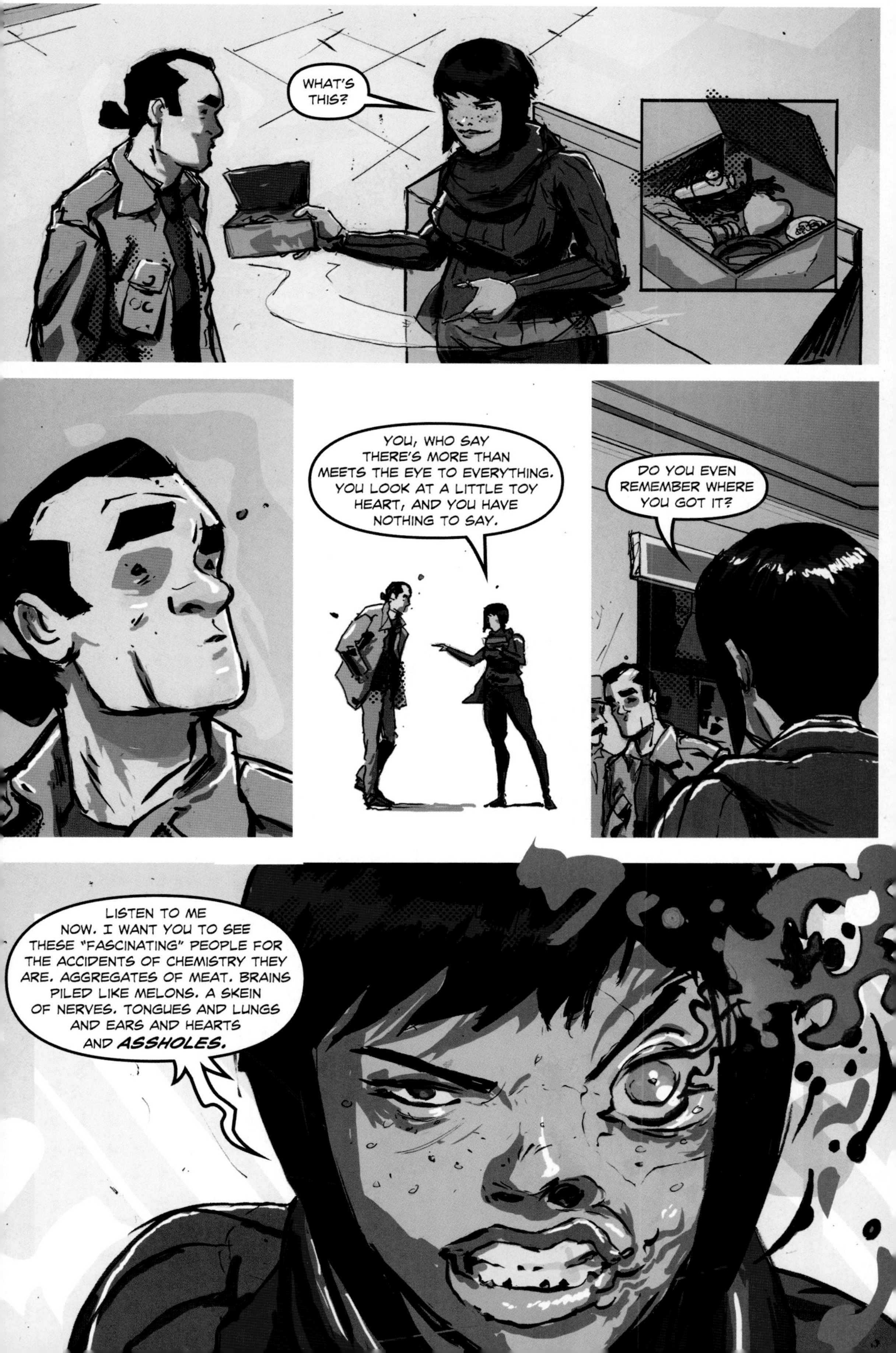
WHAT'S THIS?
YOU, WHO SAY THERE'S MORE THAN MEETS THE EYE TO EVERYTHING. YOU LOOK AT A LITTLE TOY HEART, AND YOU HAVE NOTHING TO SAY.
DO YOU EVEN REMEMBER WHERE YOU GOT IT?
LISTEN TO ME NOW. I WANT YOU TO SEE THESE "FASCINATING" PEOPLE FOR THE ACCIDENTS OF CHEMISTRY THEY ARE. AGGREGATES OF MEAT. BRAINS PILED LIKE MELONS. A SKEIN OF NERVES. TONGUES AND LUNGS AND EARS AND HEARTS AND ASSHOLES.

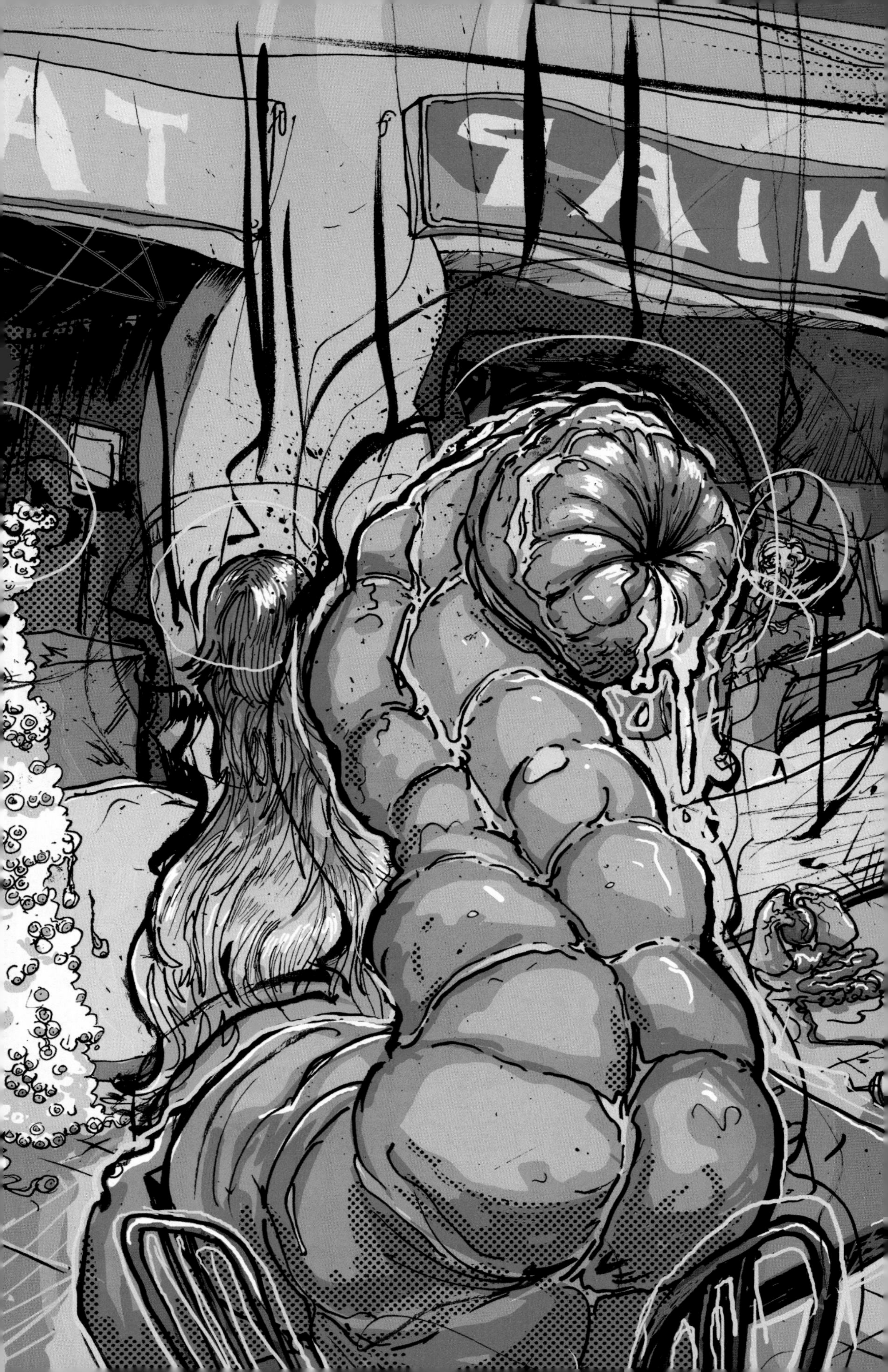

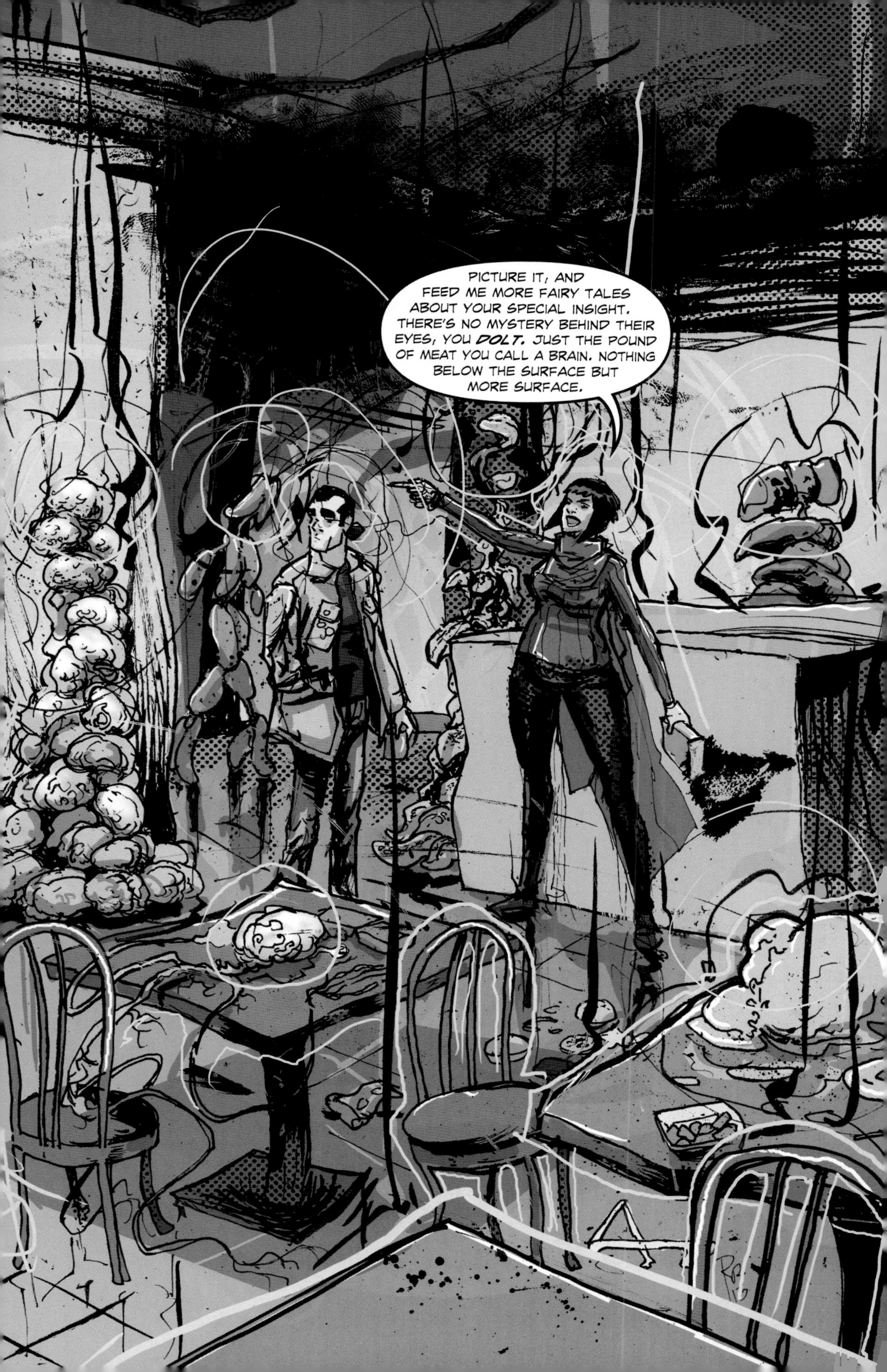
PICTURE IT, AND FEED ME MORE FAIRY TALES ABOUT YOUR SPECIAL INSIGHT. THERE'S NO MYSTERY BEHIND THEIR EYES, YOU *DOLT.* JUST THE POUND OF MEAT YOU CALL A BRAIN. NOTHING BELOW THE SURFACE BUT MORE SURFACE.

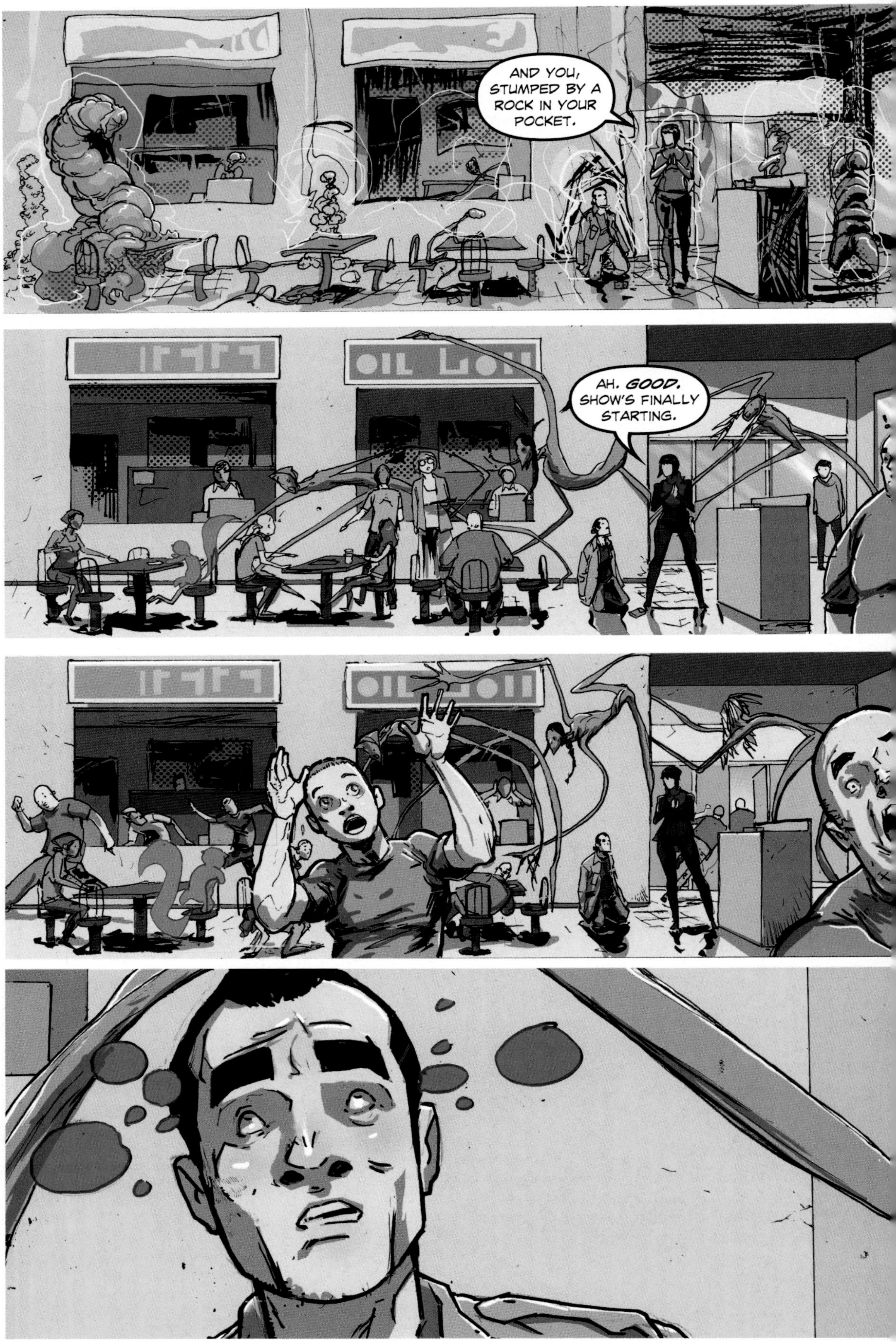
AND YOU, STUMPED BY A ROCK IN YOUR POCKET.
AH. GOOD. SHOW'S FINALLY STARTING.

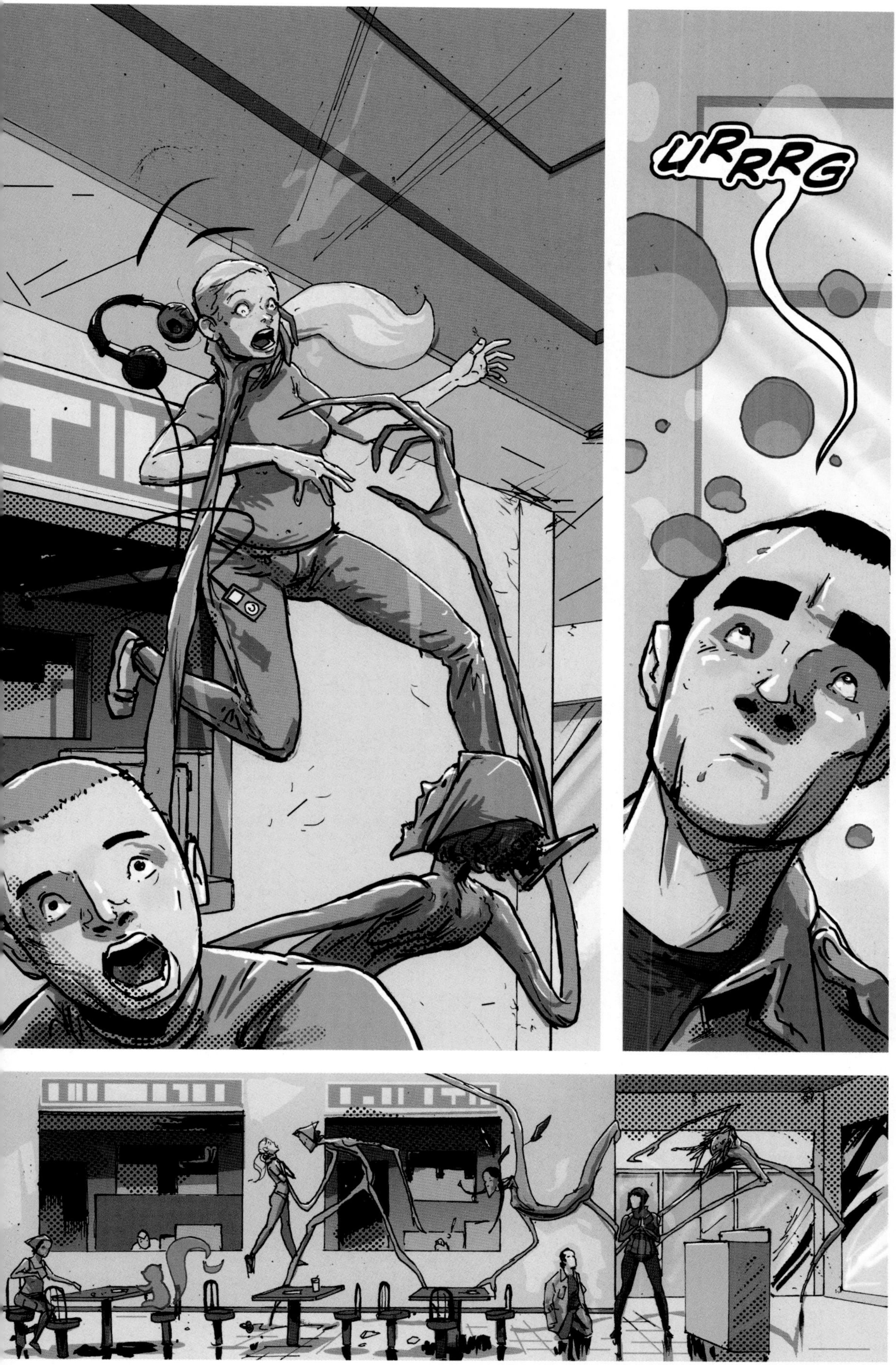
URRRG

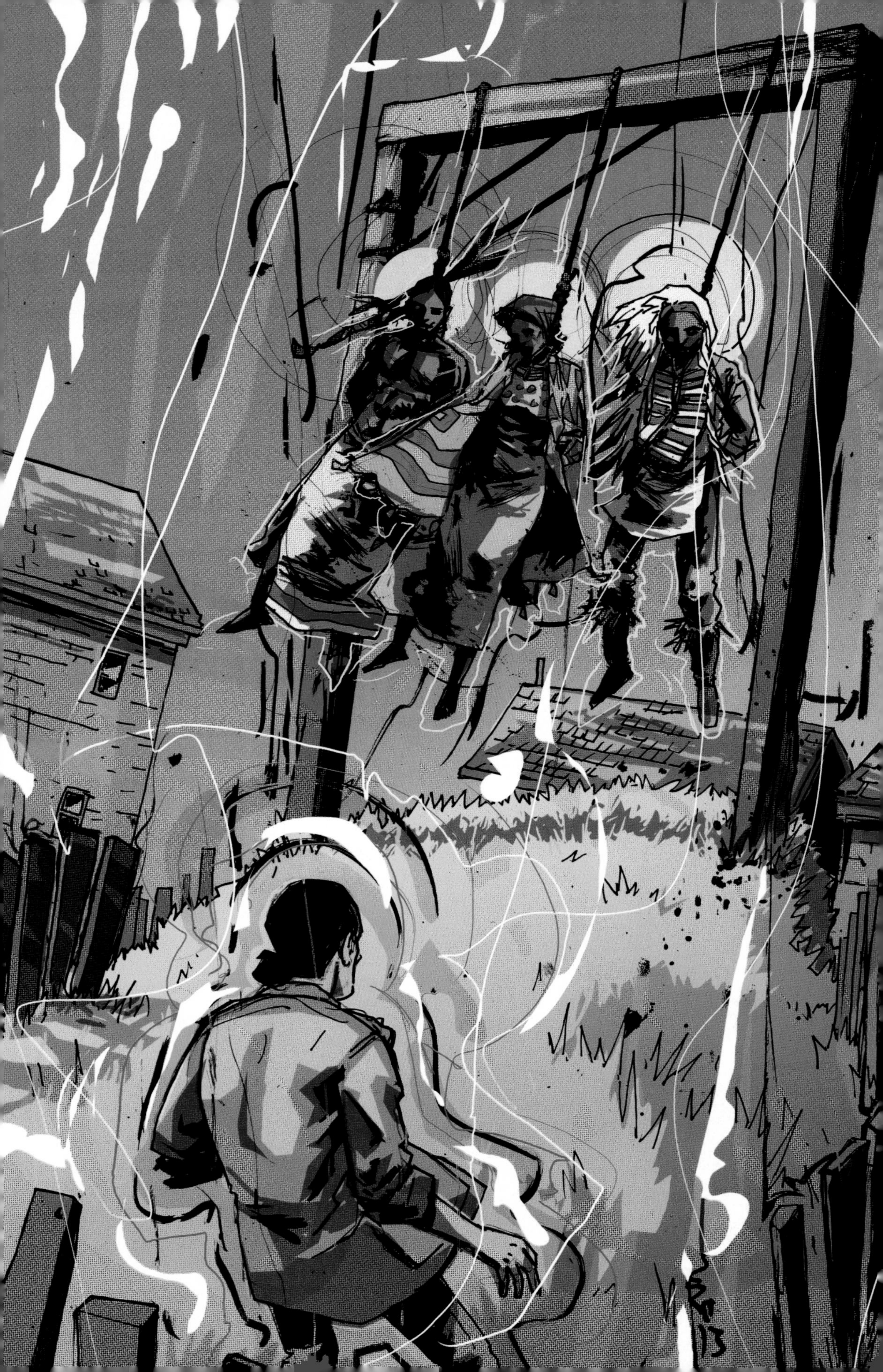

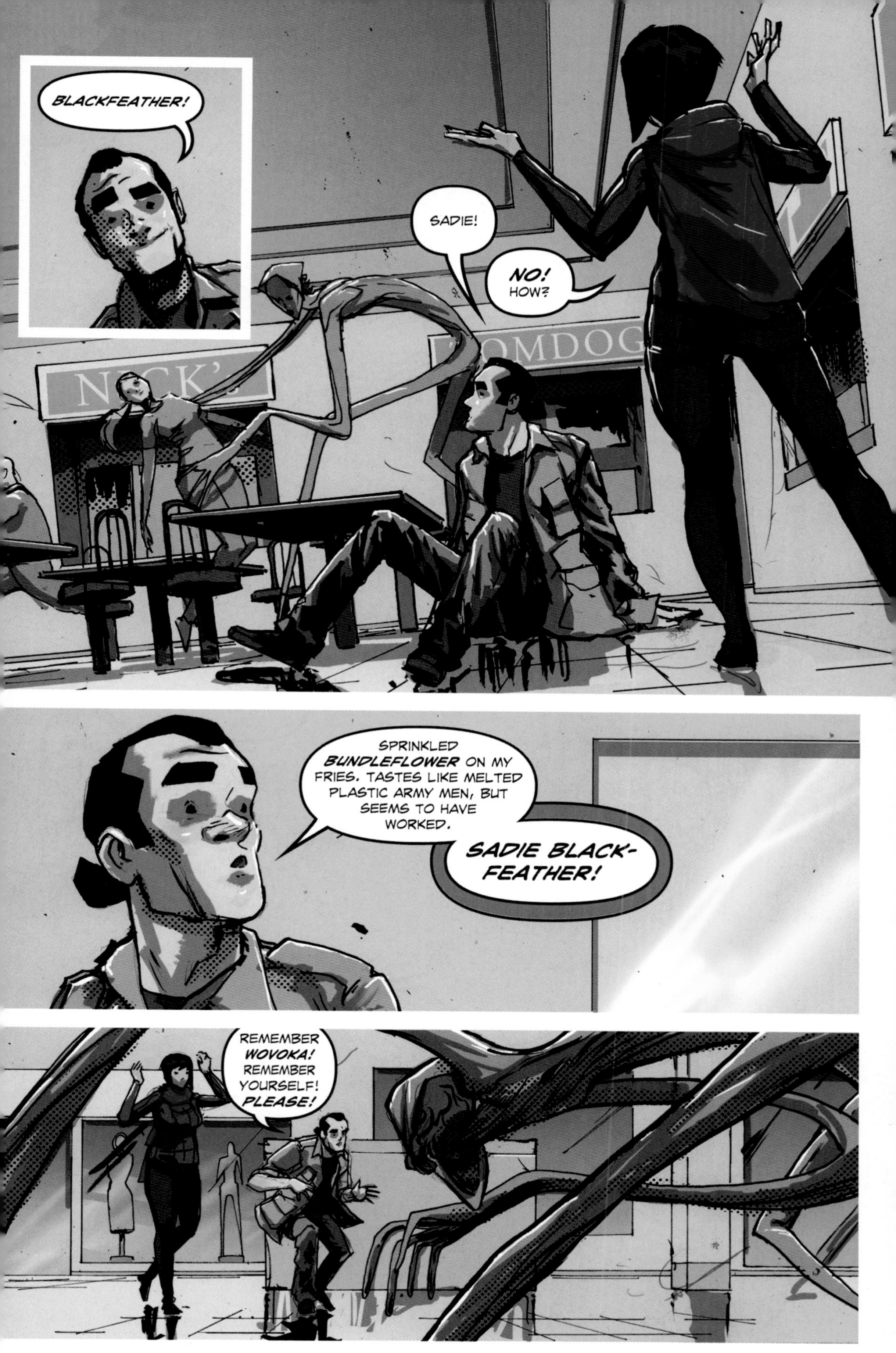
BLACKFEATHER!
SADIE!
NO! HOW?
SPRINKLED BUNDLEFLOWER ON MY FRIES. TASTES LIKE MELTED PLASTIC ARMY MEN, BUT SEEMS TO HAVE WORKED.
SADIE BLACK-FEATHER!
REMEMBER WOVOKA! REMEMBER YOURSELF! PLEASE!

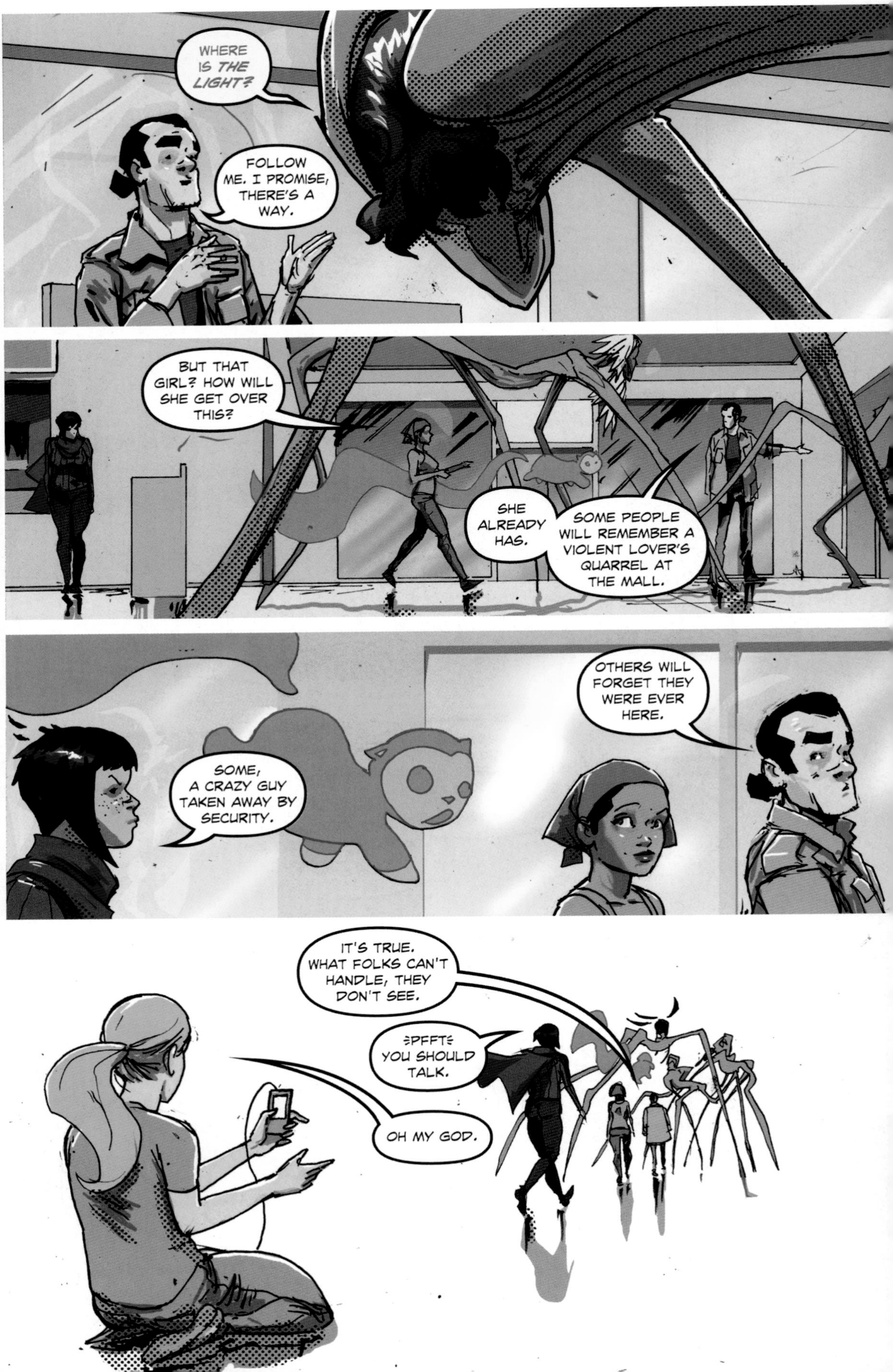
WHERE IS THE LIGHT?
FOLLOW ME. I PROMISE, THERE'S A WAY.
BUT THAT GIRL? HOW WILL SHE GET OVER THIS?
SHE ALREADY HAS.
SOME PEOPLE WILL REMEMBER A VIOLENT LOVER'S QUARREL AT THE MALL.
OTHERS WILL FORGET THEY WERE EVER HERE.
SOME, A CRAZY GUY TAKEN AWAY BY SECURITY.
IT'S TRUE. WHAT FOLKS CAN'T HANDLE, THEY DON'T SEE.
=PFFT= YOU SHOULD TALK.
OH MY GOD.

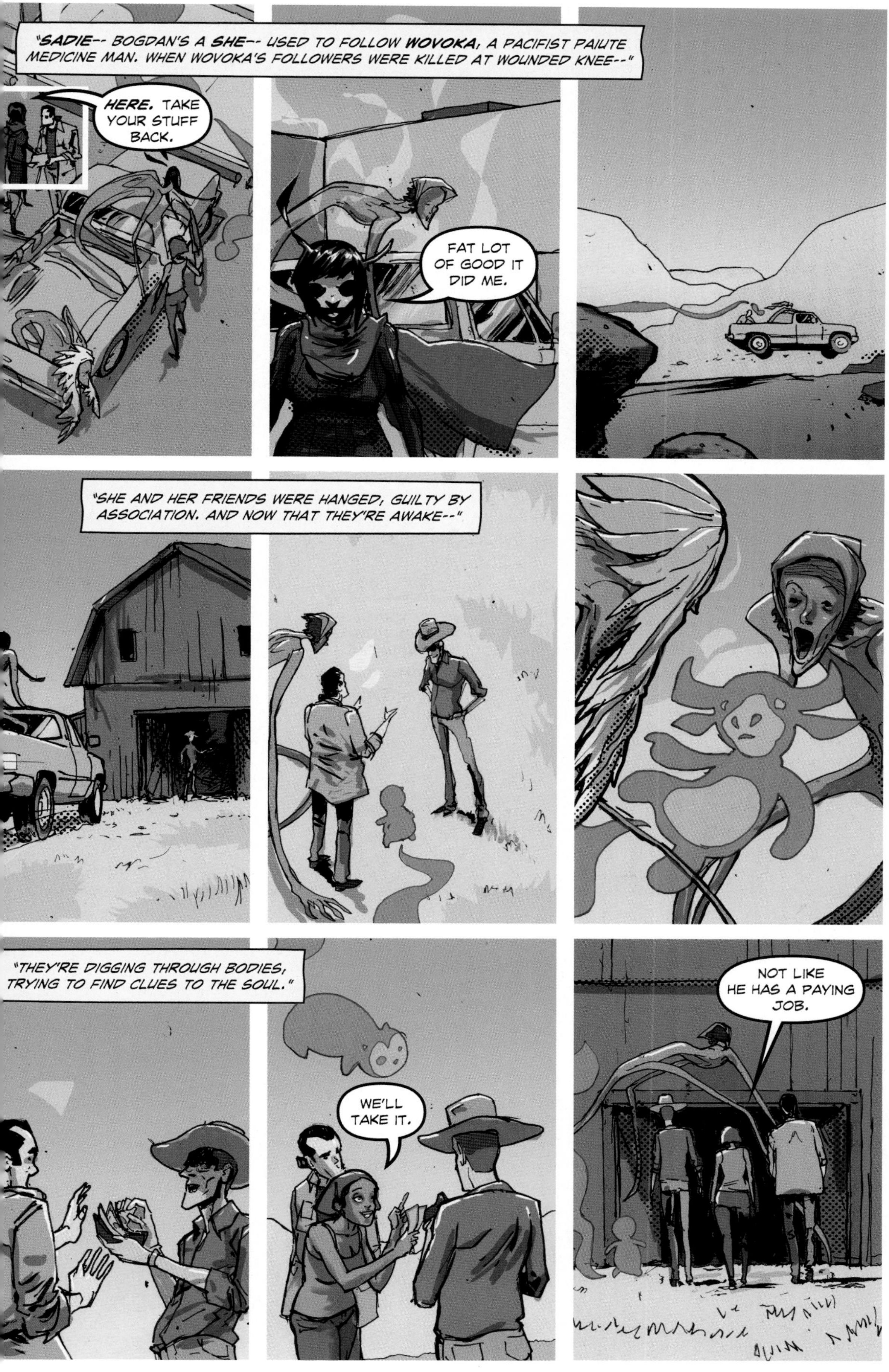
"SADIE-- BOGDAN'S A SHE-- USED TO FOLLOW WOVOKA, A PACIFIST PAIUTE MEDICINE MAN. WHEN WOVOKA'S FOLLOWERS WERE KILLED AT WOUNDED KNEE--"
HERE. TAKE YOUR STUFF BACK.
FAT LOT OF GOOD IT DID ME.
"SHE AND HER FRIENDS WERE HANGED, GUILTY BY ASSOCIATION. AND NOW THAT THEY'RE AWAKE--"
"THEY'RE DIGGING THROUGH BODIES, TRYING TO FIND CLUES TO THE SOUL."
WE'LL TAKE IT.
NOT LIKE HE HAS A PAYING JOB.

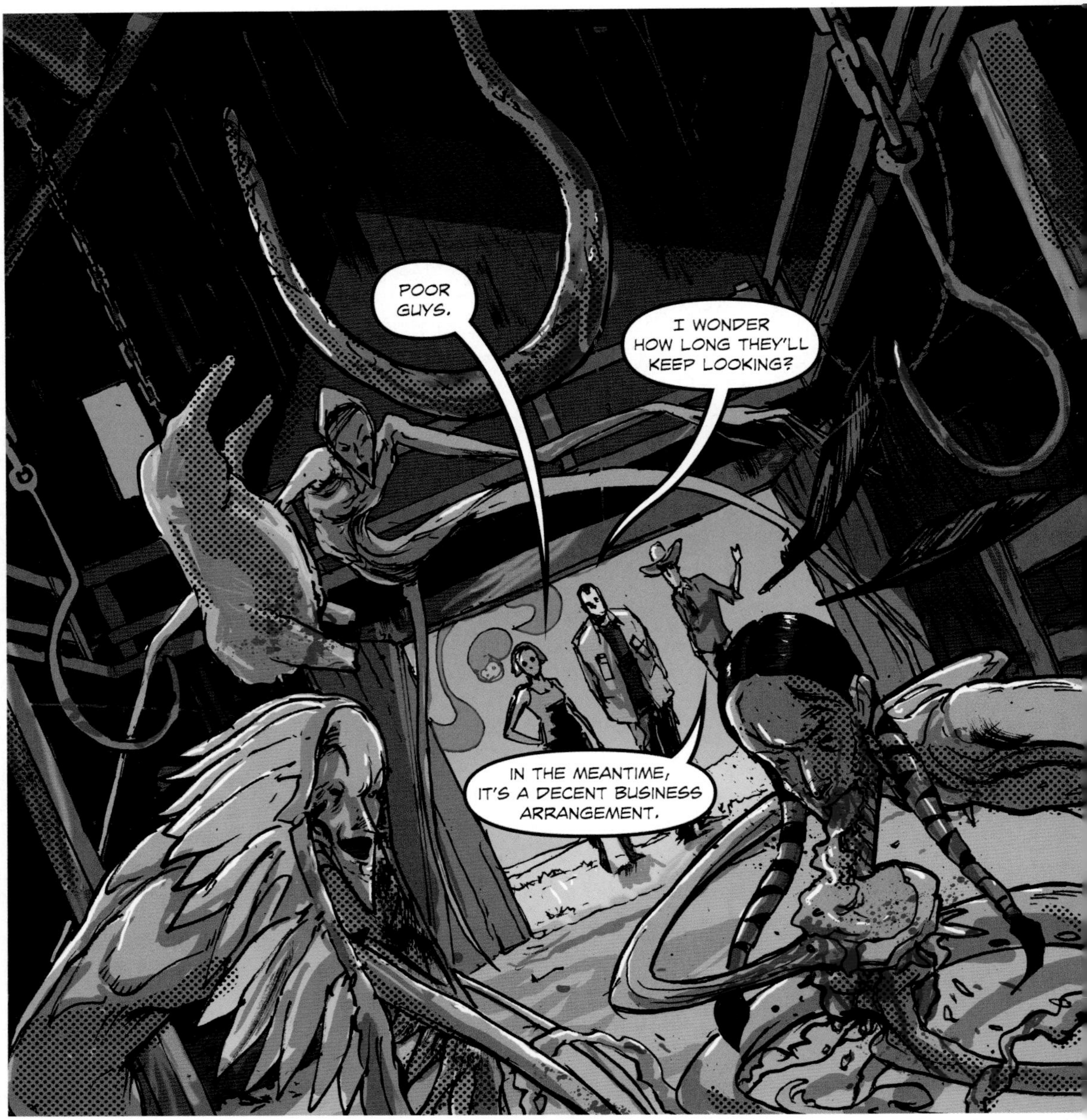
POOR GUYS.
I WONDER HOW LONG THEY'LL KEEP LOOKING?
IN THE MEANTIME, IT'S A DECENT BUSINESS ARRANGEMENT.

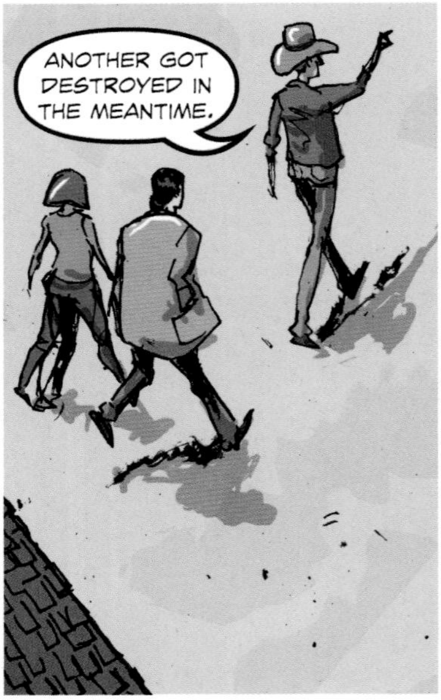
ANOTHER GOT DESTROYED IN THE MEANTIME.

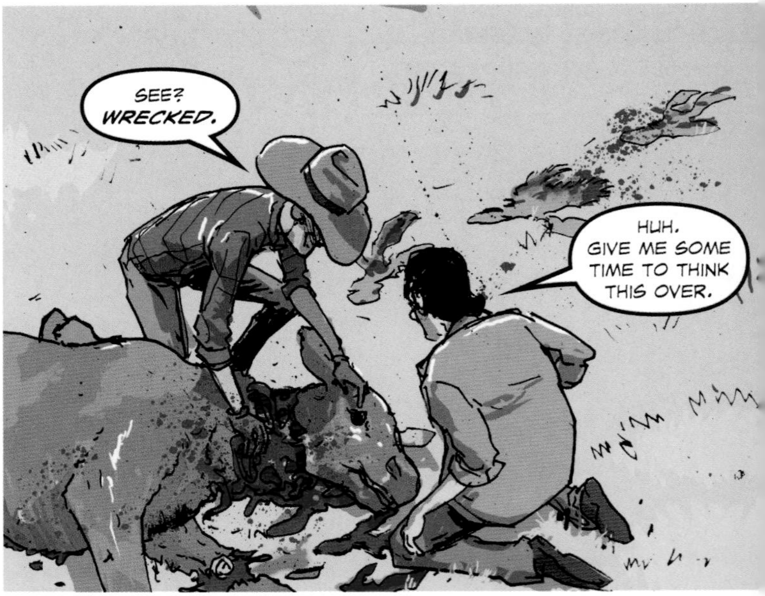
SEE? *WRECKED.*
HUH. GIVE ME SOME TIME TO THINK THIS OVER.

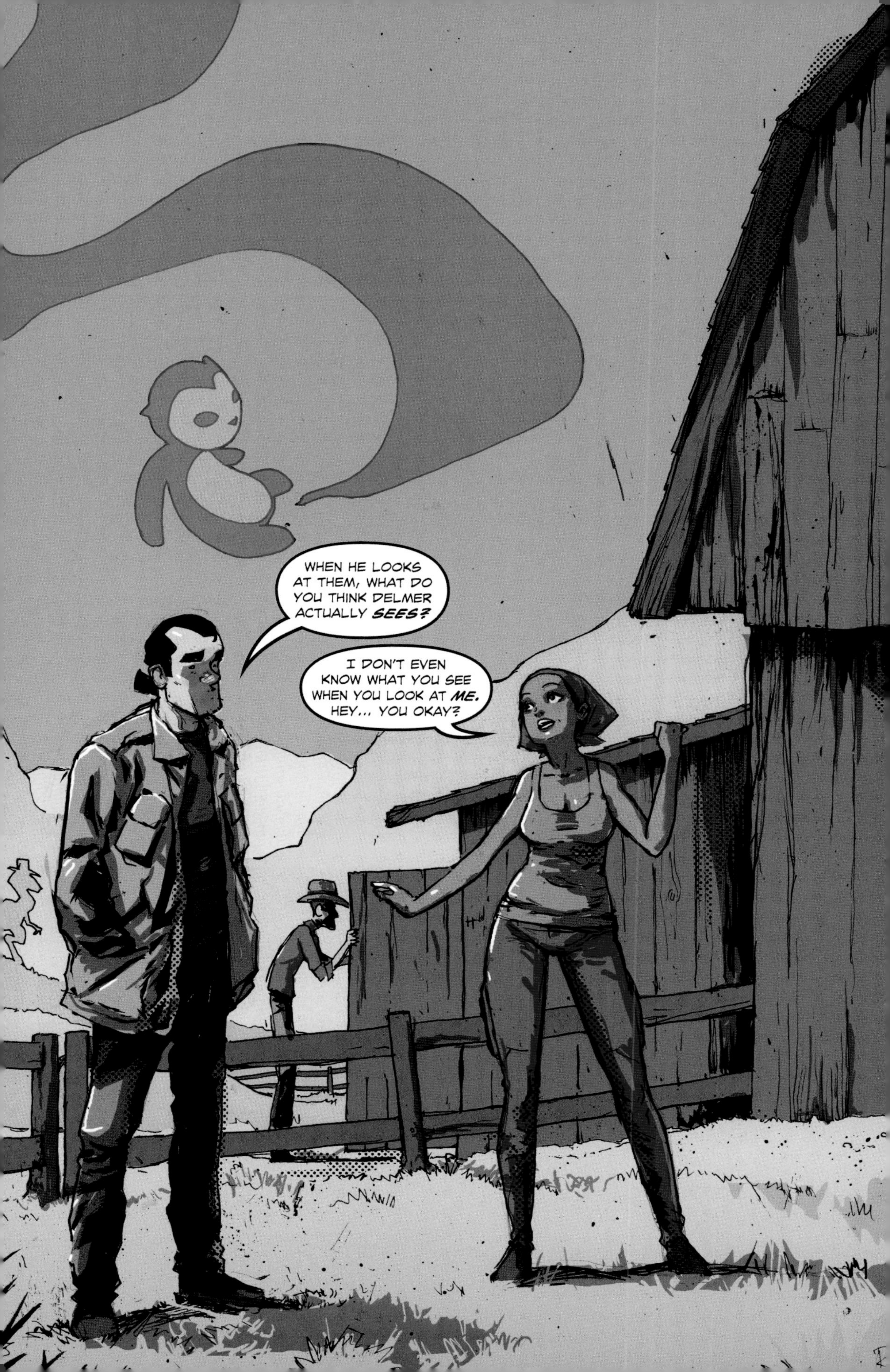
WHEN HE LOOKS AT THEM, WHAT DO YOU THINK DELMER ACTUALLY SEES?
I DON'T EVEN KNOW WHAT YOU SEE WHEN YOU LOOK AT ME. HEY... YOU OKAY?

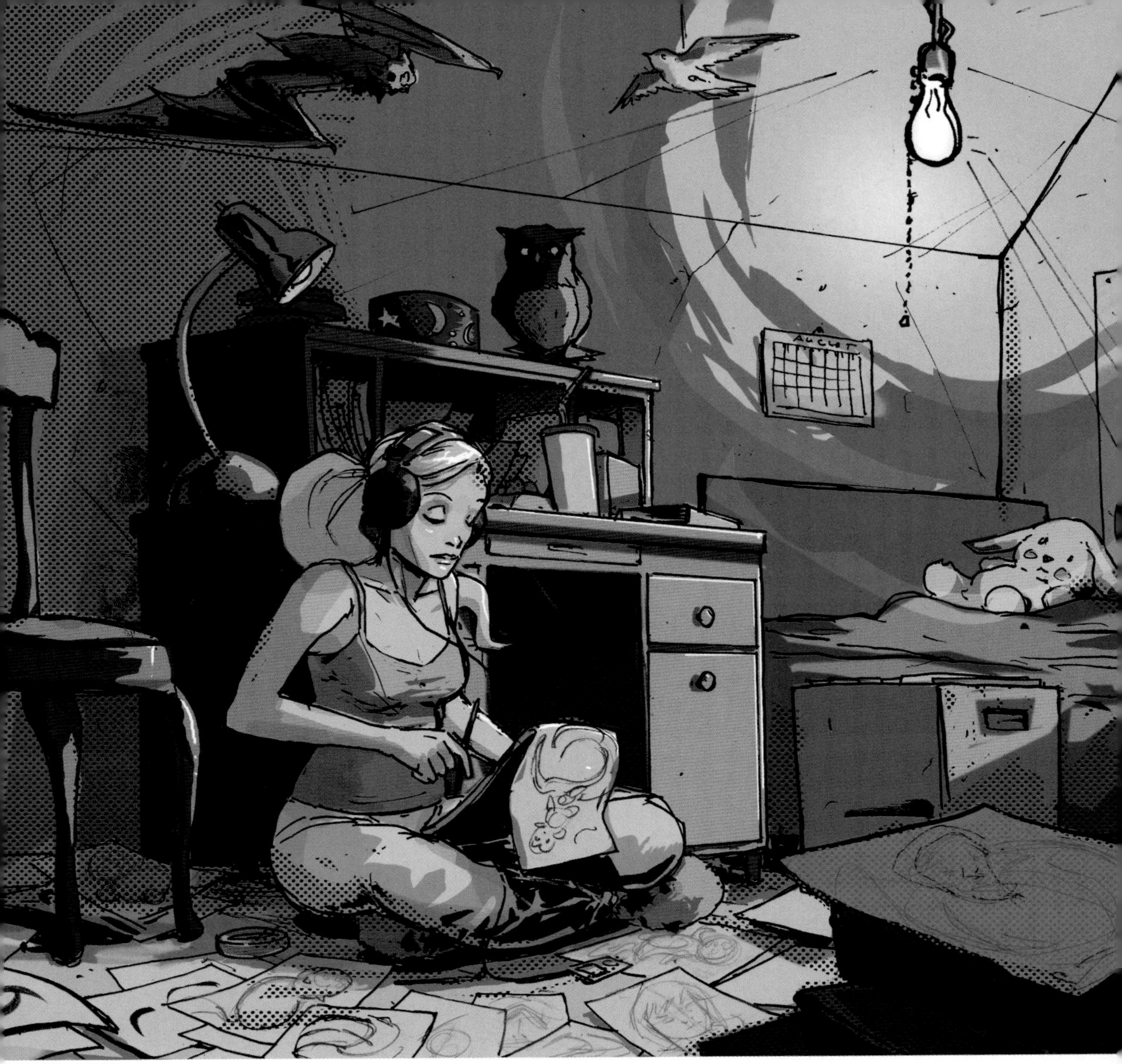
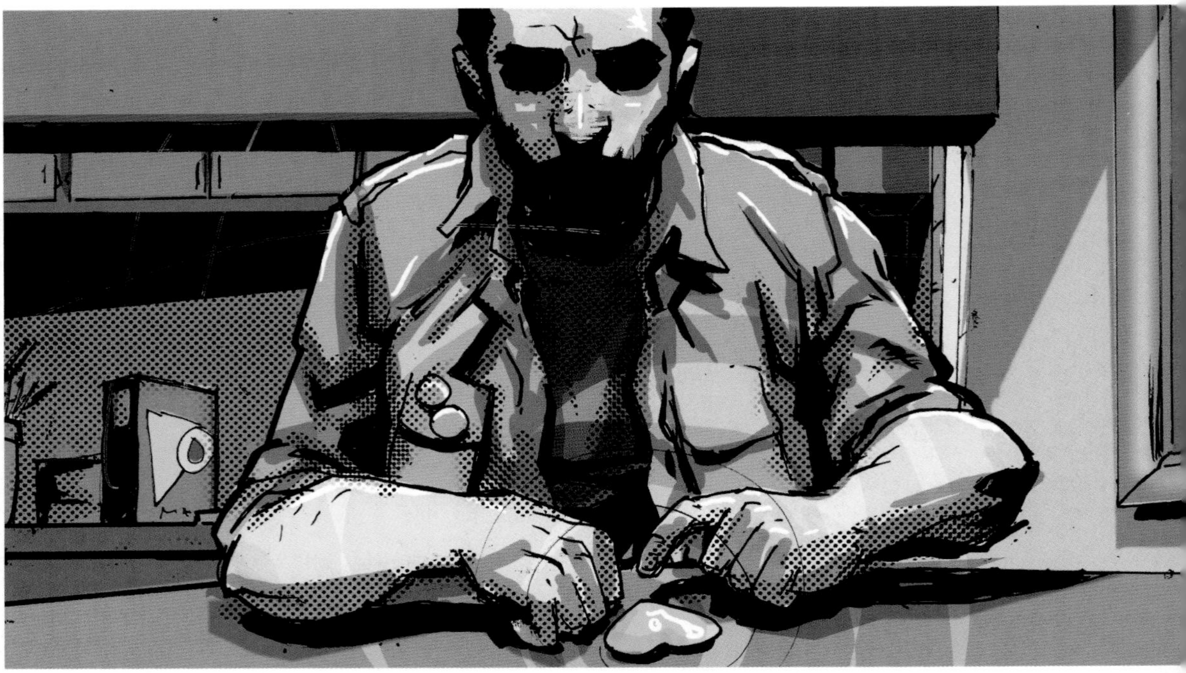

THREE

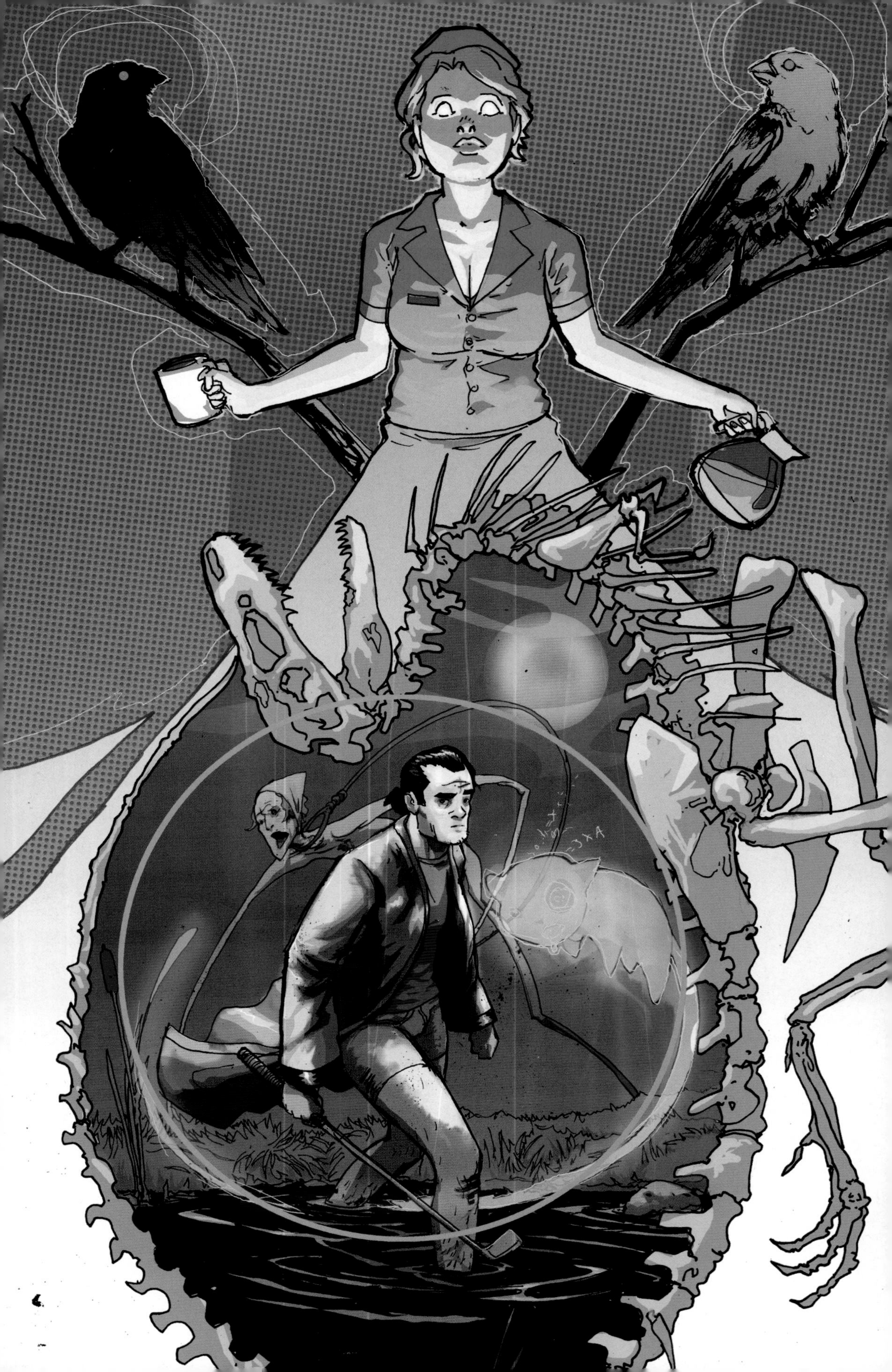

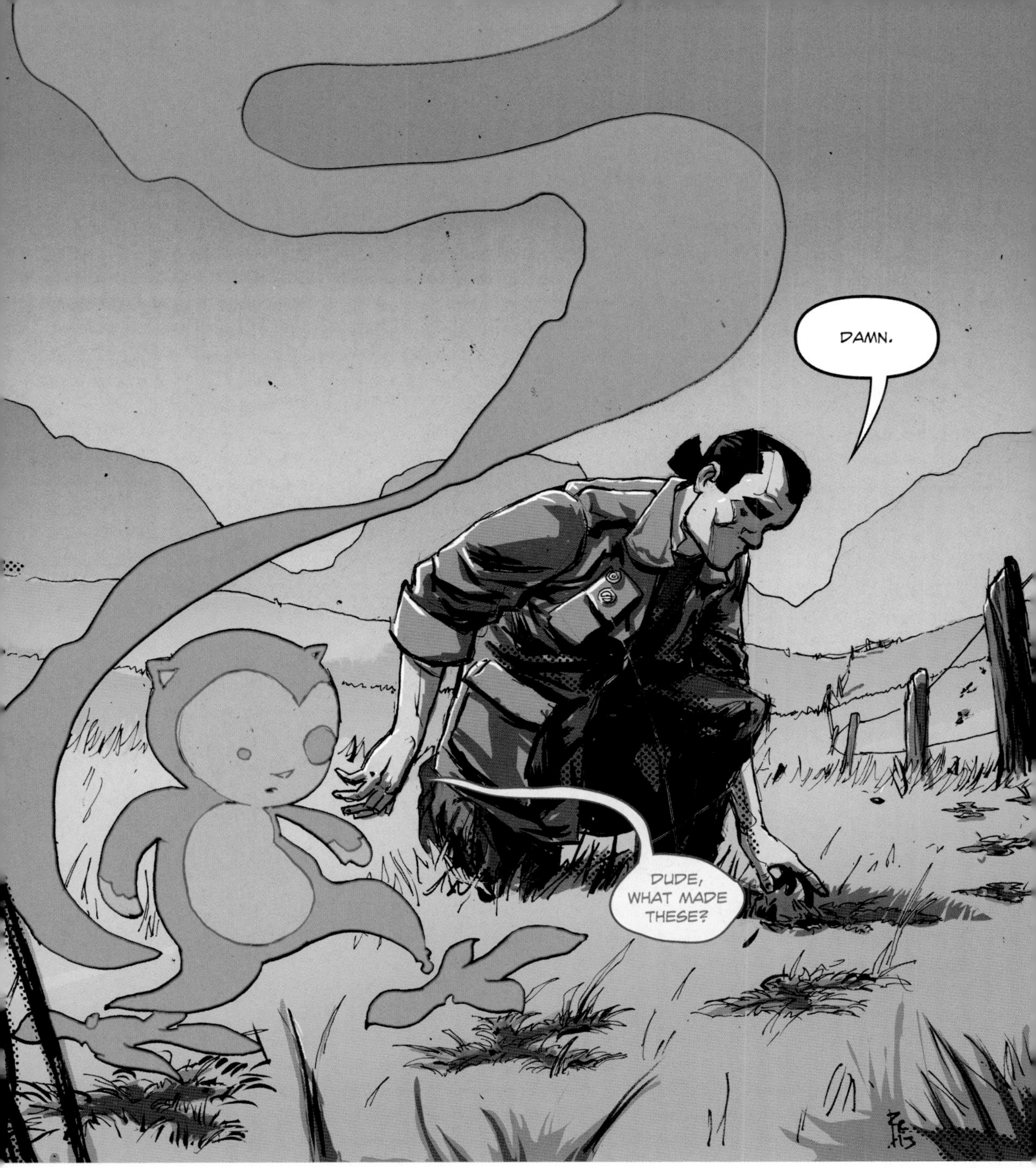
DAMN.
DUDE, WHAT MADE THESE?

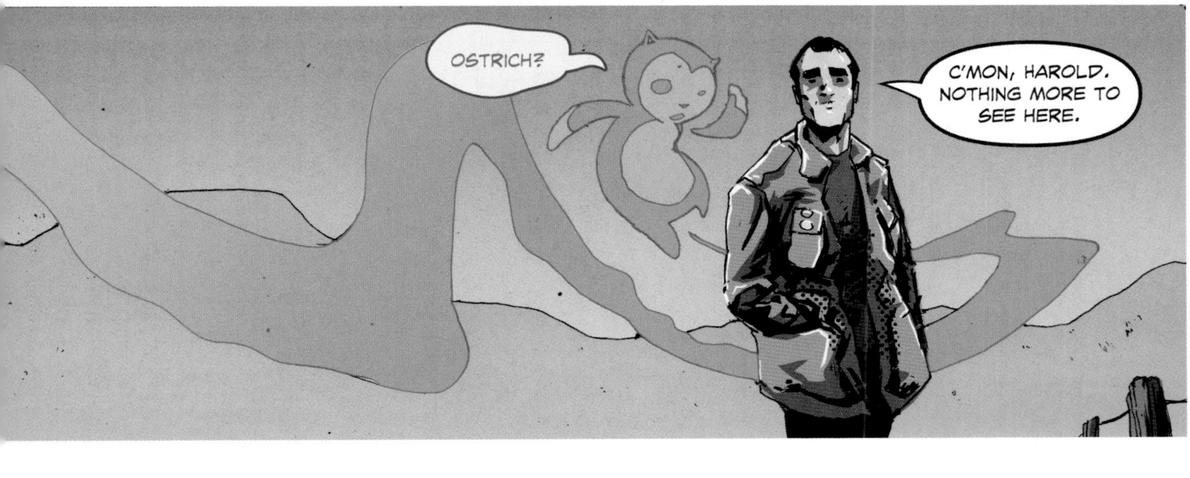
OSTRICH?
C'MON, HAROLD. NOTHING MORE TO SEE HERE.

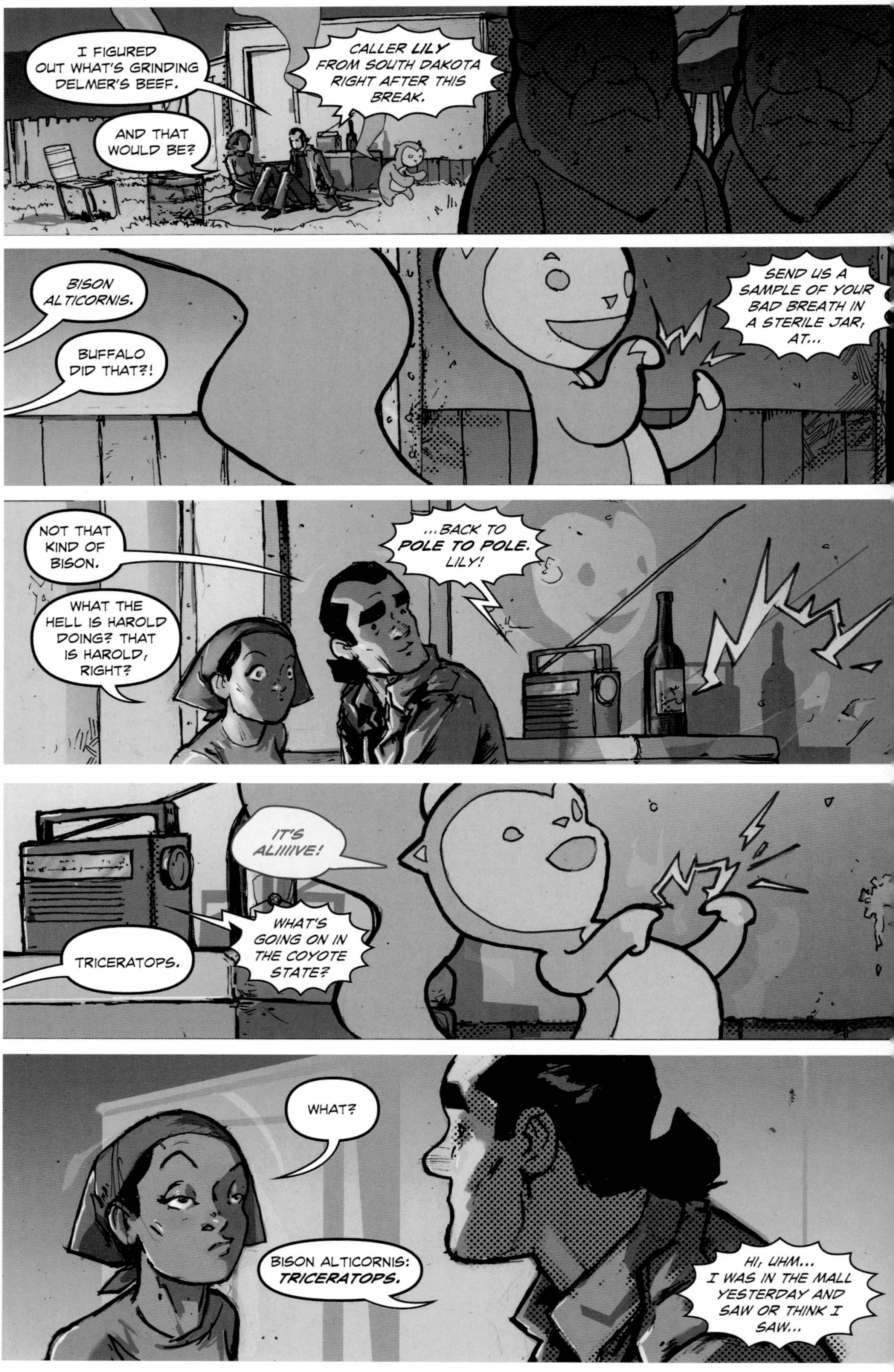
I FIGURED OUT WHAT'S GRINDING DELMER'S BEEF.
CALLER LILY FROM SOUTH DAKOTA RIGHT AFTER THIS BREAK.
AND THAT WOULD BE?
BISON ALTICORNIS.
BUFFALO DID THAT?!
SEND US A SAMPLE OF YOUR BAD BREATH IN A STERILE JAR, AT...
NOT THAT KIND OF BISON.
...BACK TO POLE TO POLE. LILY!
WHAT THE HELL IS HAROLD DOING? THAT IS HAROLD, RIGHT?
IT'S ALIIIIVE!
TRICERATOPS.
WHAT'S GOING ON IN THE COYOTE STATE?
WHAT?
BISON ALTICORNIS: TRICERATOPS.
HI, UHM... I WAS IN THE MALL YESTERDAY AND SAW OR THINK I SAW...

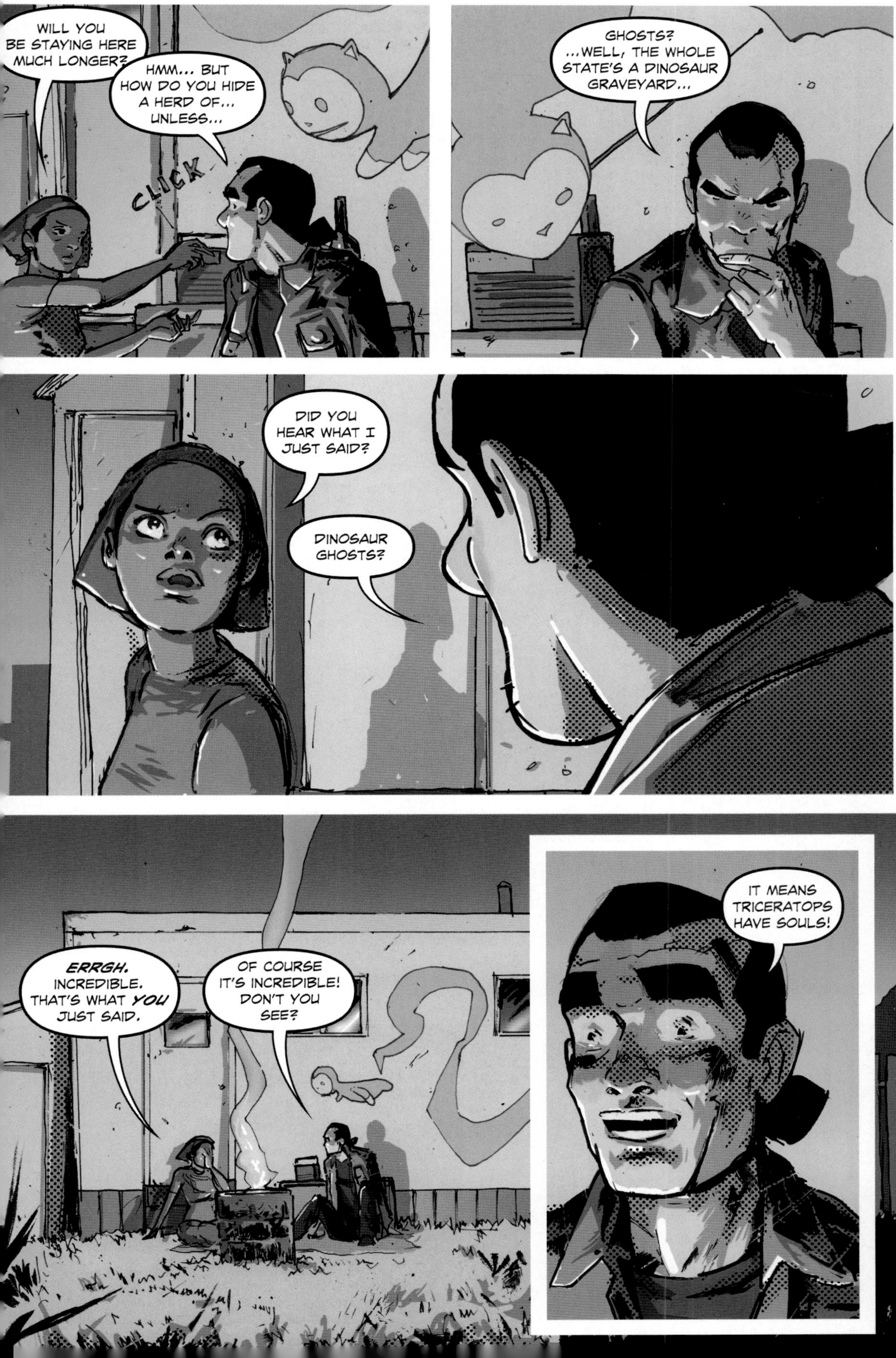
WILL YOU BE STAYING HERE MUCH LONGER?
HMM... BUT HOW DO YOU HIDE A HERD OF... UNLESS...
CLICK
GHOSTS? ...WELL, THE WHOLE STATE'S A DINOSAUR GRAVEYARD...
DID YOU HEAR WHAT I JUST SAID?
DINOSAUR GHOSTS?
ERRGH. INCREDIBLE. THAT'S WHAT YOU JUST SAID.
OF COURSE IT'S INCREDIBLE! DON'T YOU SEE?
IT MEANS TRICERATOPS HAVE SOULS!

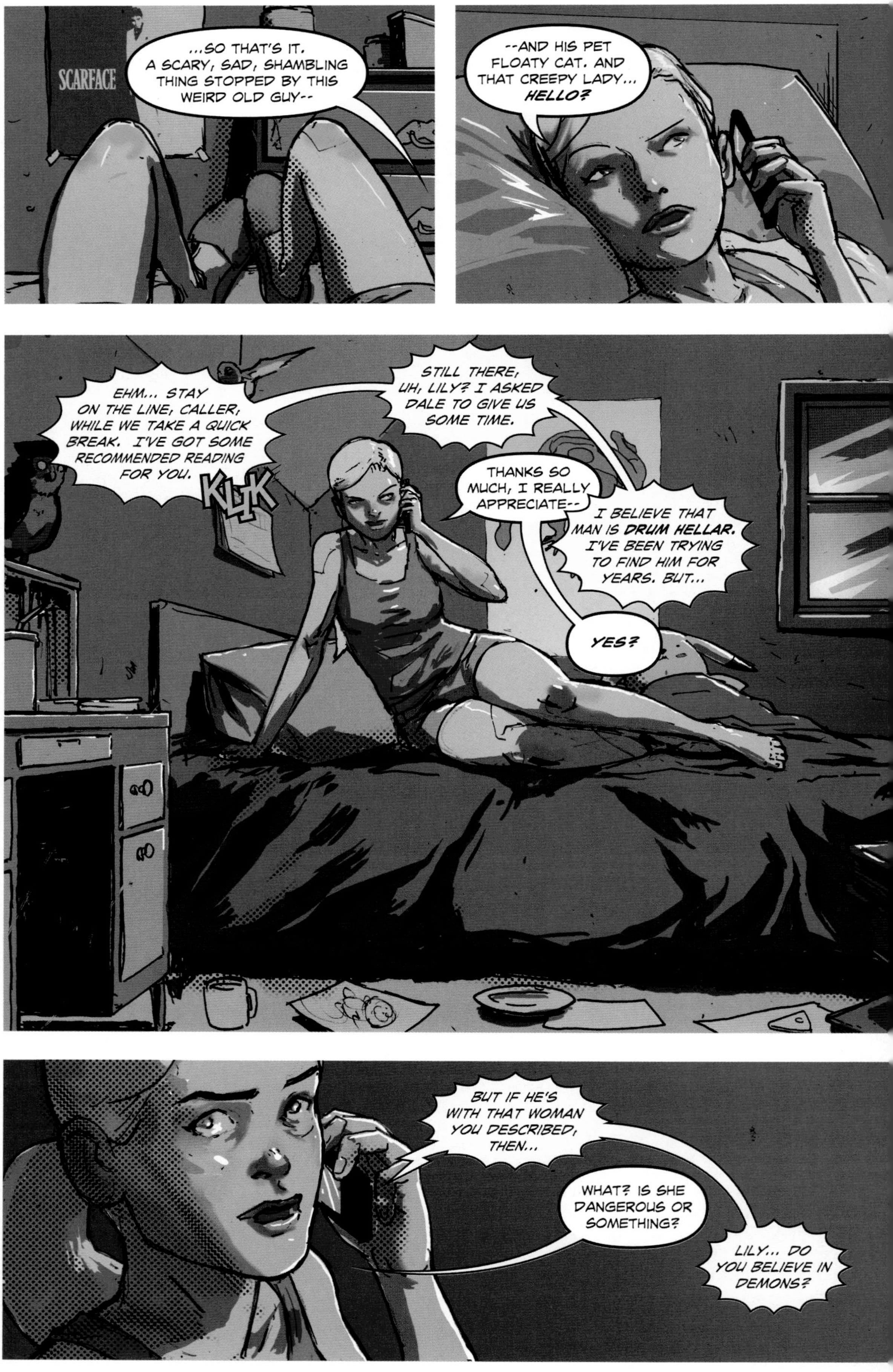

...SO THAT'S IT. A SCARY, SAD, SHAMBLING THING STOPPED BY THIS WEIRD OLD GUY--
SCARFACE
--AND HIS PET FLOATY CAT. AND THAT CREEPY LADY... HELLO?
EHM... STAY ON THE LINE, CALLER, WHILE WE TAKE A QUICK BREAK. I'VE GOT SOME RECOMMENDED READING FOR YOU.
KLIK
STILL THERE, UH, LILY? I ASKED DALE TO GIVE US SOME TIME.
THANKS SO MUCH, I REALLY APPRECIATE--
I BELIEVE THAT MAN IS DRUM HELLAR. I'VE BEEN TRYING TO FIND HIM FOR YEARS. BUT...
YES?
BUT IF HE'S WITH THAT WOMAN YOU DESCRIBED, THEN...
WHAT? IS SHE DANGEROUS OR SOMETHING?
LILY... DO YOU BELIEVE IN DEMONS?

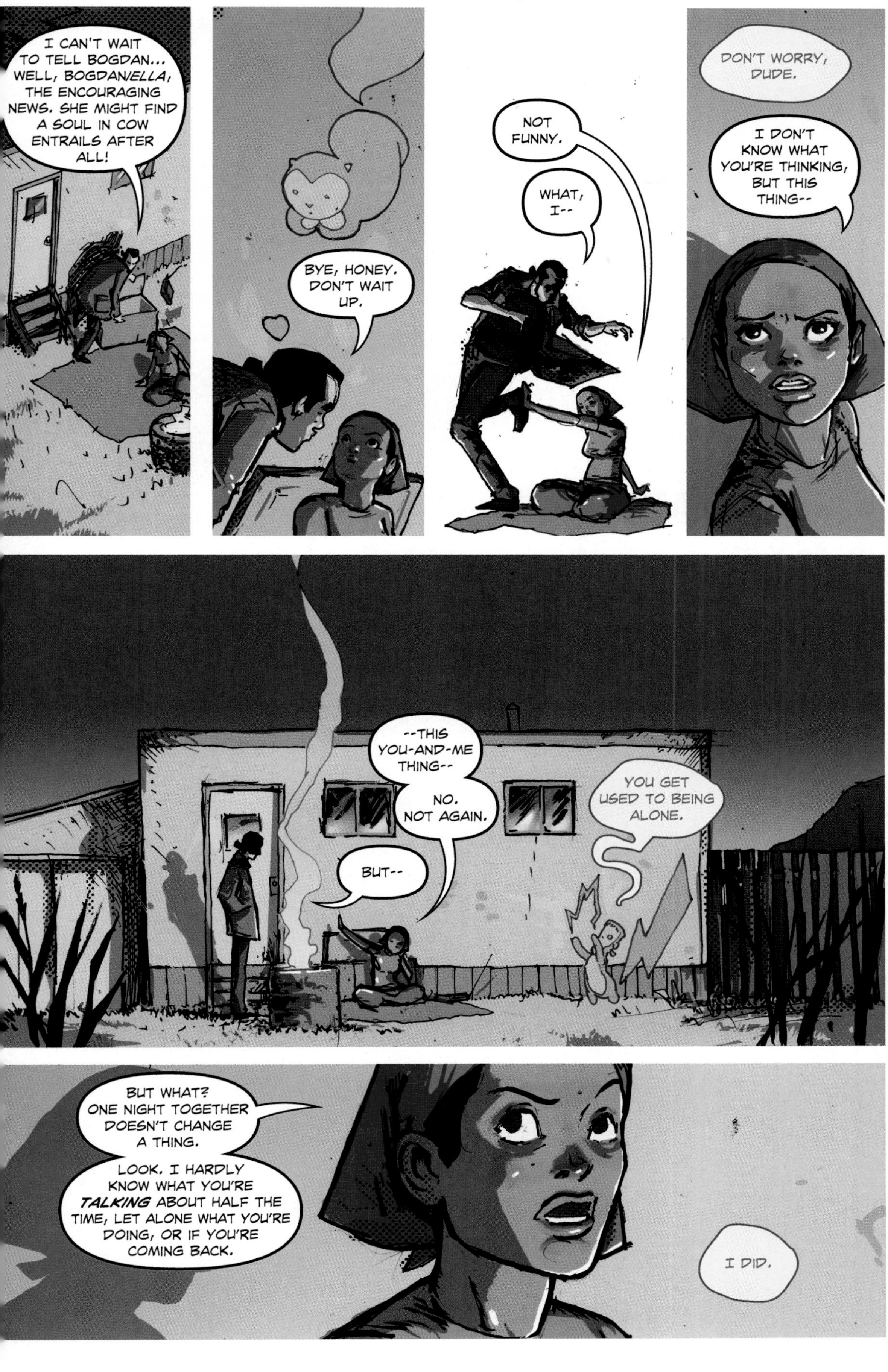
I CAN'T WAIT TO TELL BOGDAN... WELL, BOGDAN/ELLA, THE ENCOURAGING NEWS. SHE MIGHT FIND A SOUL IN COW ENTRAILS AFTER ALL!
BYE, HONEY. DON'T WAIT UP.
NOT FUNNY.
WHAT, I--
DON'T WORRY, DUDE.
I DON'T KNOW WHAT YOU'RE THINKING, BUT THIS THING--
--THIS YOU-AND-ME THING--
NO. NOT AGAIN.
BUT--
YOU GET USED TO BEING ALONE.
BUT WHAT? ONE NIGHT TOGETHER DOESN'T CHANGE A THING.
LOOK. I HARDLY KNOW WHAT YOU'RE TALKING ABOUT HALF THE TIME, LET ALONE WHAT YOU'RE DOING, OR IF YOU'RE COMING BACK.
I DID.

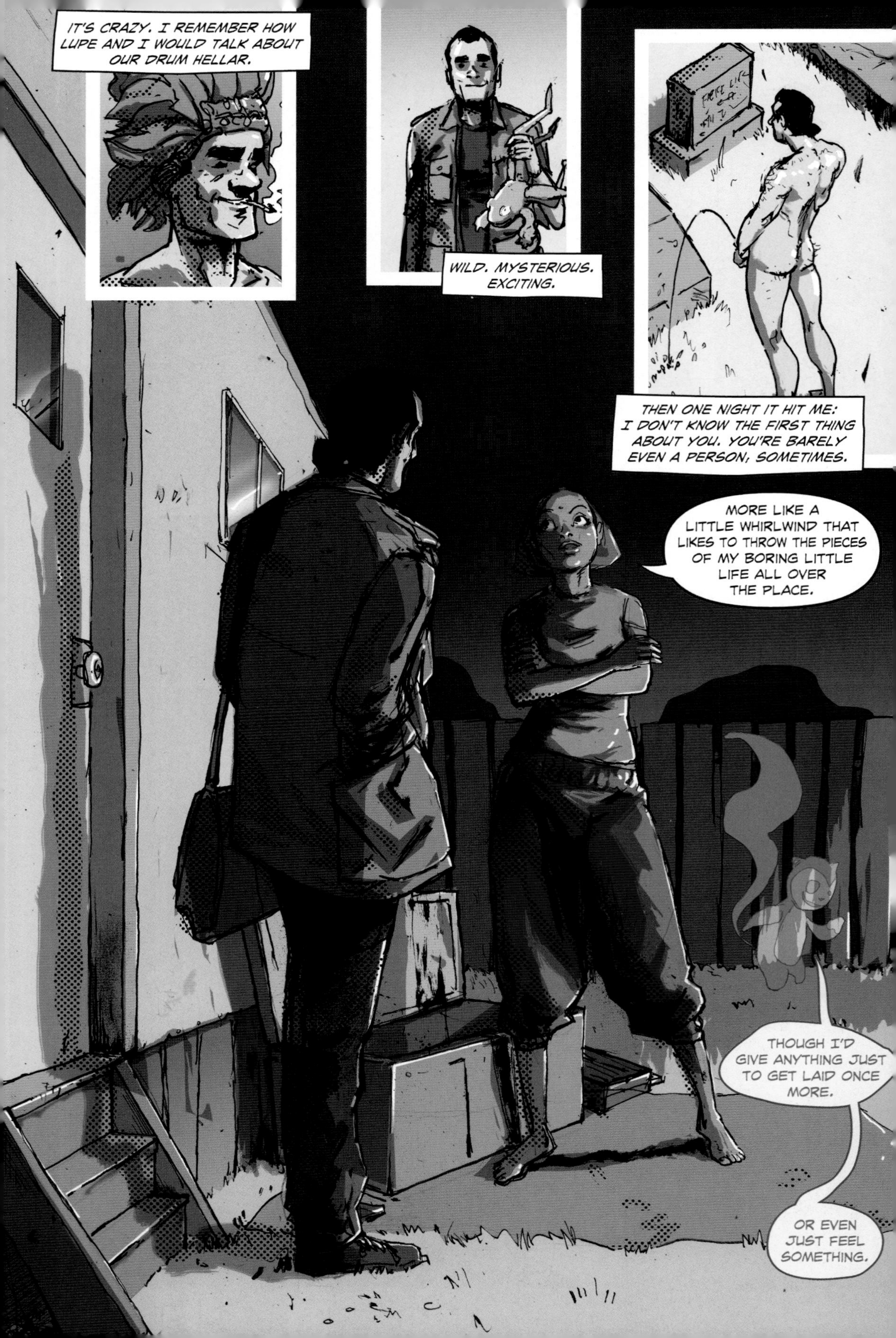
IT'S CRAZY. I REMEMBER HOW LUPE AND I WOULD TALK ABOUT OUR DRUM HELLAR.
WILD. MYSTERIOUS. EXCITING.
THEN ONE NIGHT IT HIT ME: I DON'T KNOW THE FIRST THING ABOUT YOU. YOU'RE BARELY EVEN A PERSON, SOMETIMES.
MORE LIKE A LITTLE WHIRLWIND THAT LIKES TO THROW THE PIECES OF MY BORING LITTLE LIFE ALL OVER THE PLACE.
THOUGH I'D GIVE ANYTHING JUST TO GET LAID ONCE MORE.
OR EVEN JUST FEEL SOMETHING.

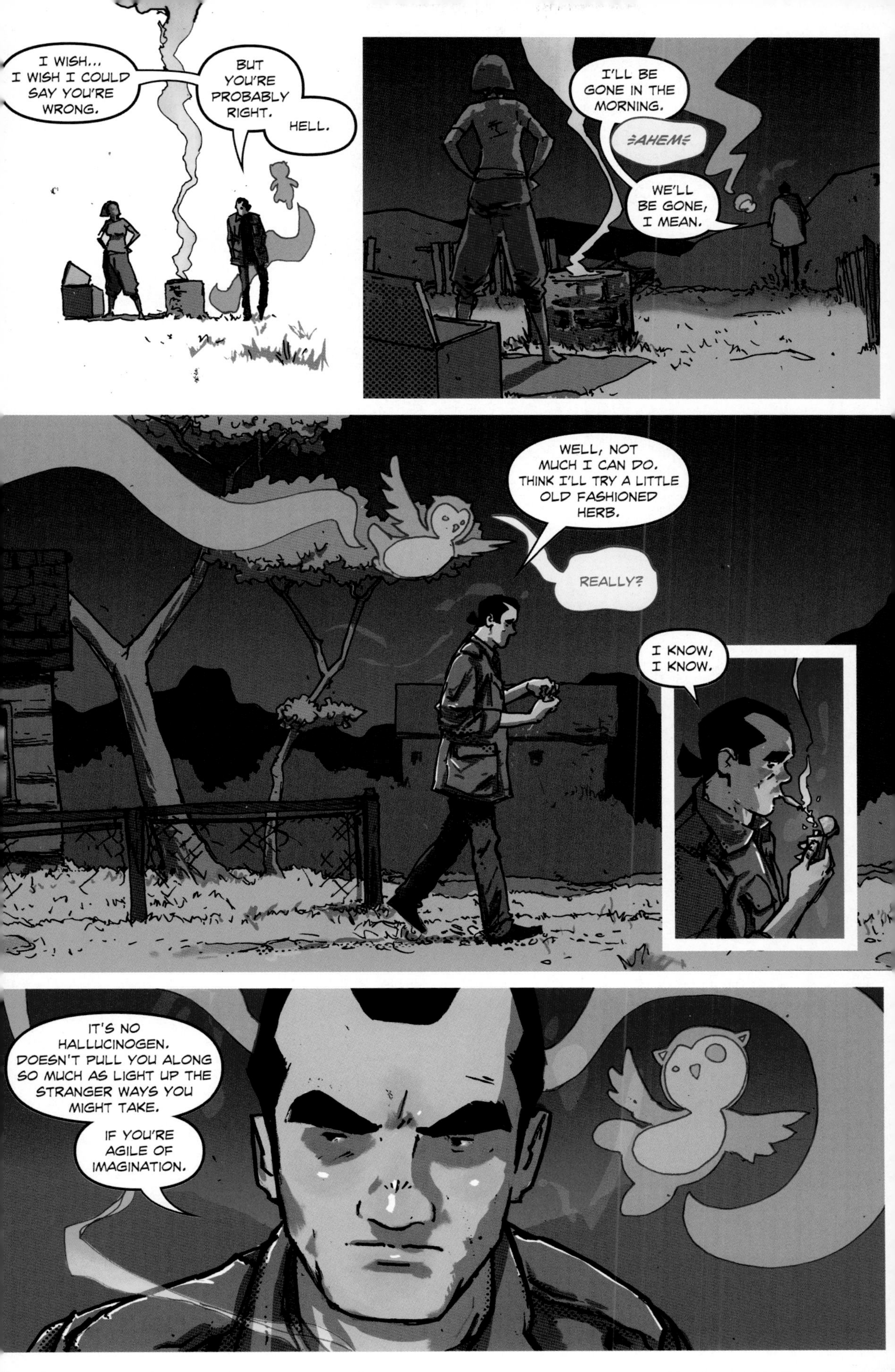
I WISH... I WISH I COULD SAY YOU'RE WRONG.
BUT YOU'RE PROBABLY RIGHT.
HELL.
I'LL BE GONE IN THE MORNING.
AHEM
WE'LL BE GONE, I MEAN.
WELL, NOT MUCH I CAN DO. THINK I'LL TRY A LITTLE OLD FASHIONED HERB.
REALLY?
I KNOW, I KNOW.
IT'S NO HALLUCINOGEN. DOESN'T PULL YOU ALONG SO MUCH AS LIGHT UP THE STRANGER WAYS YOU MIGHT TAKE.
IF YOU'RE AGILE OF IMAGINATION.

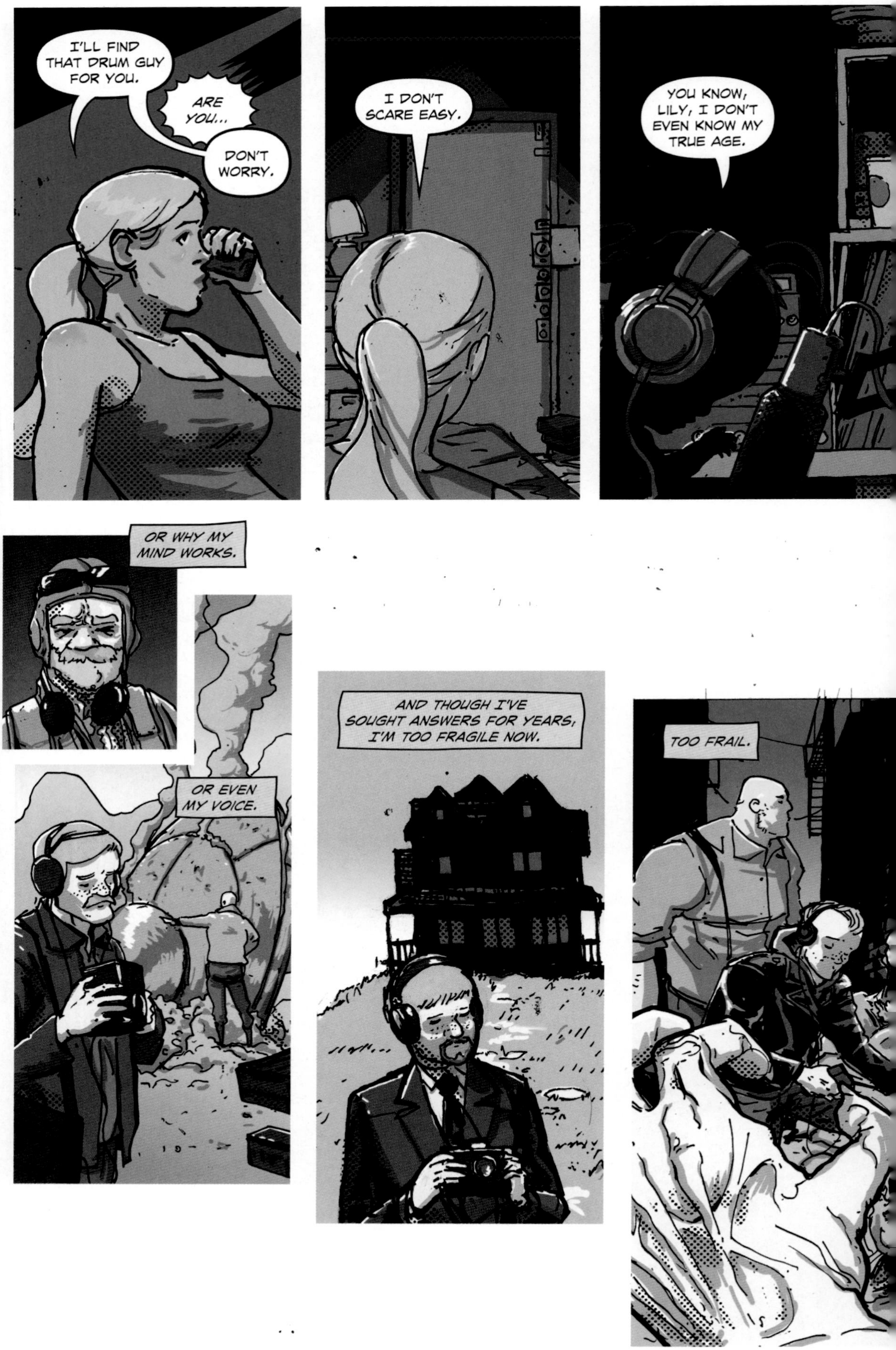
I'LL FIND THAT DRUM GUY FOR YOU.
ARE YOU...
DON'T WORRY.
I DON'T SCARE EASY.
YOU KNOW, LILY, I DON'T EVEN KNOW MY TRUE AGE.
OR WHY MY MIND WORKS.
OR EVEN MY VOICE.
AND THOUGH I'VE SOUGHT ANSWERS FOR YEARS, I'M TOO FRAGILE NOW.
TOO FRAIL.

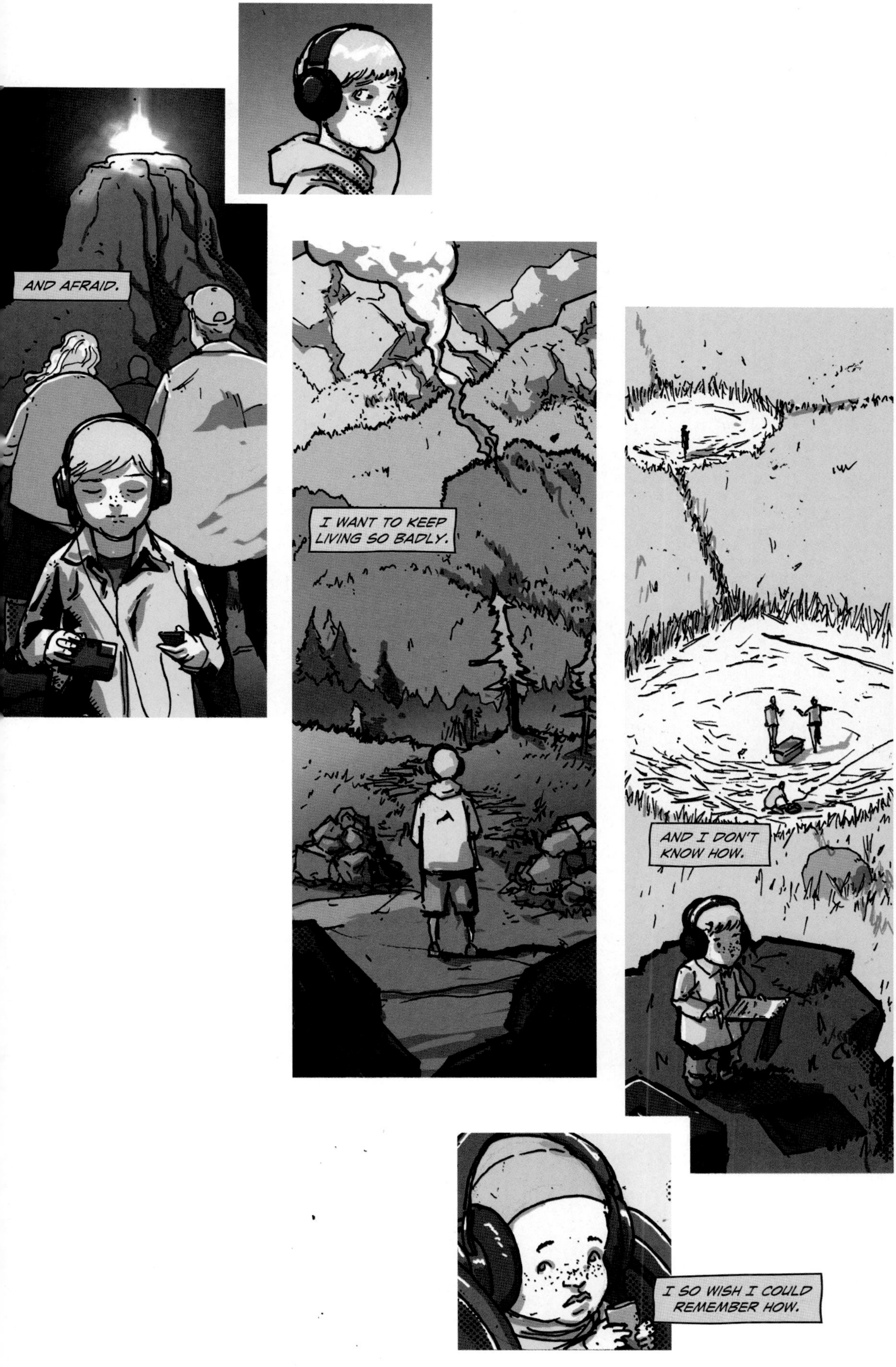
AND AFRAID.
I WANT TO KEEP LIVING SO BADLY.
AND I DON'T KNOW HOW.
I SO WISH I COULD REMEMBER HOW.

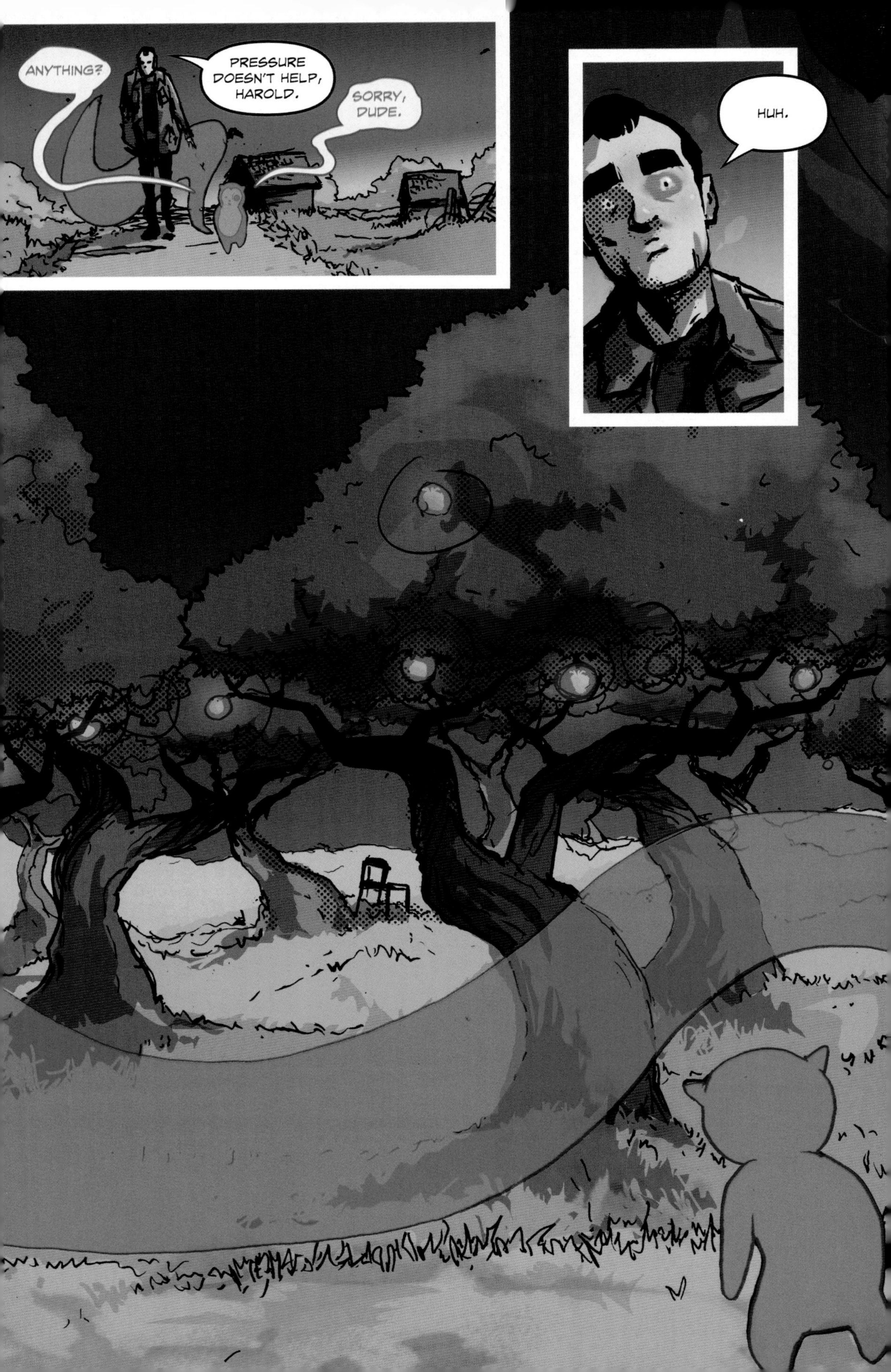
ANYTHING?
PRESSURE DOESN'T HELP, HAROLD.
SORRY, DUDE.
HUH.

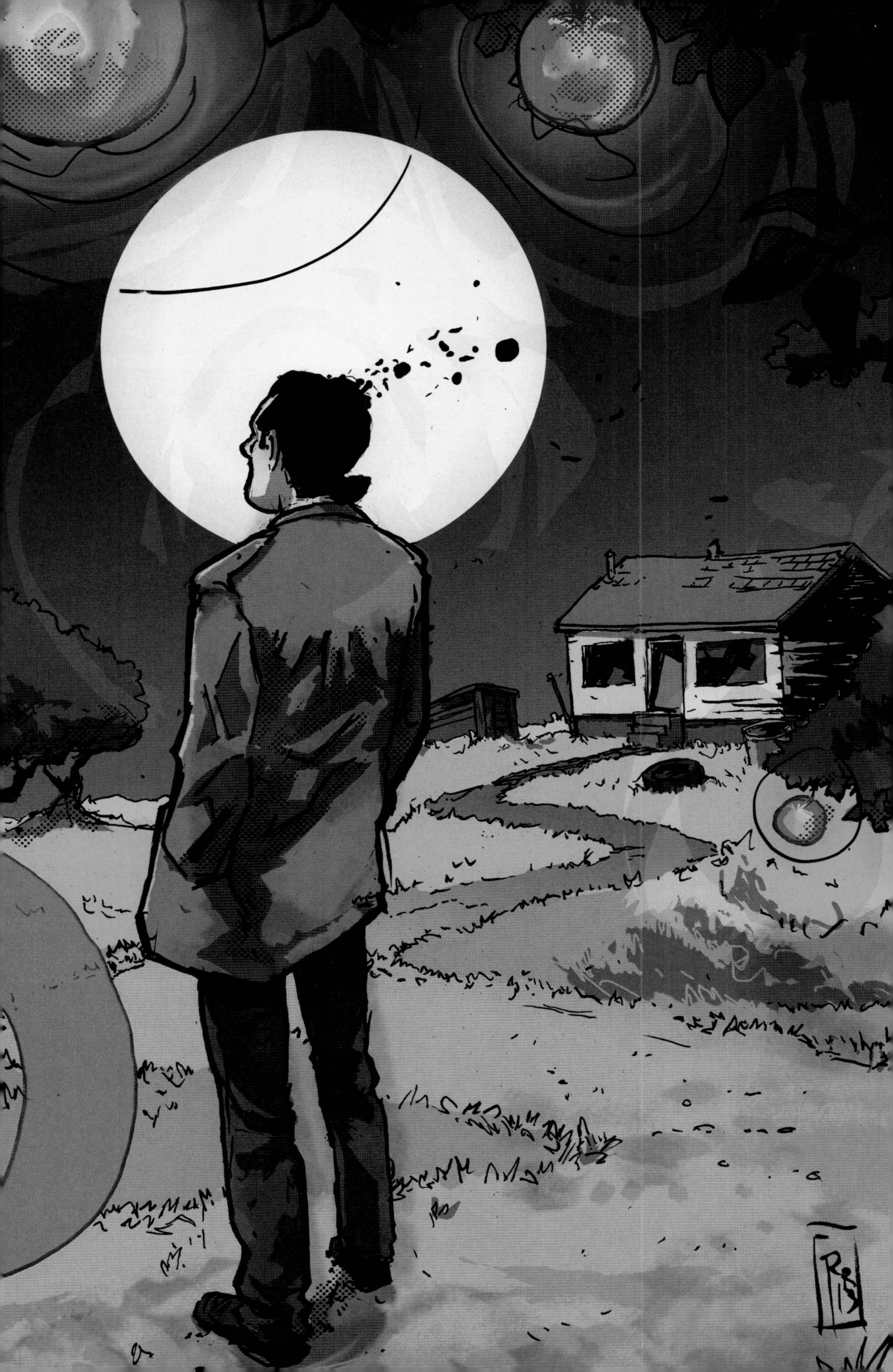

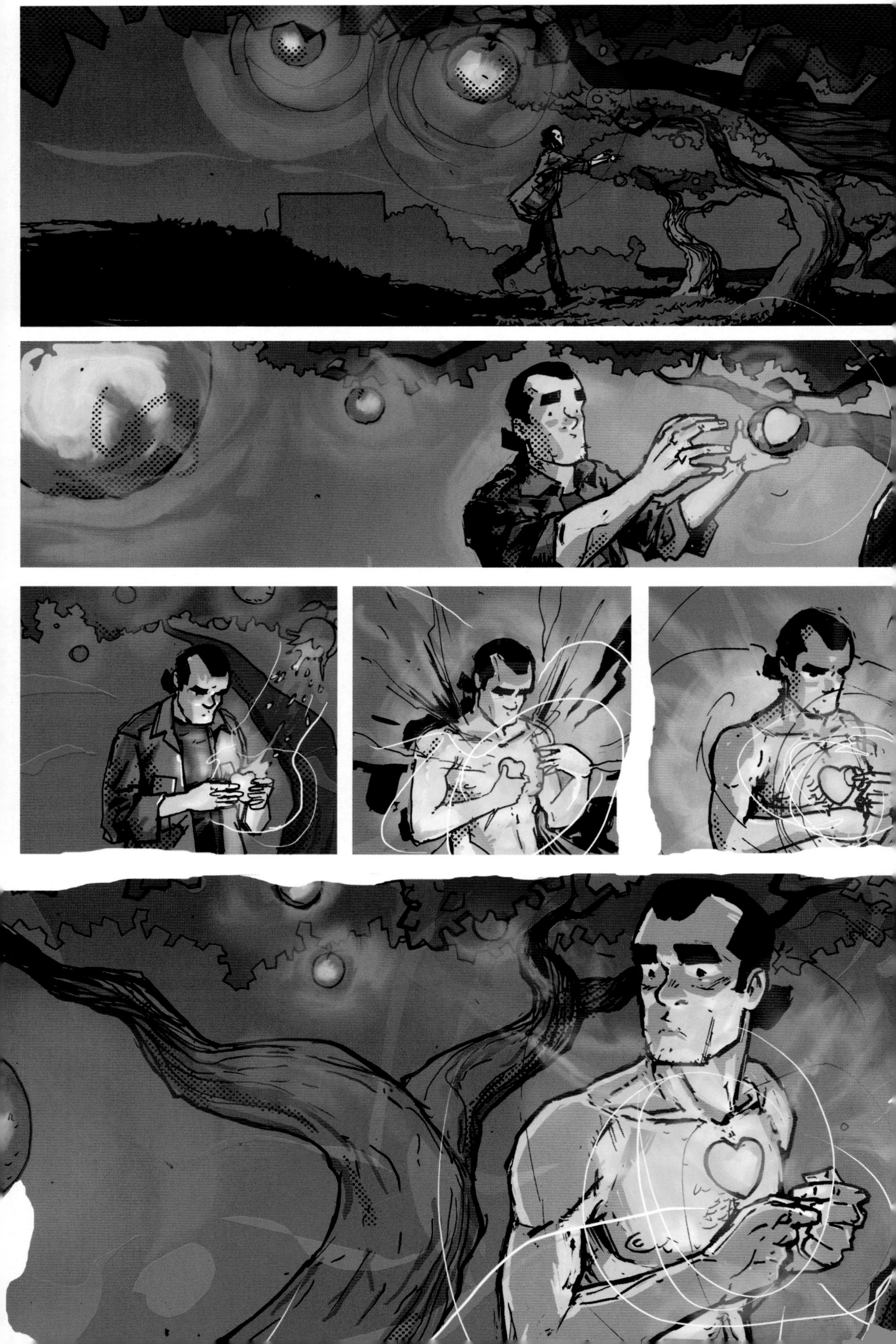

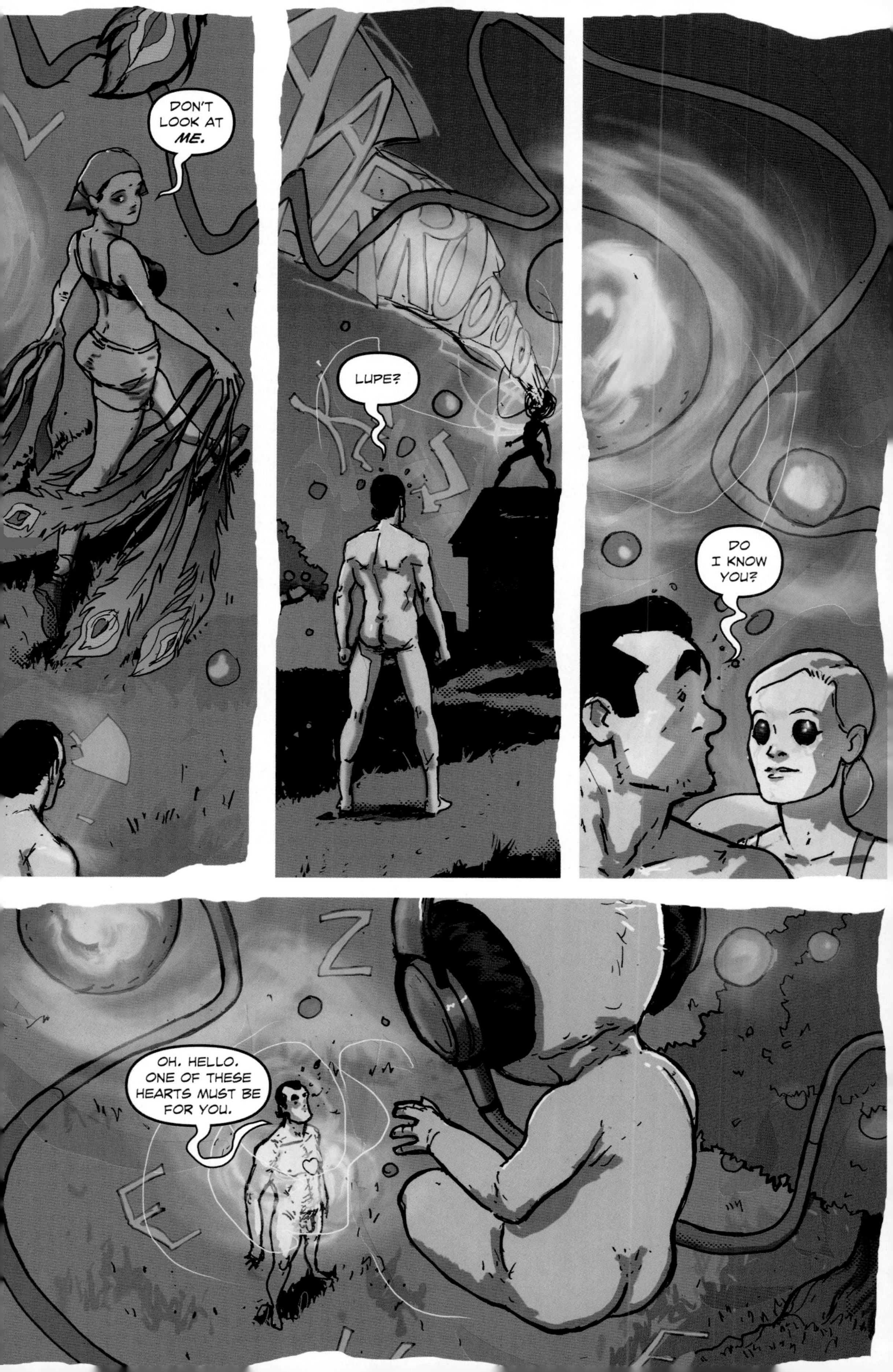
DON'T LOOK AT *ME.*
LUPE?
DO I KNOW YOU?
OH. HELLO. ONE OF THESE HEARTS MUST BE FOR YOU.

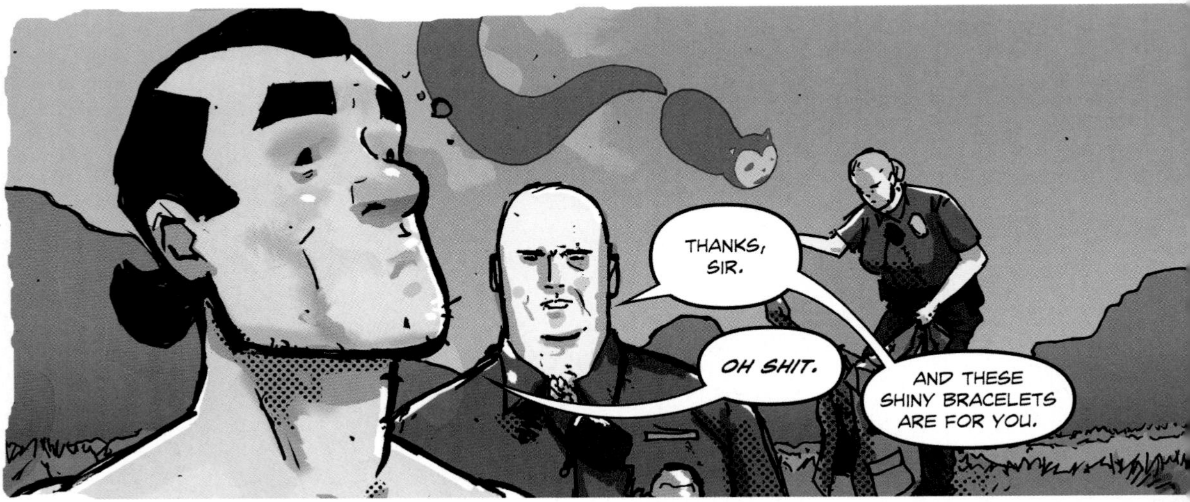
THANKS, SIR.
OH SHIT.
AND THESE SHINY BRACELETS ARE FOR YOU.

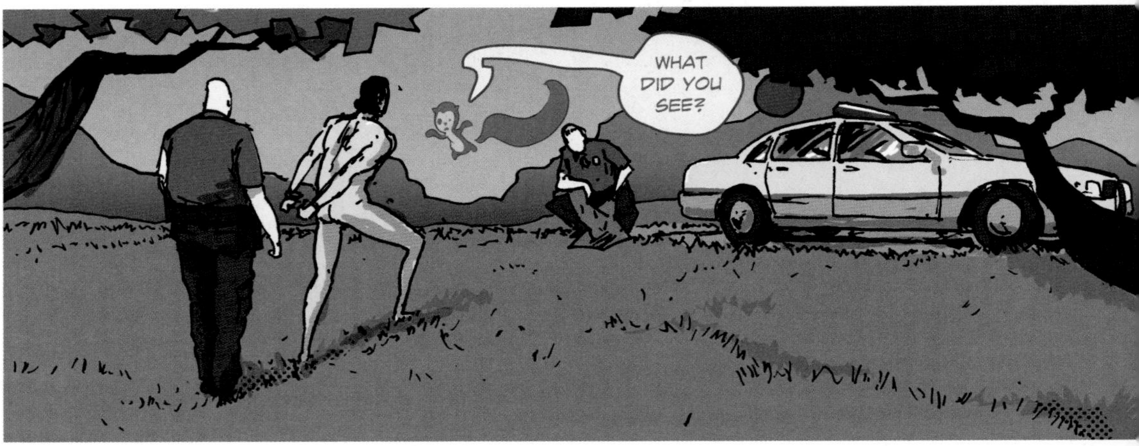
WHAT DID YOU SEE?

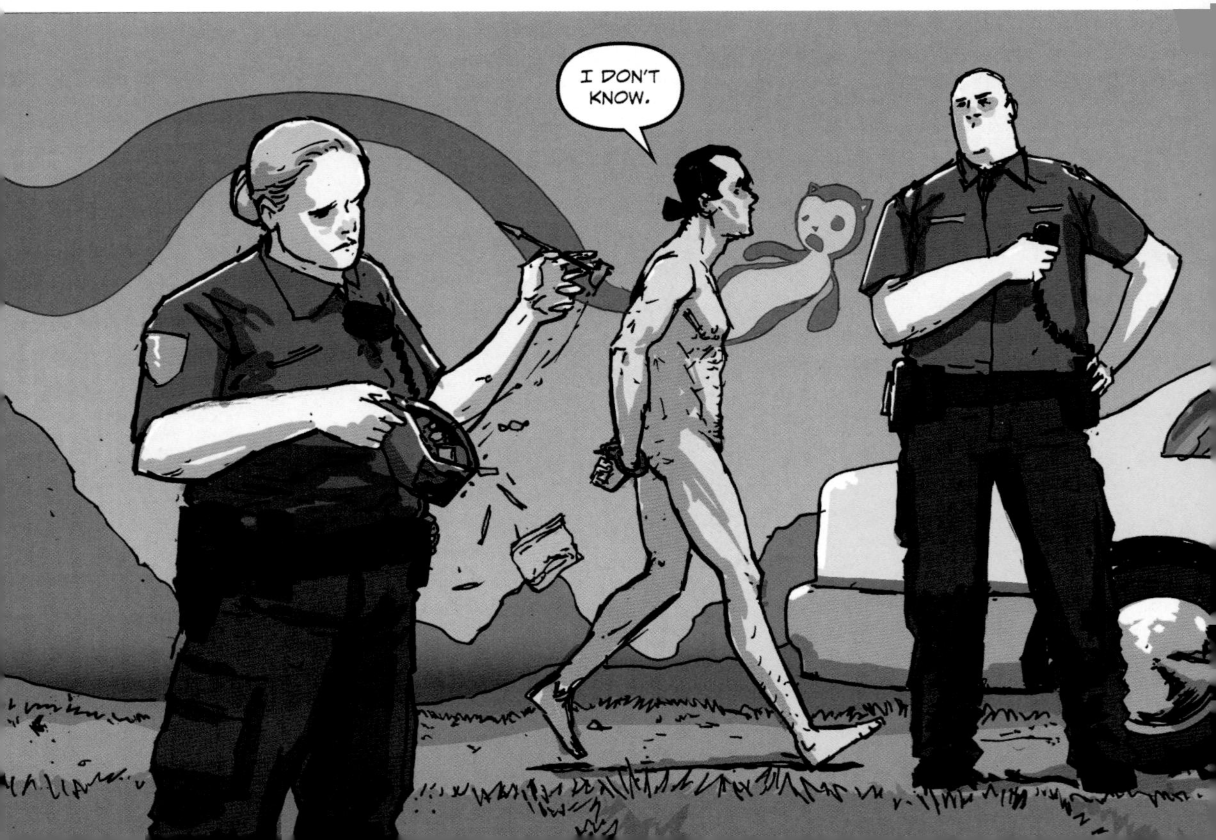
I DON'T KNOW.

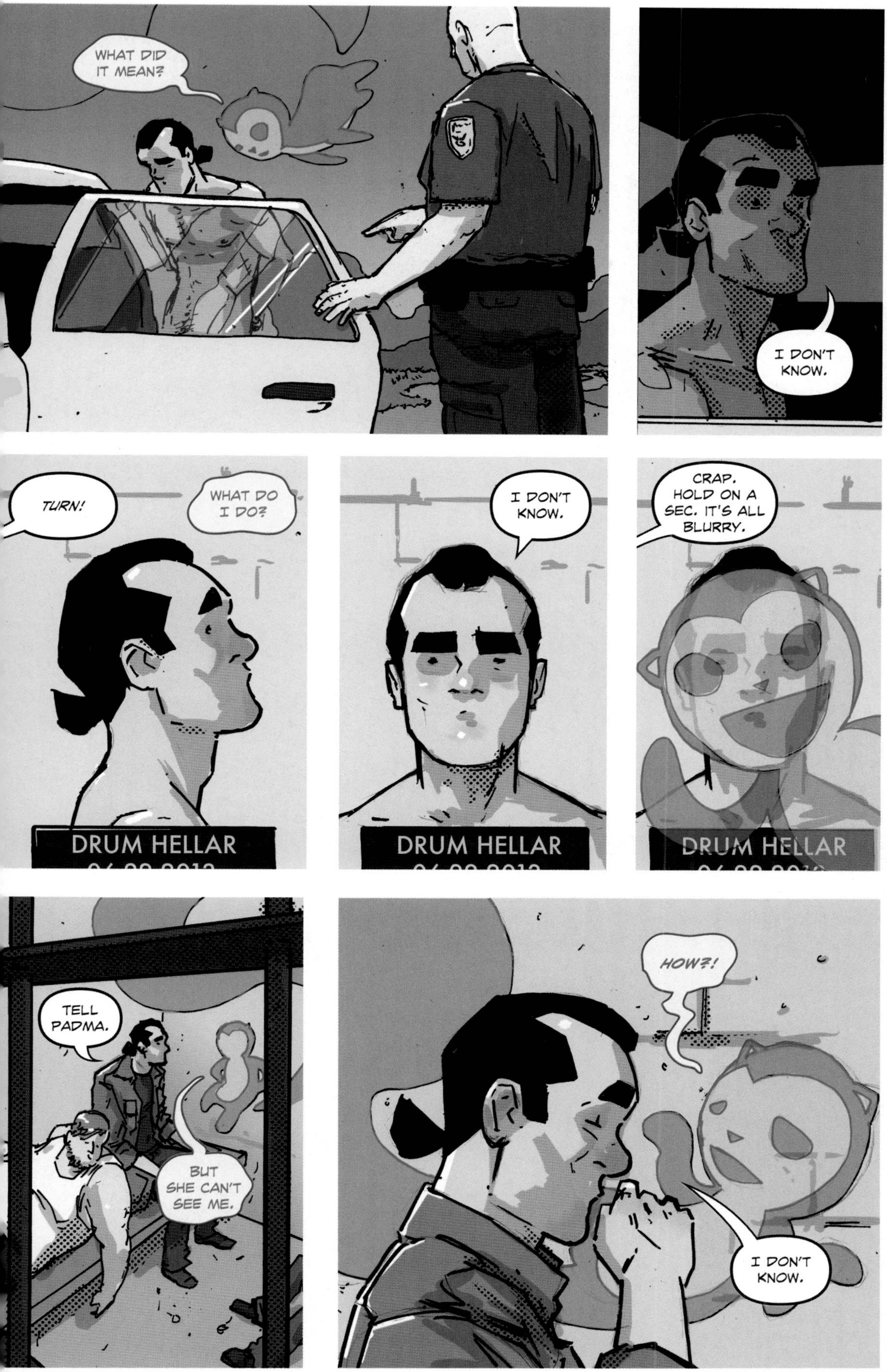
WHAT DID IT MEAN?
I DON'T KNOW.
TURN!
WHAT DO I DO?
DRUM HELLAR
I DON'T KNOW.
DRUM HELLAR
CRAP. HOLD ON A SEC. IT'S ALL BLURRY.
DRUM HELLAR
TELL PADMA.
BUT SHE CAN'T SEE ME.
HOW?!
I DON'T KNOW.

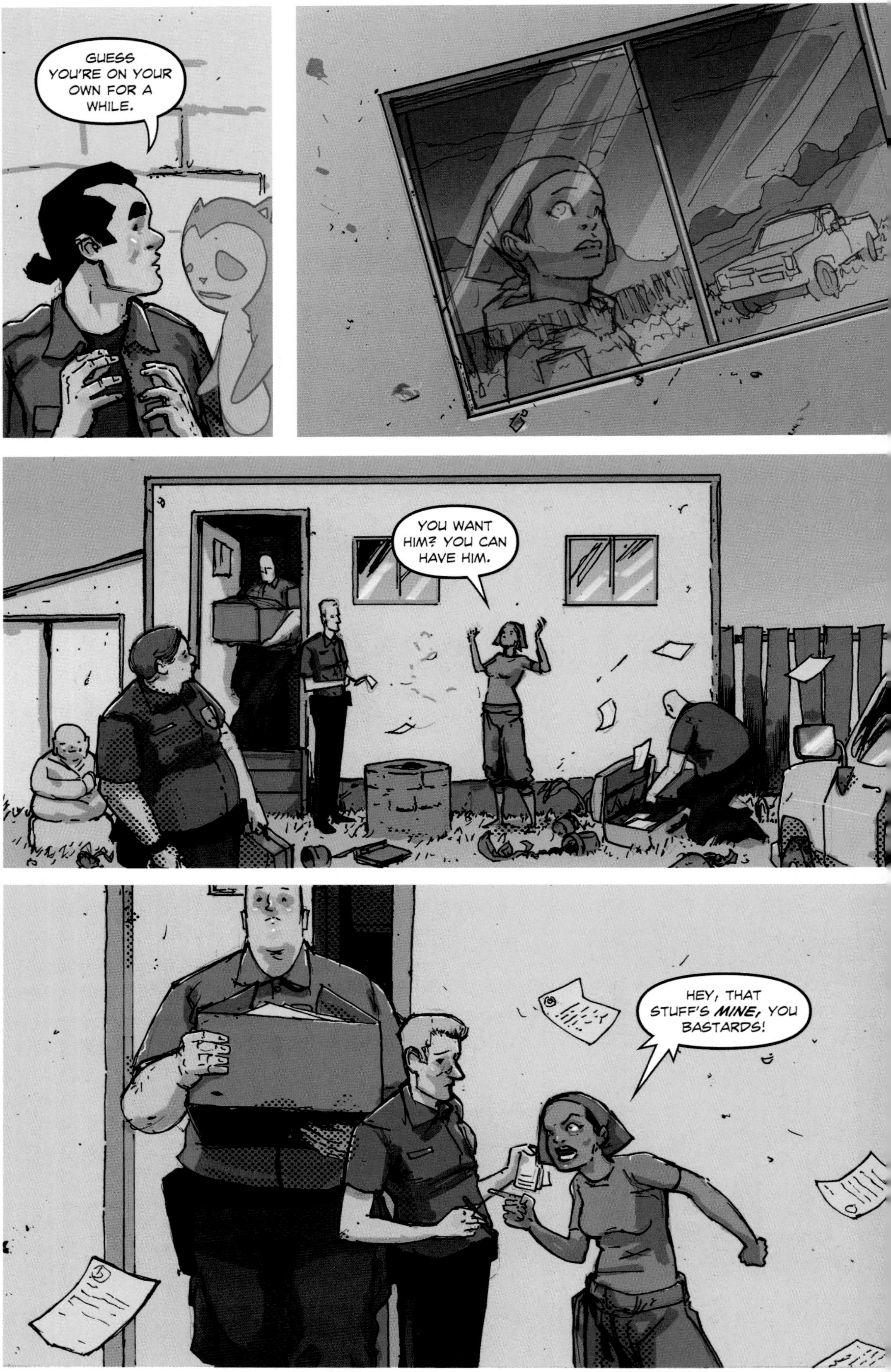
GUESS YOU'RE ON YOUR OWN FOR A WHILE.
YOU WANT HIM? YOU CAN HAVE HIM.
HEY, THAT STUFF'S *MINE,* YOU BASTARDS!

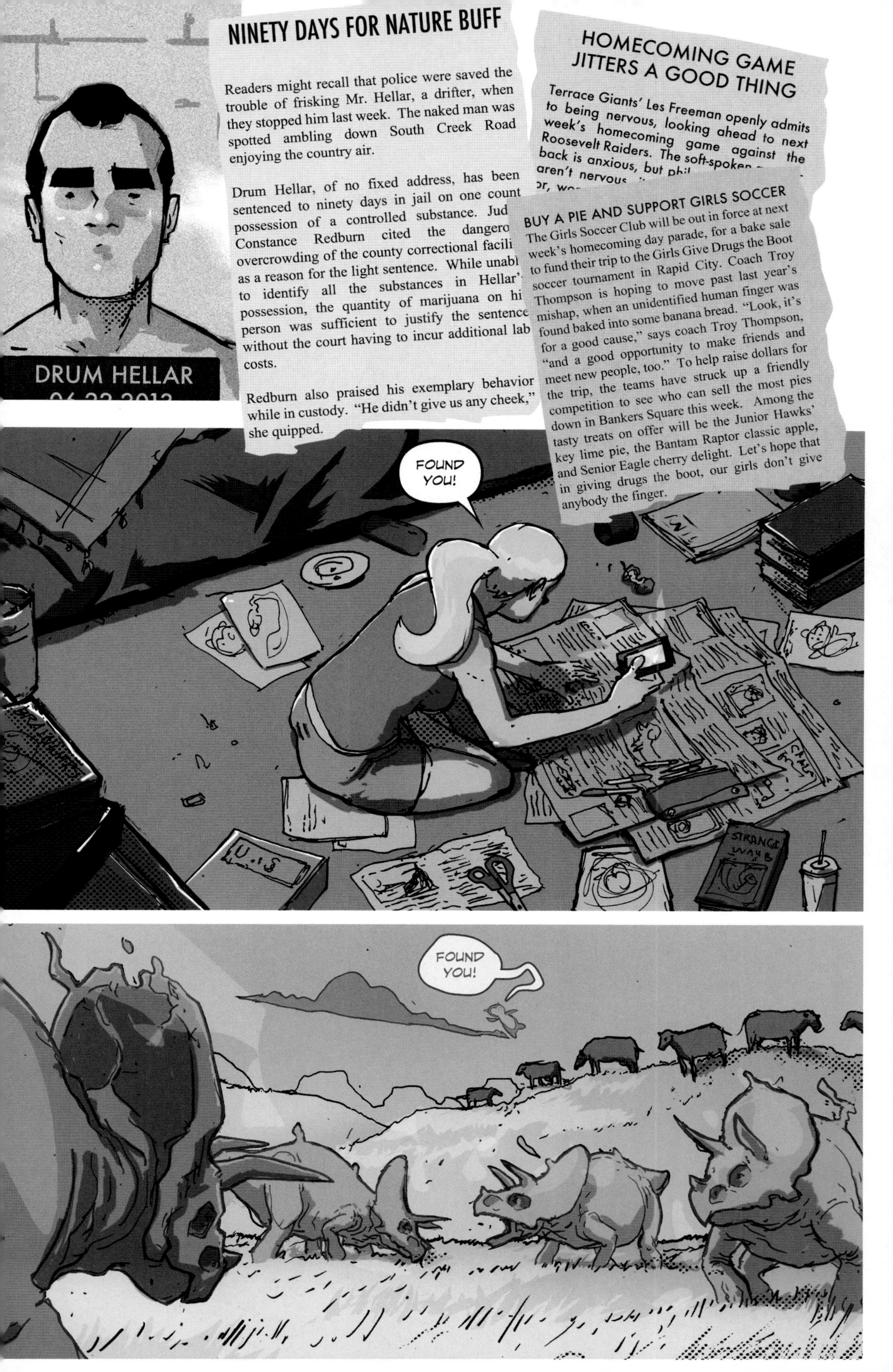
DRUM HELLAR
NINETY DAYS FOR NATURE BUFF
Readers might recall that police were saved the trouble of frisking Mr. Hellar, a drifter, when they stopped him last week. The naked man was spotted ambling down South Creek Road enjoying the country air.
Drum Hellar, of no fixed address, has been sentenced to ninety days in jail on one count possession of a controlled substance. Jud Constance Redburn cited the dangero overcrowding of the county correctional facili as a reason for the light sentence. While unabl to identify all the substances in Hellar' possession, the quantity of marijuana on hi person was sufficient to justify the sentence without the court having to incur additional lab costs.
Redburn also praised his exemplary behavior while in custody. "He didn't give us any cheek," she quipped.
HOMECOMING GAME JITTERS A GOOD THING
Terrace Giants' Les Freeman openly admits to being nervous, looking ahead to next week's homecoming game against the Roosevelt Raiders. The soft-spoken
back is anxious, but phil
aren't nervous
BUY A PIE AND SUPPORT GIRLS SOCCER
The Girls Soccer Club will be out in force at next week's homecoming day parade, for a bake sale to fund their trip to the Girls Give Drugs the Boot soccer tournament in Rapid City. Coach Troy Thompson is hoping to move past last year's mishap, when an unidentified human finger was found baked into some banana bread. "Look, it's for a good cause," says coach Troy Thompson, "and a good opportunity to make friends and meet new people, too." To help raise dollars for the trip, the teams have struck up a friendly competition to see who can sell the most pies down in Bankers Square this week. Among the tasty treats on offer will be the Junior Hawks' key lime pie, the Bantam Raptor classic apple, and Senior Eagle cherry delight. Let's hope that in giving drugs the boot, our girls don't give anybody the finger.
FOUND YOU!
STRANGE
FOUND YOU!

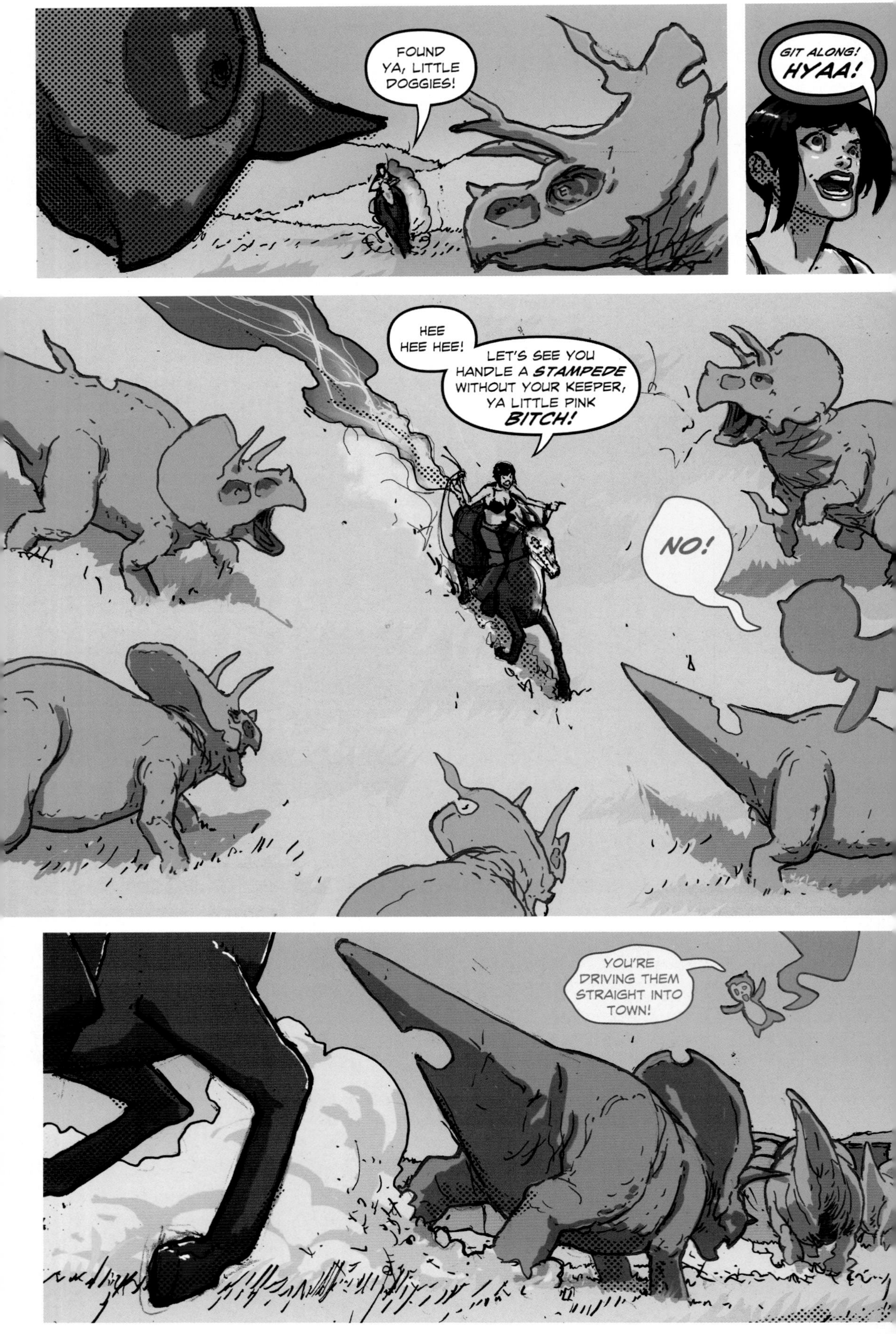
FOUND YA, LITTLE DOGGIES!
GIT ALONG! HYAA!
HEE HEE HEE!
LET'S SEE YOU HANDLE A STAMPEDE WITHOUT YOUR KEEPER, YA LITTLE PINK BITCH!
NO!
YOU'RE DRIVING THEM STRAIGHT INTO TOWN!

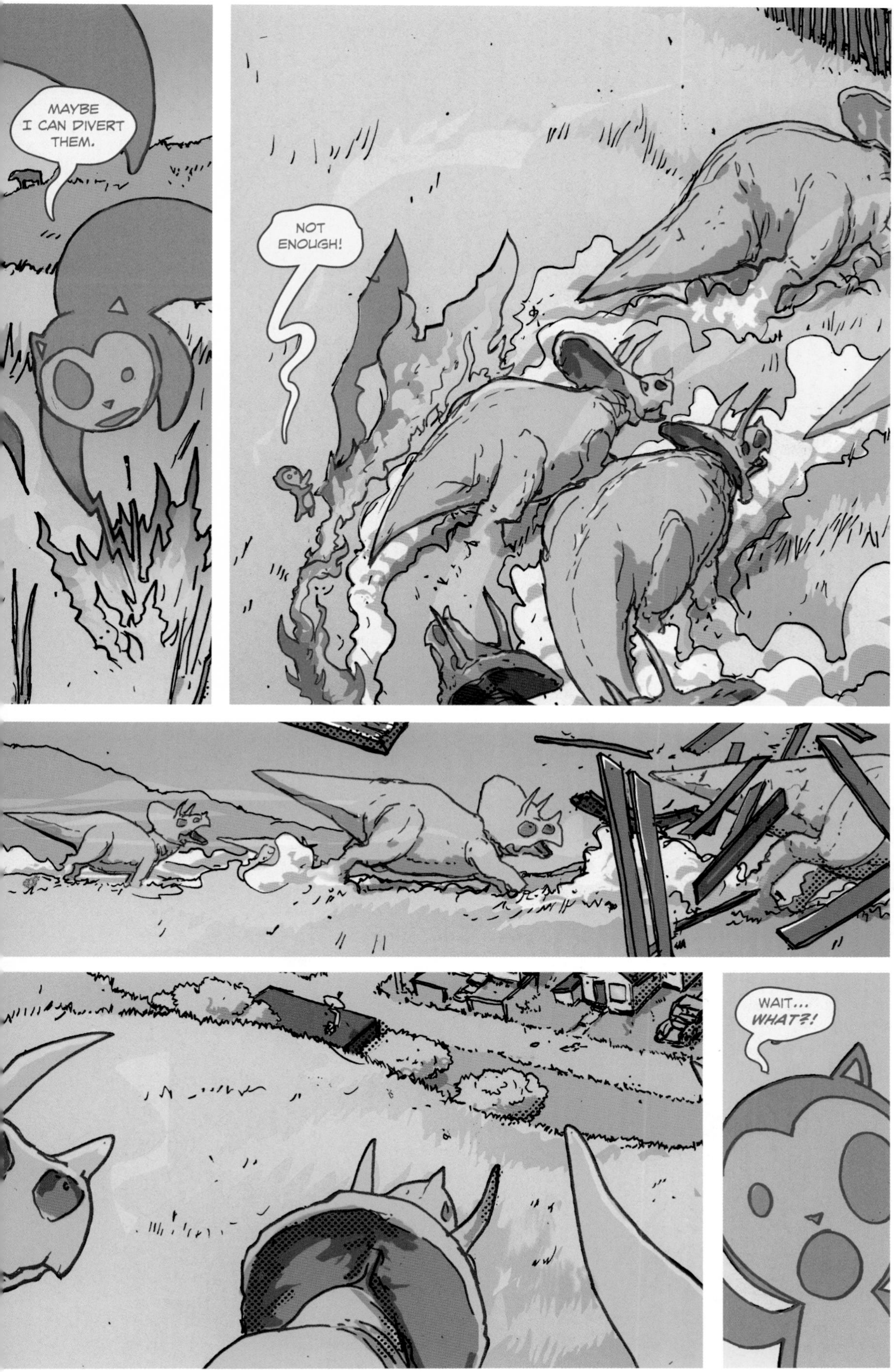
MAYBE I CAN DIVERT THEM.
NOT ENOUGH!
WAIT... WHAT?!

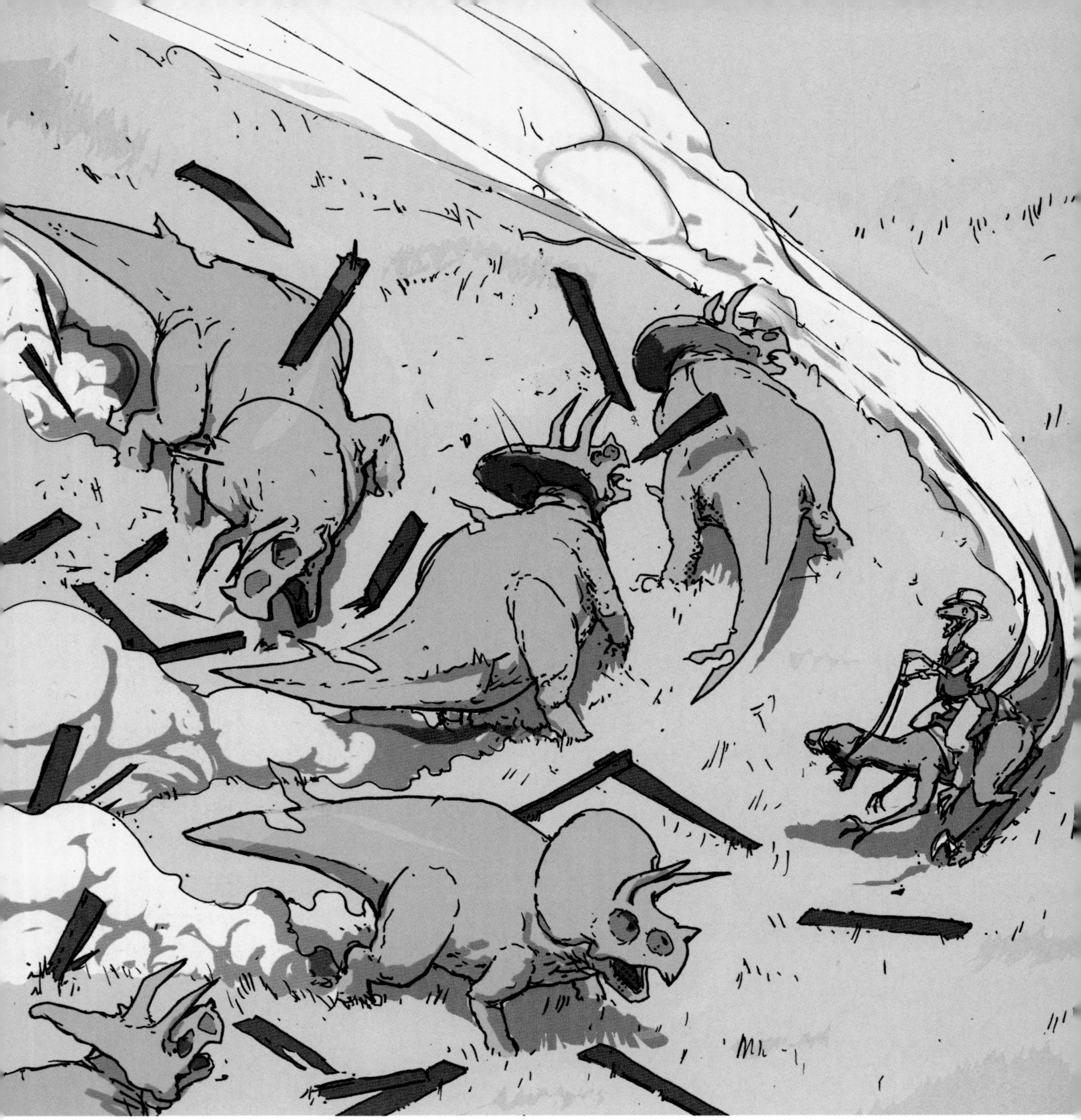

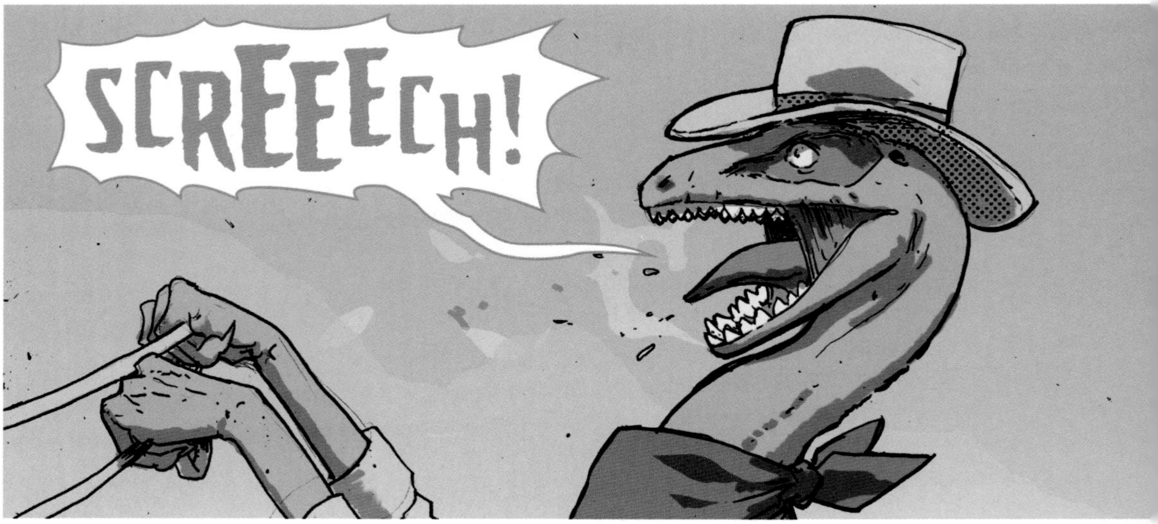
SCREEECH!

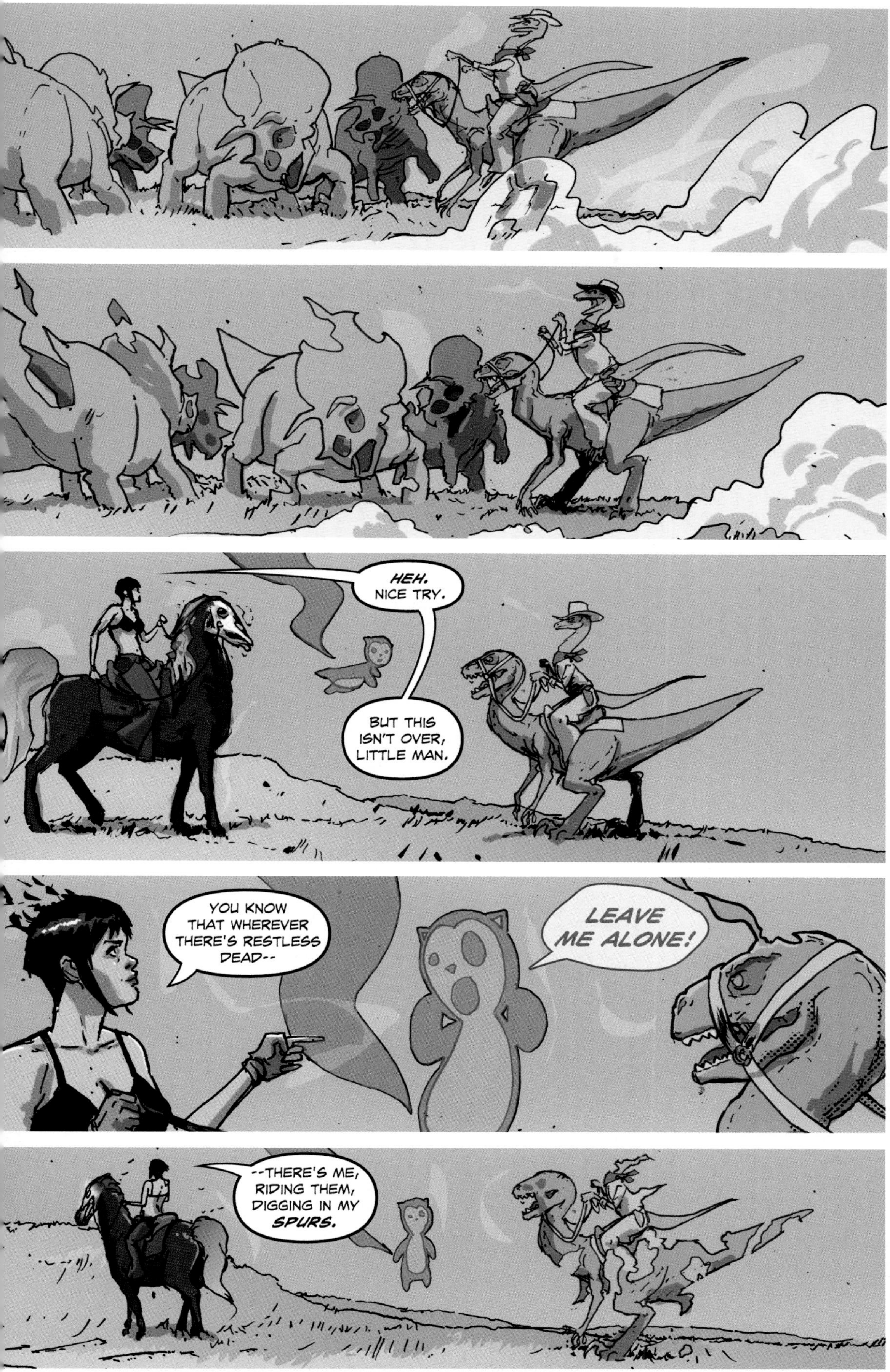
HEH. NICE TRY.
BUT THIS ISN'T OVER, LITTLE MAN.
YOU KNOW THAT WHEREVER THERE'S RESTLESS DEAD--
LEAVE ME ALONE!
--THERE'S ME, RIDING THEM, DIGGING IN MY SPURS.

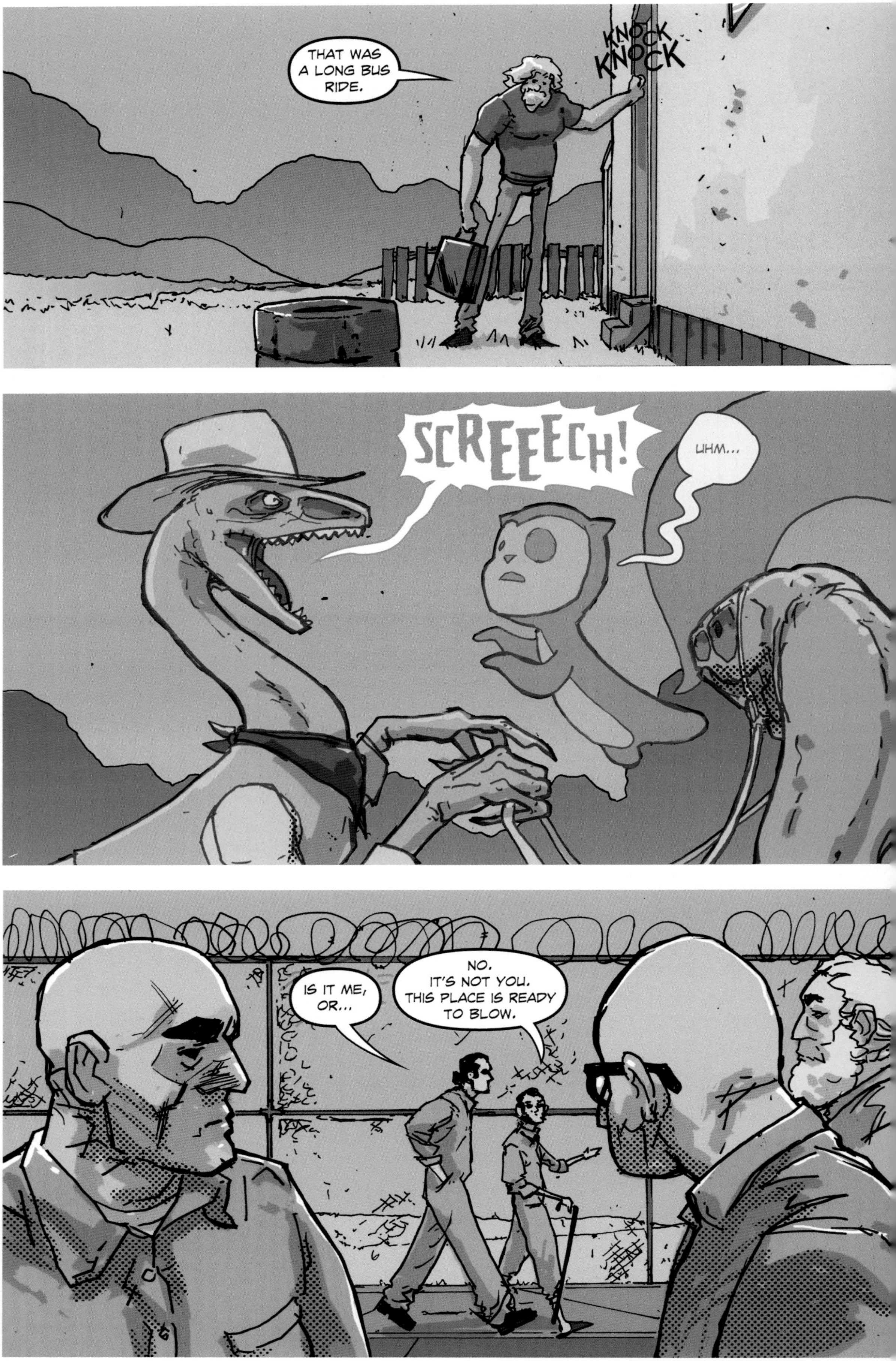
THAT WAS A LONG BUS RIDE.
KNOCK KNOCK
SCREEECH!
UHM...
IS IT ME, OR...
NO. IT'S NOT YOU. THIS PLACE IS READY TO BLOW.

FOUR

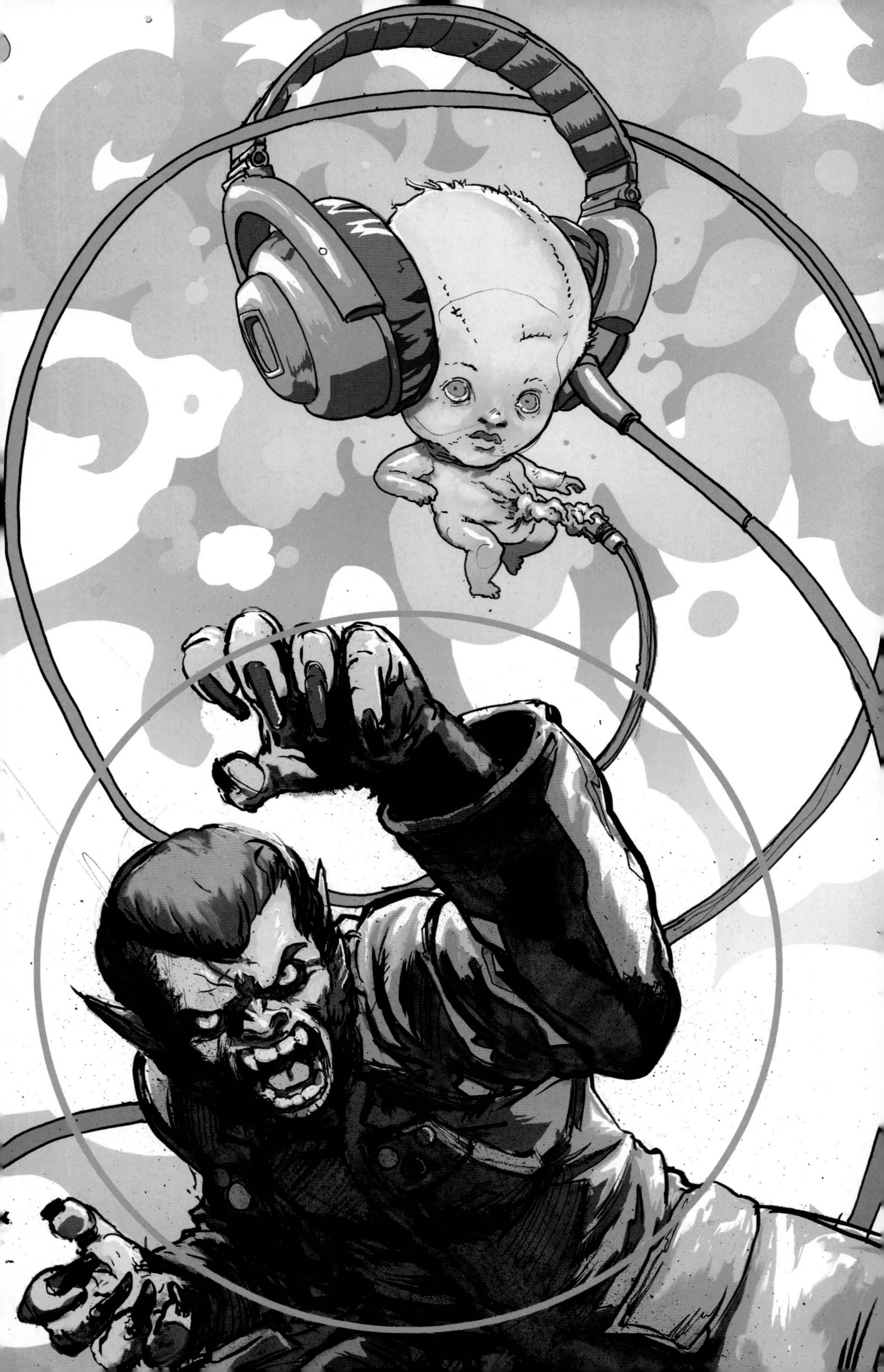

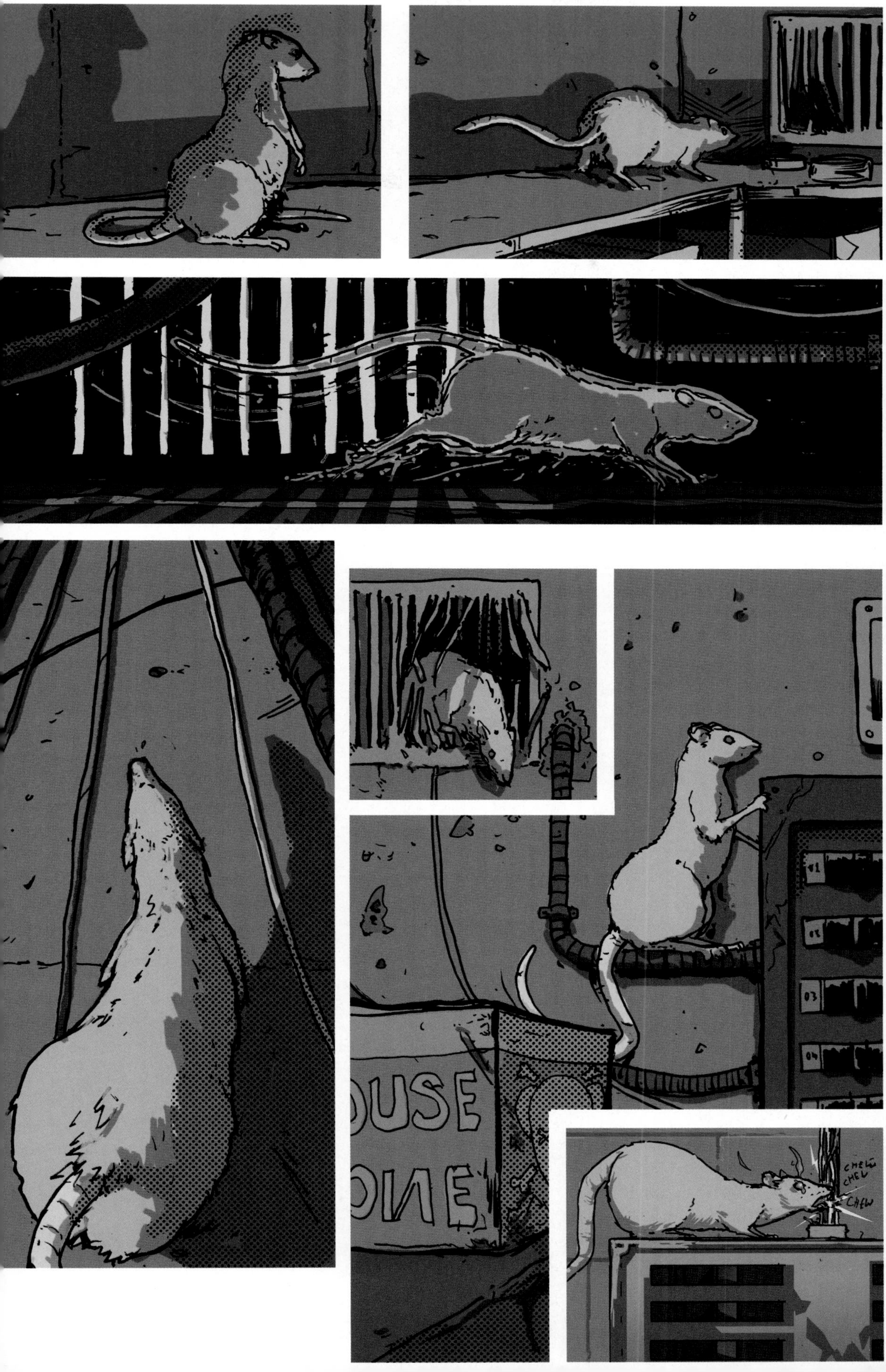
01
02
03
04
OUSE
ONE
CHEW
CHEW
CHEW

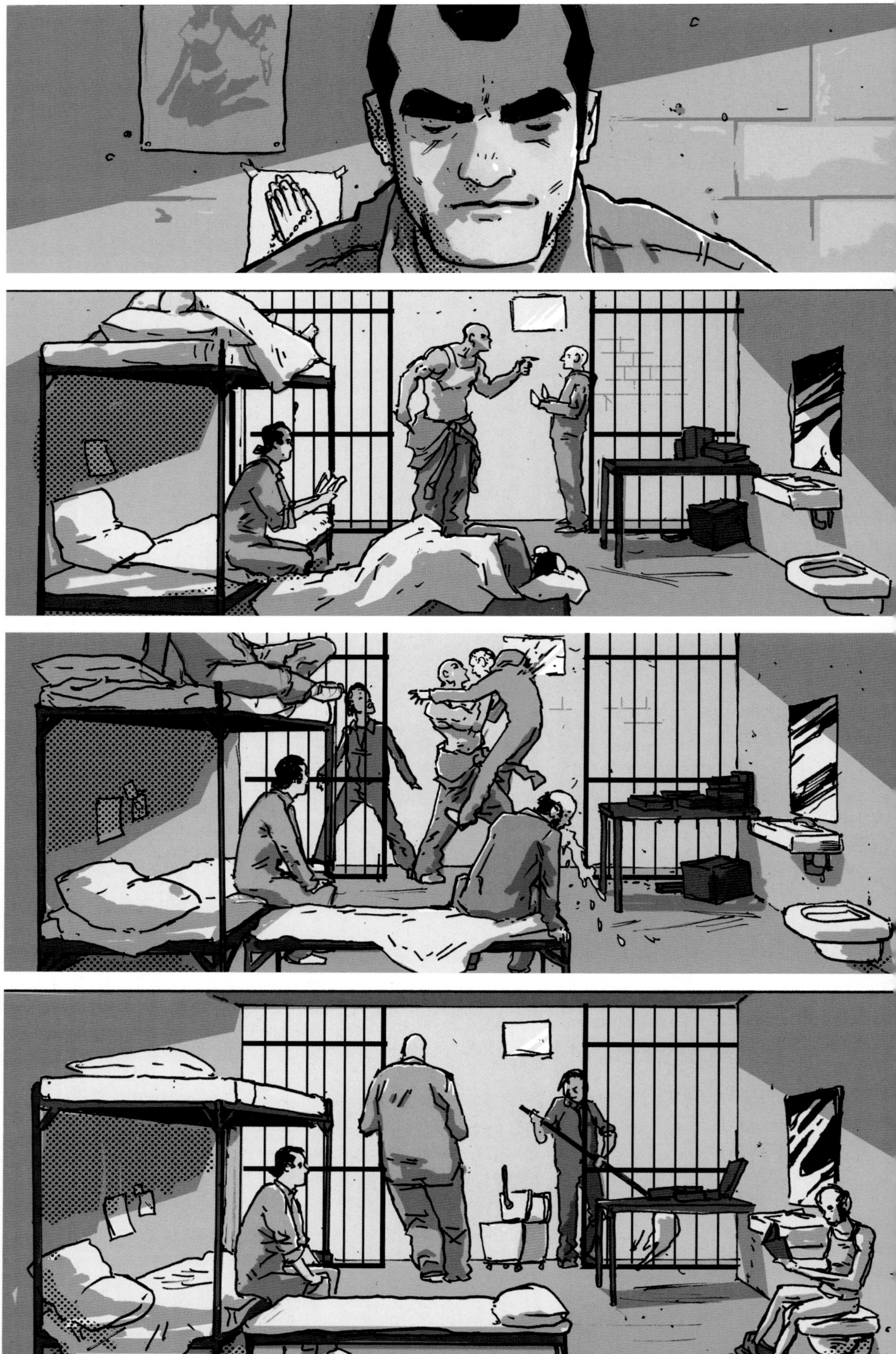

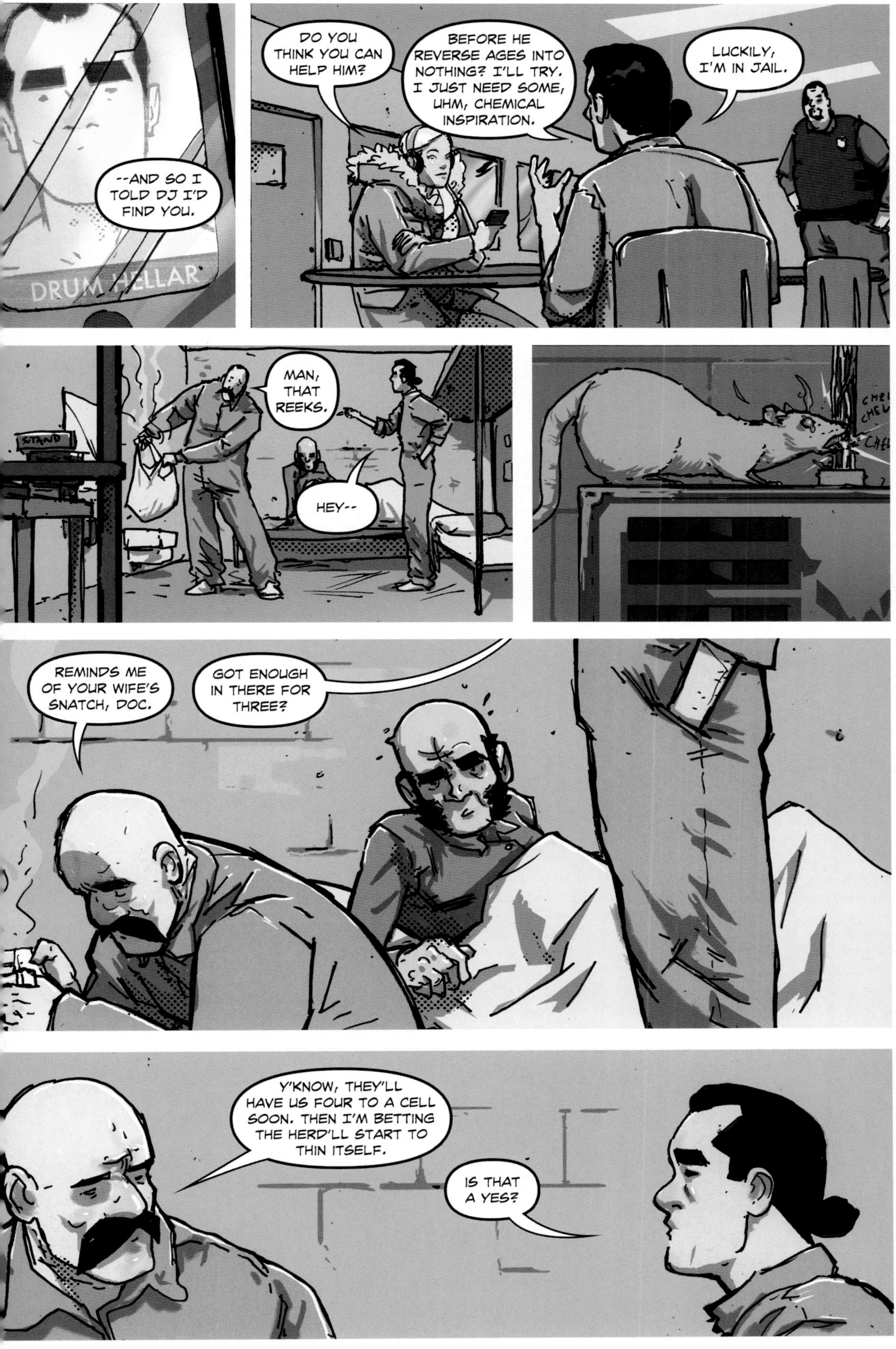
DRUM HELLAR
--AND SO I TOLD DJ I'D FIND YOU.
DO YOU THINK YOU CAN HELP HIM?
BEFORE HE REVERSE AGES INTO NOTHING? I'LL TRY. I JUST NEED SOME, UHM, CHEMICAL INSPIRATION.
LUCKILY, I'M IN JAIL.
STAND
MAN, THAT REEKS.
HEY--
REMINDS ME OF YOUR WIFE'S SNATCH, DOC.
GOT ENOUGH IN THERE FOR THREE?
Y'KNOW, THEY'LL HAVE US FOUR TO A CELL SOON. THEN I'M BETTING THE HERD'LL START TO THIN ITSELF.
IS THAT A YES?

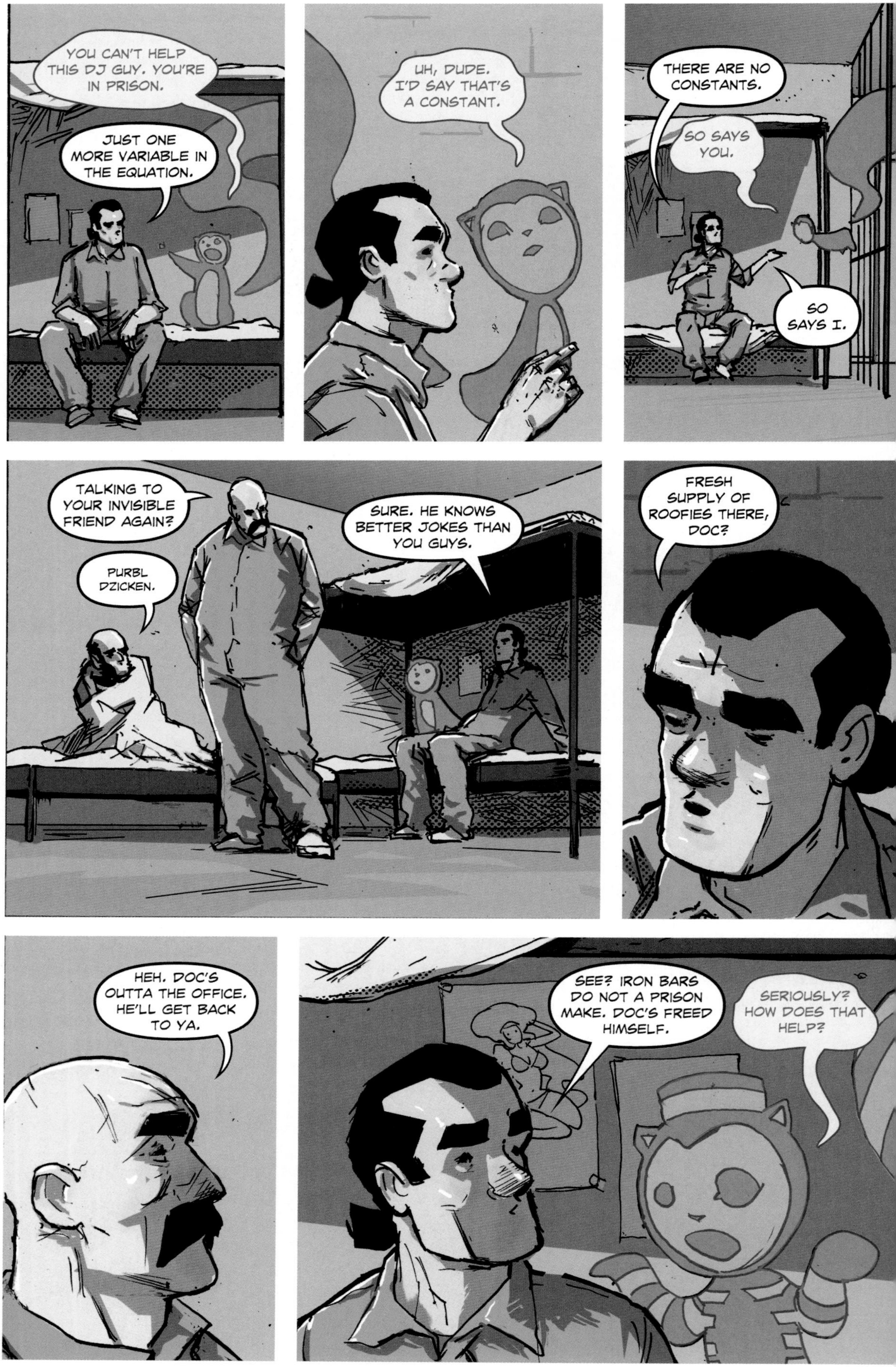
YOU CAN'T HELP THIS DJ GUY. YOU'RE IN PRISON.
JUST ONE MORE VARIABLE IN THE EQUATION.
UH, DUDE. I'D SAY THAT'S A CONSTANT.
THERE ARE NO CONSTANTS.
SO SAYS YOU.
SO SAYS I.
TALKING TO YOUR INVISIBLE FRIEND AGAIN?
PURBL DZICKEN.
SURE. HE KNOWS BETTER JOKES THAN YOU GUYS.
FRESH SUPPLY OF ROOFIES THERE, DOC?
HEH. DOC'S OUTTA THE OFFICE. HE'LL GET BACK TO YA.
SEE? IRON BARS DO NOT A PRISON MAKE. DOC'S FREED HIMSELF.
SERIOUSLY? HOW DOES THAT HELP?

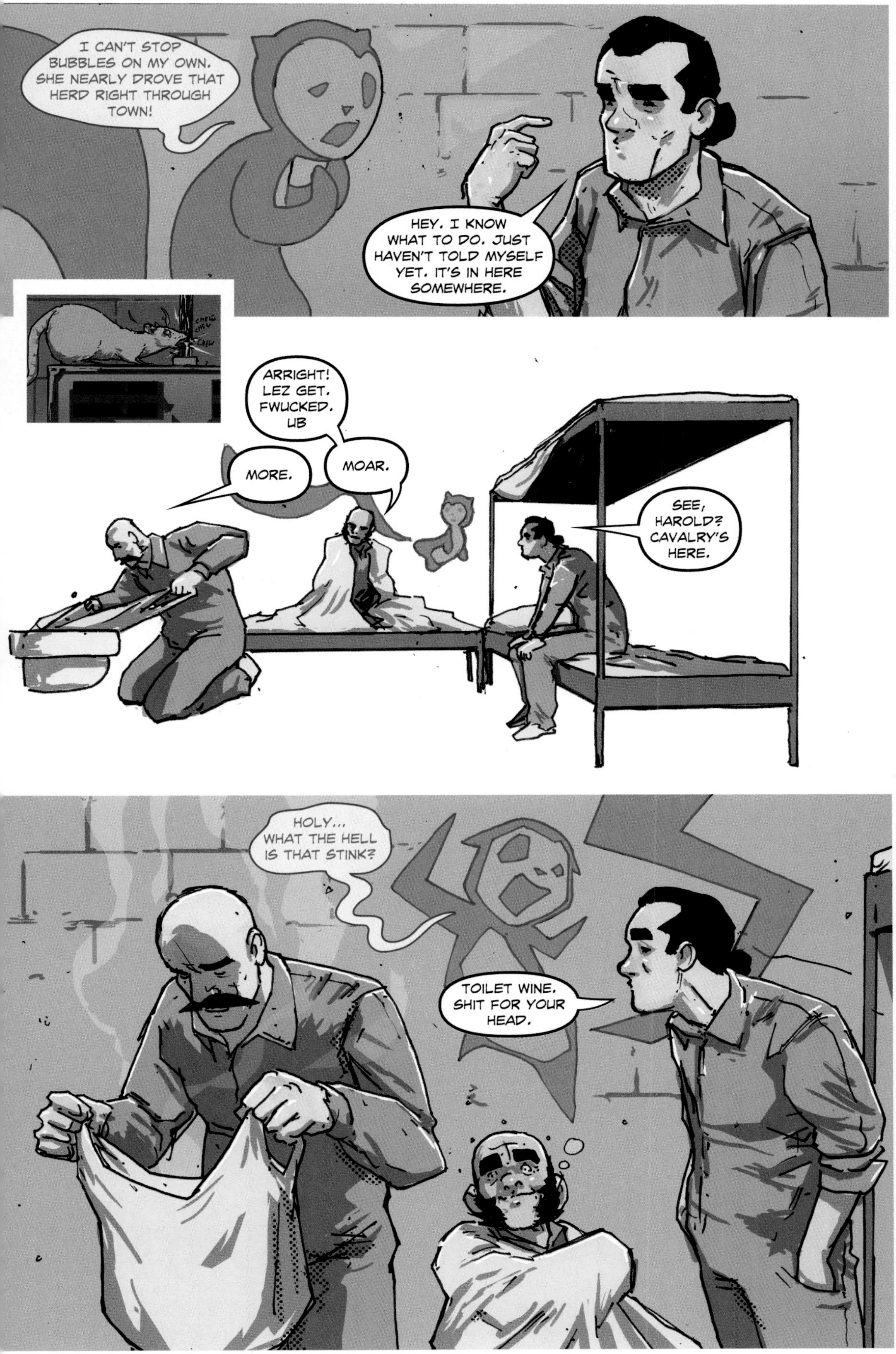
I CAN'T STOP BUBBLES ON MY OWN. SHE NEARLY DROVE THAT HERD RIGHT THROUGH TOWN!
HEY. I KNOW WHAT TO DO. JUST HAVEN'T TOLD MYSELF YET. IT'S IN HERE SOMEWHERE.
CHEW CHEW CHEW
ARRIGHT! LEZ GET. FWUCKED. UB
MORE.
MOAR.
SEE, HAROLD? CAVALRY'S HERE.
HOLY... WHAT THE HELL IS THAT STINK?
TOILET WINE. SHIT FOR YOUR HEAD.

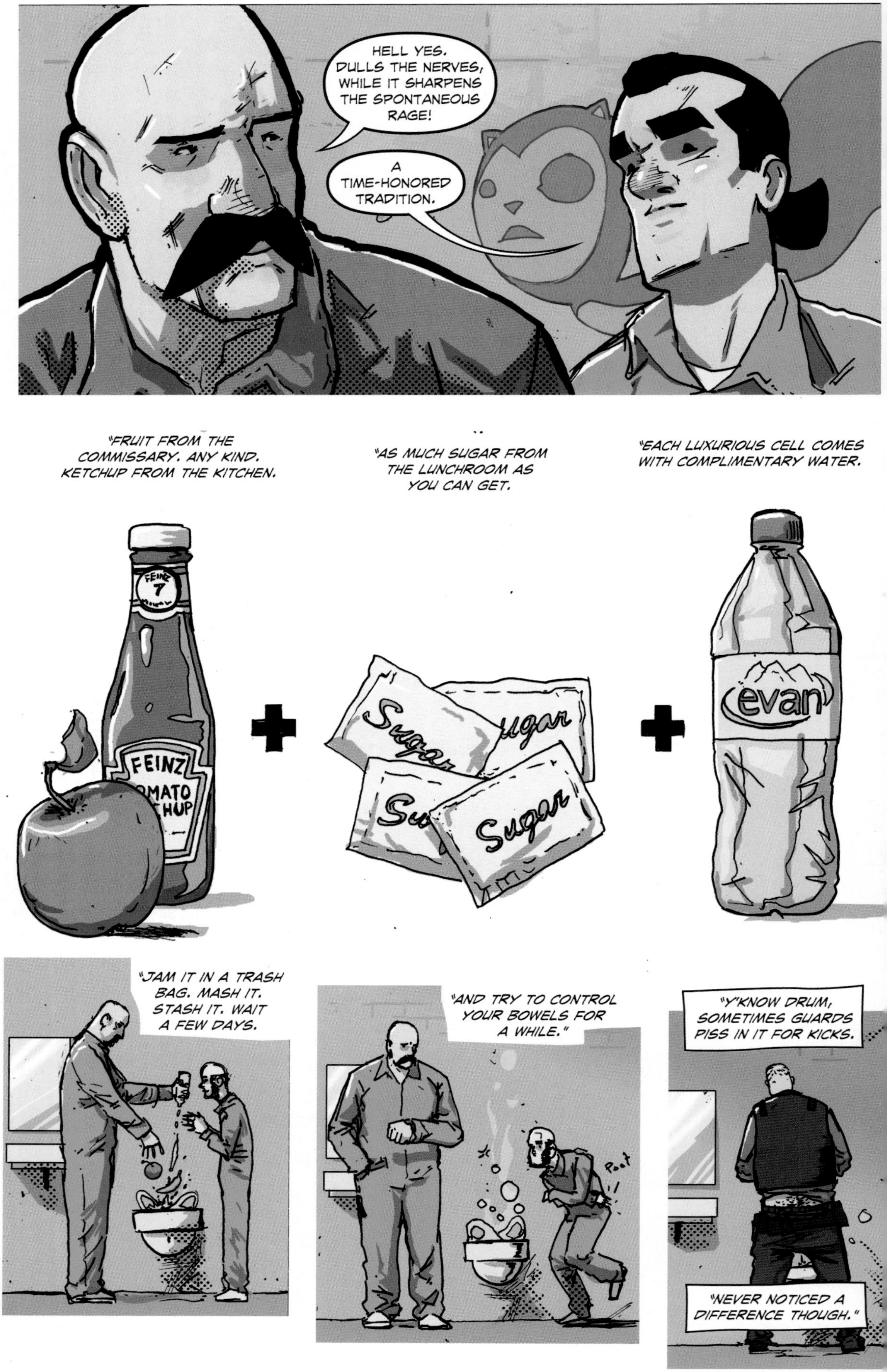
HELL YES. DULLS THE NERVES, WHILE IT SHARPENS THE SPONTANEOUS RAGE!
A TIME-HONORED TRADITION.
"FRUIT FROM THE COMMISSARY. ANY KIND. KETCHUP FROM THE KITCHEN.
"AS MUCH SUGAR FROM THE LUNCHROOM AS YOU CAN GET.
"EACH LUXURIOUS CELL COMES WITH COMPLIMENTARY WATER.
FEINZ
Sugar
evan
"JAM IT IN A TRASH BAG. MASH IT. STASH IT. WAIT A FEW DAYS.
"AND TRY TO CONTROL YOUR BOWELS FOR A WHILE."
Poot
"Y'KNOW DRUM, SOMETIMES GUARDS PISS IN IT FOR KICKS.
"NEVER NOTICED A DIFFERENCE THOUGH."

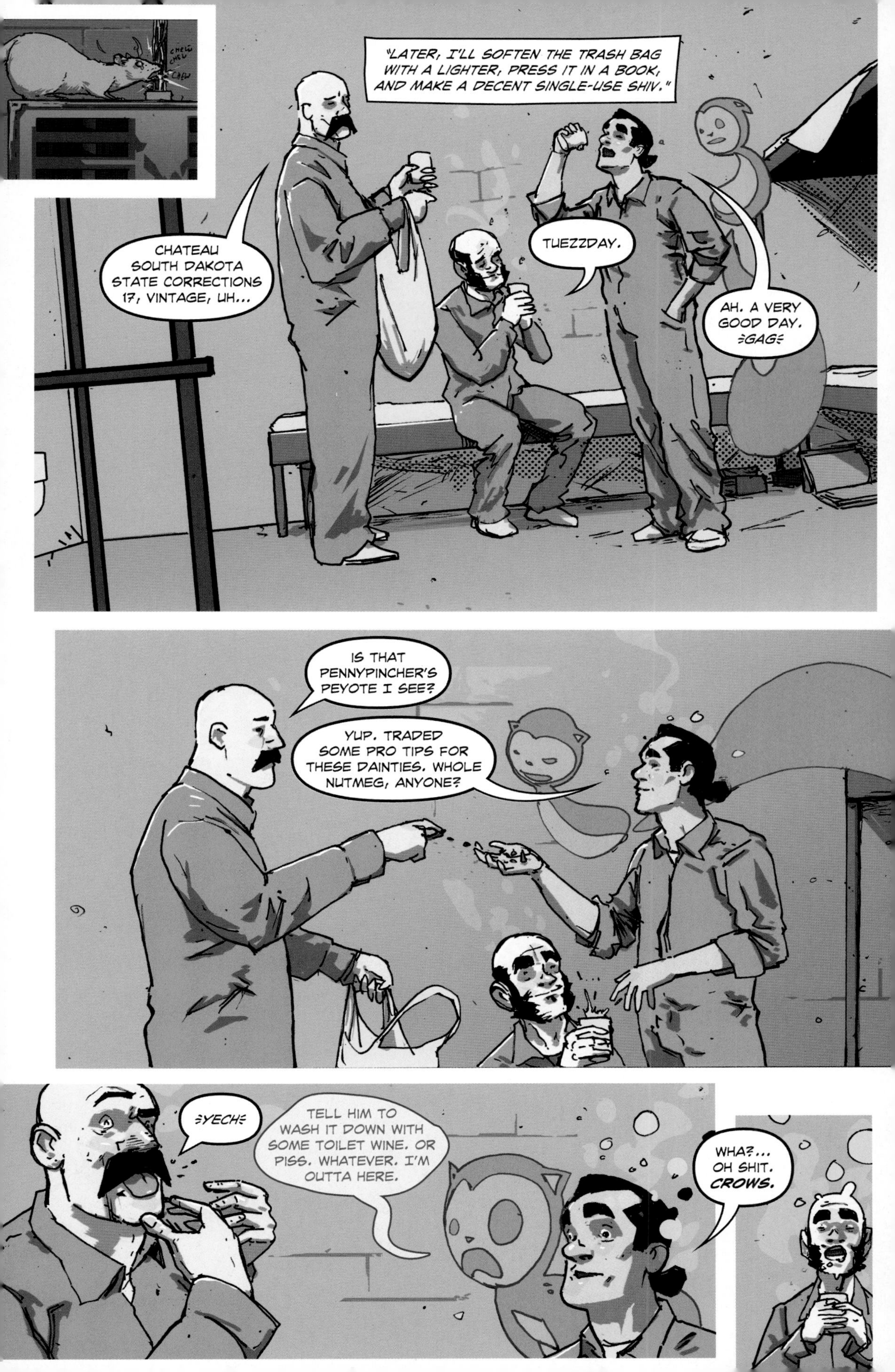
CHEW CHEW
CHEW
"LATER, I'LL SOFTEN THE TRASH BAG WITH A LIGHTER, PRESS IT IN A BOOK, AND MAKE A DECENT SINGLE-USE SHIV."
CHATEAU SOUTH DAKOTA STATE CORRECTIONS 17, VINTAGE, UH...
TUEZZDAY.
AH. A VERY GOOD DAY. ≶GAG≶
IS THAT PENNYPINCHER'S PEYOTE I SEE?
YUP. TRADED SOME PRO TIPS FOR THESE DAINTIES. WHOLE NUTMEG, ANYONE?
...
≶YECH≶
TELL HIM TO WASH IT DOWN WITH SOME TOILET WINE. OR PISS. WHATEVER. I'M OUTTA HERE.
WHA?... OH SHIT. *CROWS.*

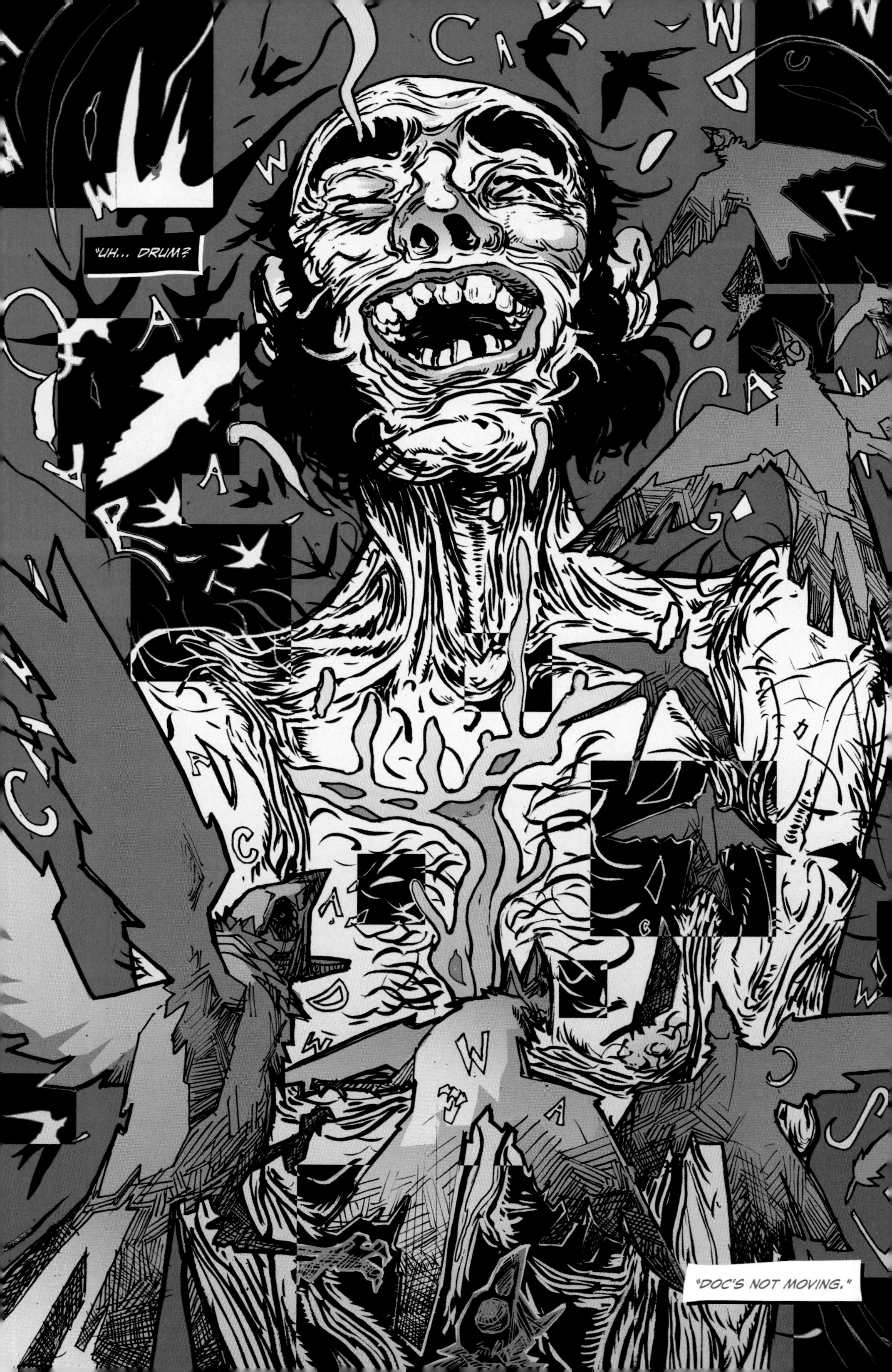
"UH... DRUM?
"DOC'S NOT MOVING."

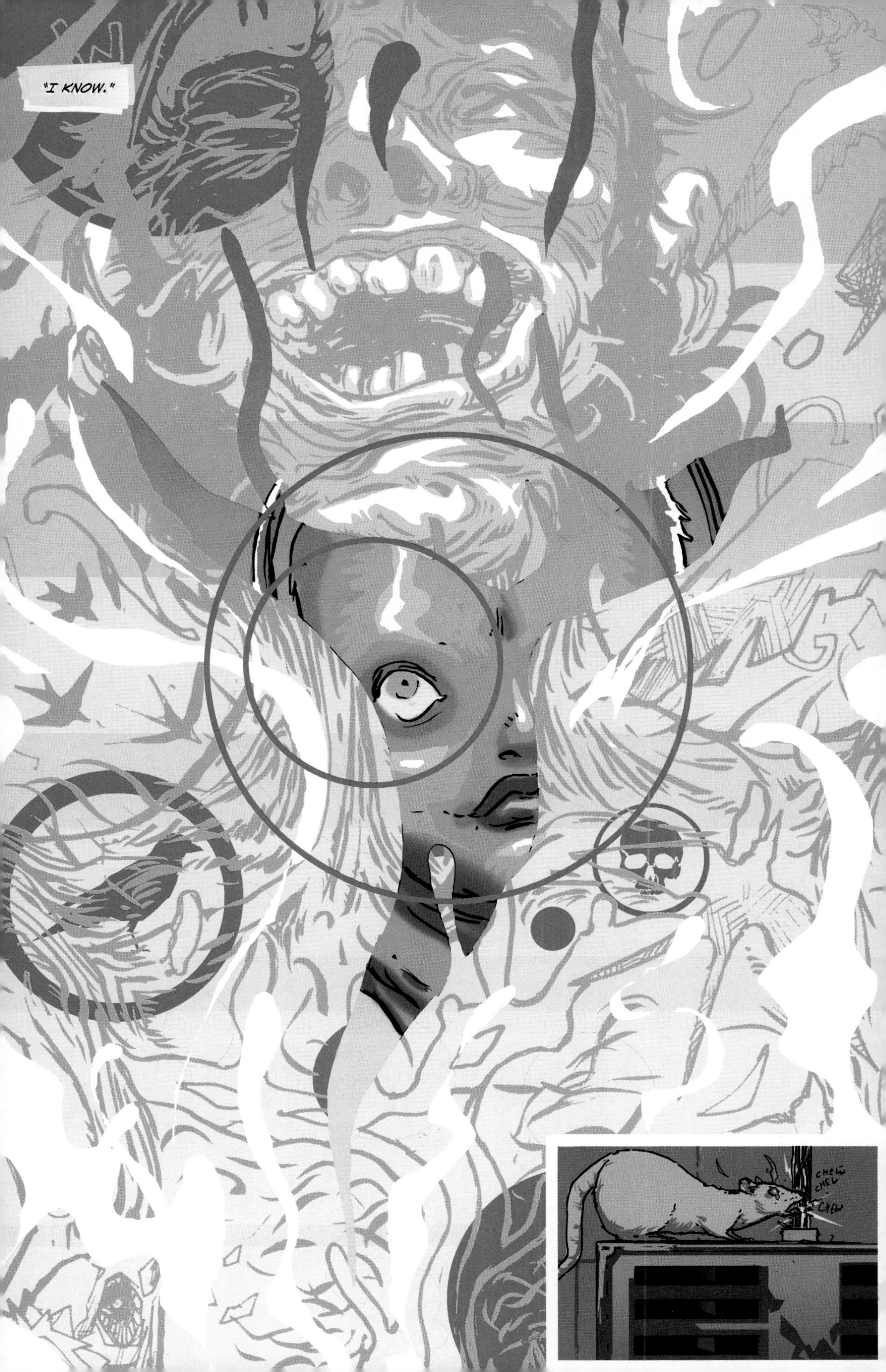
"I KNOW."
CHEW
CHEW
CHEW

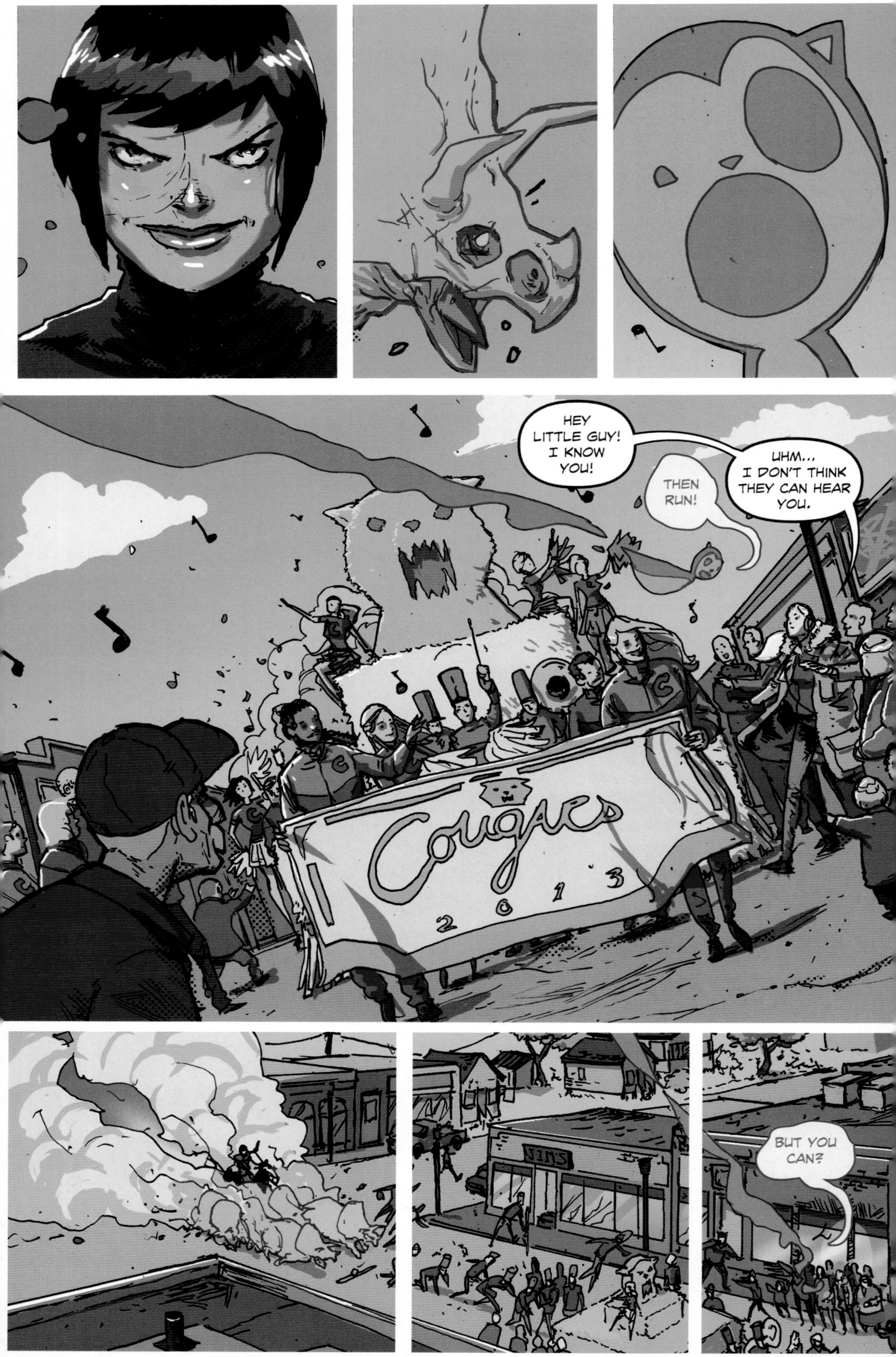
HEY LITTLE GUY! I KNOW YOU!
THEN RUN!
UHM... I DON'T THINK THEY CAN HEAR YOU.
Cougars
2013
SIMS
BUT YOU CAN?

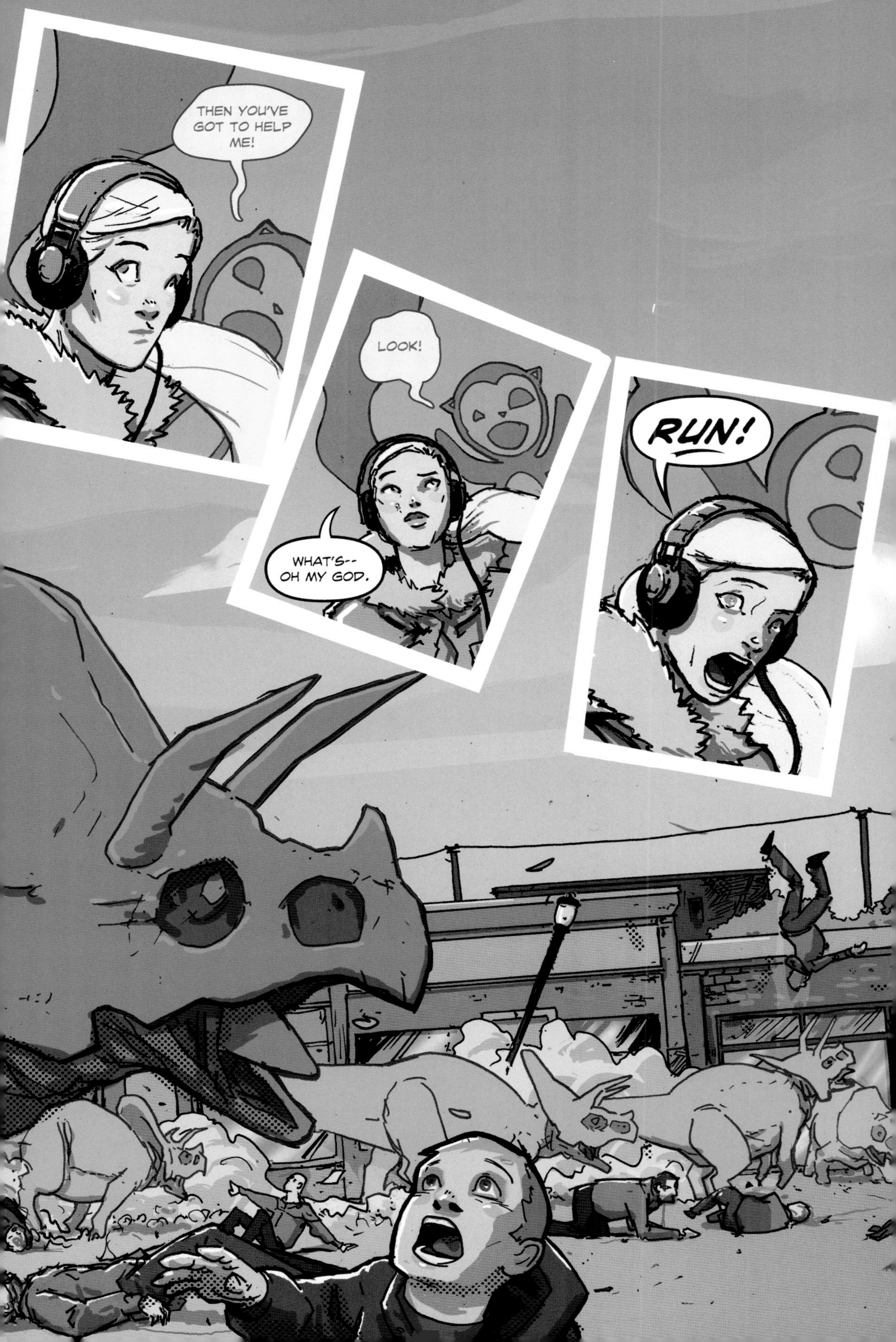
THEN YOU'VE GOT TO HELP ME!
LOOK!
WHAT'S-- OH MY GOD.
RUN!

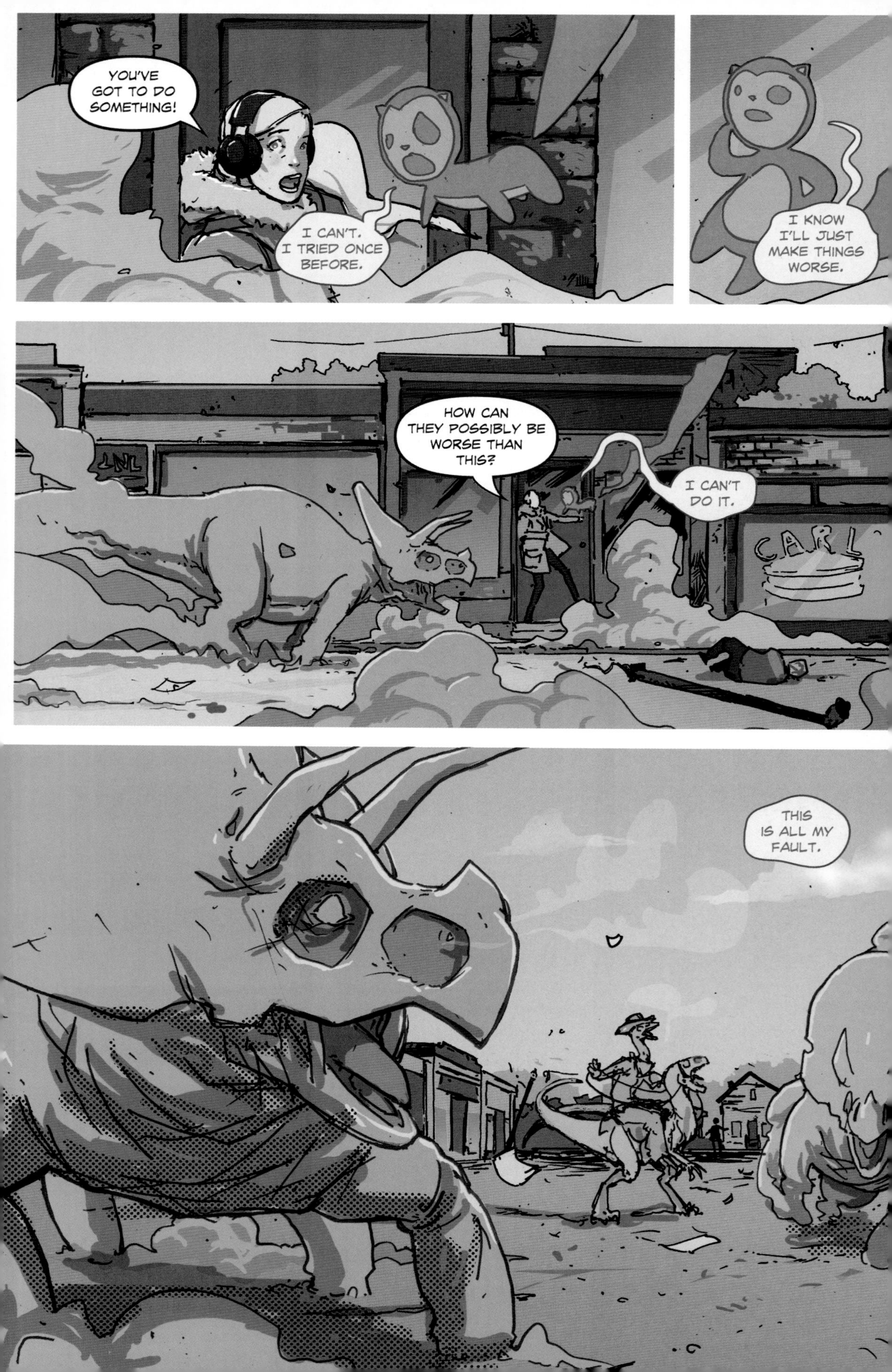
YOU'VE GOT TO DO SOMETHING!
I CAN'T. I TRIED ONCE BEFORE.
I KNOW I'LL JUST MAKE THINGS WORSE.
HOW CAN THEY POSSIBLY BE WORSE THAN THIS?
I CAN'T DO IT.
CARL
THIS IS ALL MY FAULT.

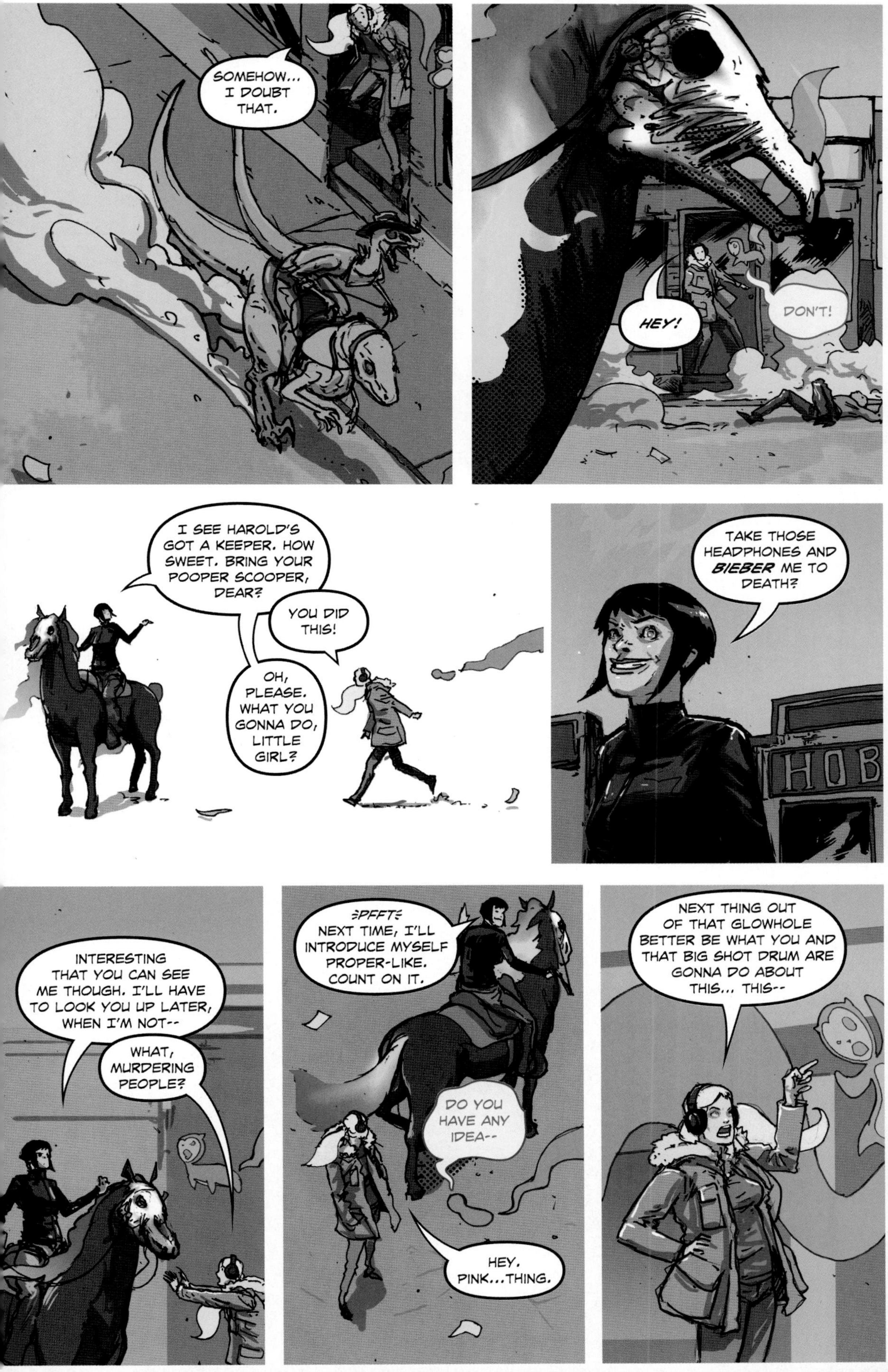
SOMEHOW... I DOUBT THAT.
HEY!
DON'T!
I SEE HAROLD'S GOT A KEEPER. HOW SWEET. BRING YOUR POOPER SCOOPER, DEAR?
YOU DID THIS!
OH, PLEASE. WHAT YOU GONNA DO, LITTLE GIRL?
TAKE THOSE HEADPHONES AND BIEBER ME TO DEATH?
HOB
INTERESTING THAT YOU CAN SEE ME THOUGH. I'LL HAVE TO LOOK YOU UP LATER, WHEN I'M NOT--
WHAT, MURDERING PEOPLE?
PFFT
NEXT TIME, I'LL INTRODUCE MYSELF PROPER-LIKE. COUNT ON IT.
DO YOU HAVE ANY IDEA--
HEY. PINK...THING.
NEXT THING OUT OF THAT GLOWHOLE BETTER BE WHAT YOU AND THAT BIG SHOT DRUM ARE GONNA DO ABOUT THIS... THIS--

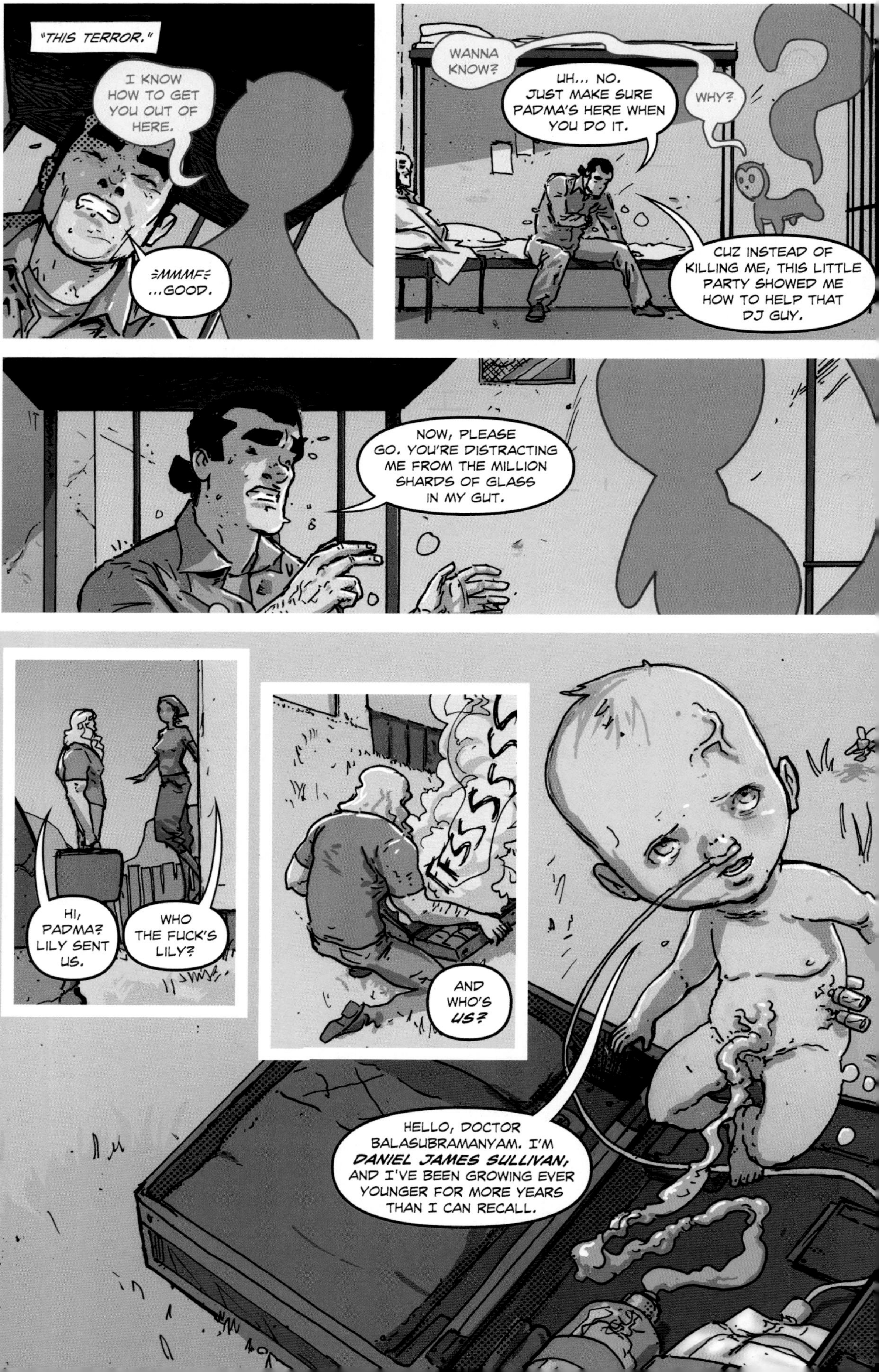
"THIS TERROR."
I KNOW HOW TO GET YOU OUT OF HERE.
MMMF ...GOOD.
WANNA KNOW?
UH... NO. JUST MAKE SURE PADMA'S HERE WHEN YOU DO IT.
WHY?
CUZ INSTEAD OF KILLING ME, THIS LITTLE PARTY SHOWED ME HOW TO HELP THAT DJ GUY.
NOW, PLEASE GO. YOU'RE DISTRACTING ME FROM THE MILLION SHARDS OF GLASS IN MY GUT.
HI, PADMA? LILY SENT US.
WHO THE FUCK'S LILY?
AND WHO'S *US?*
HELLO, DOCTOR BALASUBRAMANYAM. I'M ***DANIEL JAMES SULLIVAN,*** AND I'VE BEEN GROWING EVER YOUNGER FOR MORE YEARS THAN I CAN RECALL.

I WAS TOLD WE WOULD BE SAFE HERE. I TAKE IT MISTER HELLAR DIDN'T FULLY BRIEF YOU.
I'M SORRY FOR THAT.
WELL--
RING
PERHAPS THAT'S HIM NOW.
HI, IT'S RAY OVER AT THE SDSC17 MORGUE. I GOT A STIFF.
THINK YOU COULD HELP ME CLEAR HIS PAPERWORK BEFORE HE HEADS TO POTTER'S FIELD?
IT LOOKS LIKE AN ADVERSE ROHYP-NUTMEG INTERACTION, BUT I'D LIKE A NUT AND BERRY TYPE LIKE YOURSELF TO SIGN OFF ON HIM FOR CORROBORATION.
GEE, THANKS.
AW, DON'T BE LIKE THAT. PLEASE?
SIGH YEAH, SURE. I'LL DO IT RIGHT NOW.
I NEED TO GET OUT OF THE HOUSE ANYWAY.

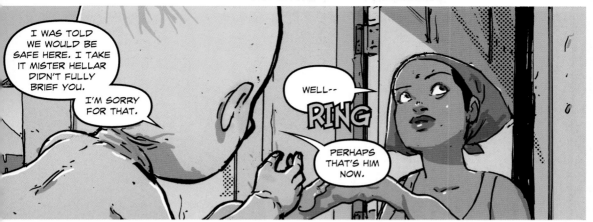

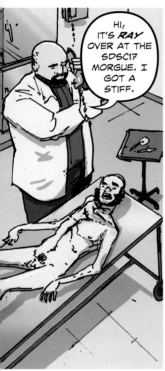

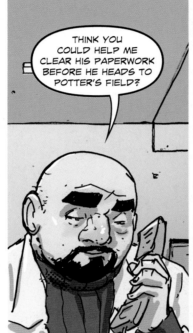

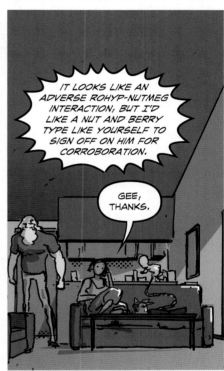

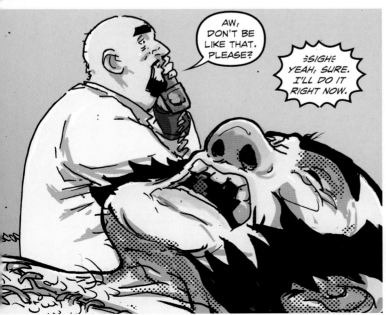

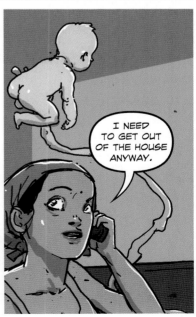

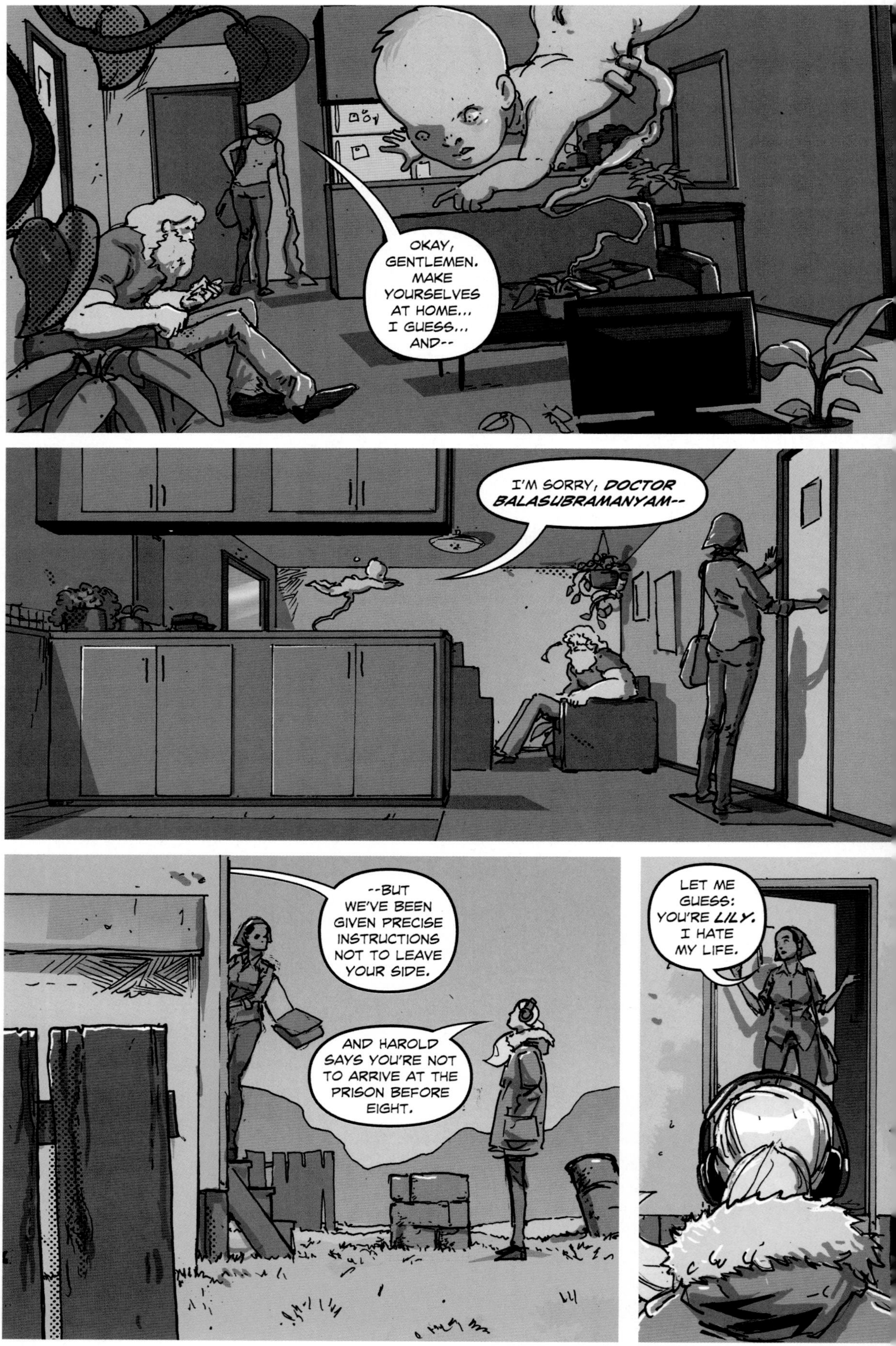

OKAY, GENTLEMEN. MAKE YOURSELVES AT HOME... I GUESS... AND--
I'M SORRY, DOCTOR BALASUBRAMANYAM--
--BUT WE'VE BEEN GIVEN PRECISE INSTRUCTIONS NOT TO LEAVE YOUR SIDE.
AND HAROLD SAYS YOU'RE NOT TO ARRIVE AT THE PRISON BEFORE EIGHT.
LET ME GUESS: YOU'RE LILY. I HATE MY LIFE.

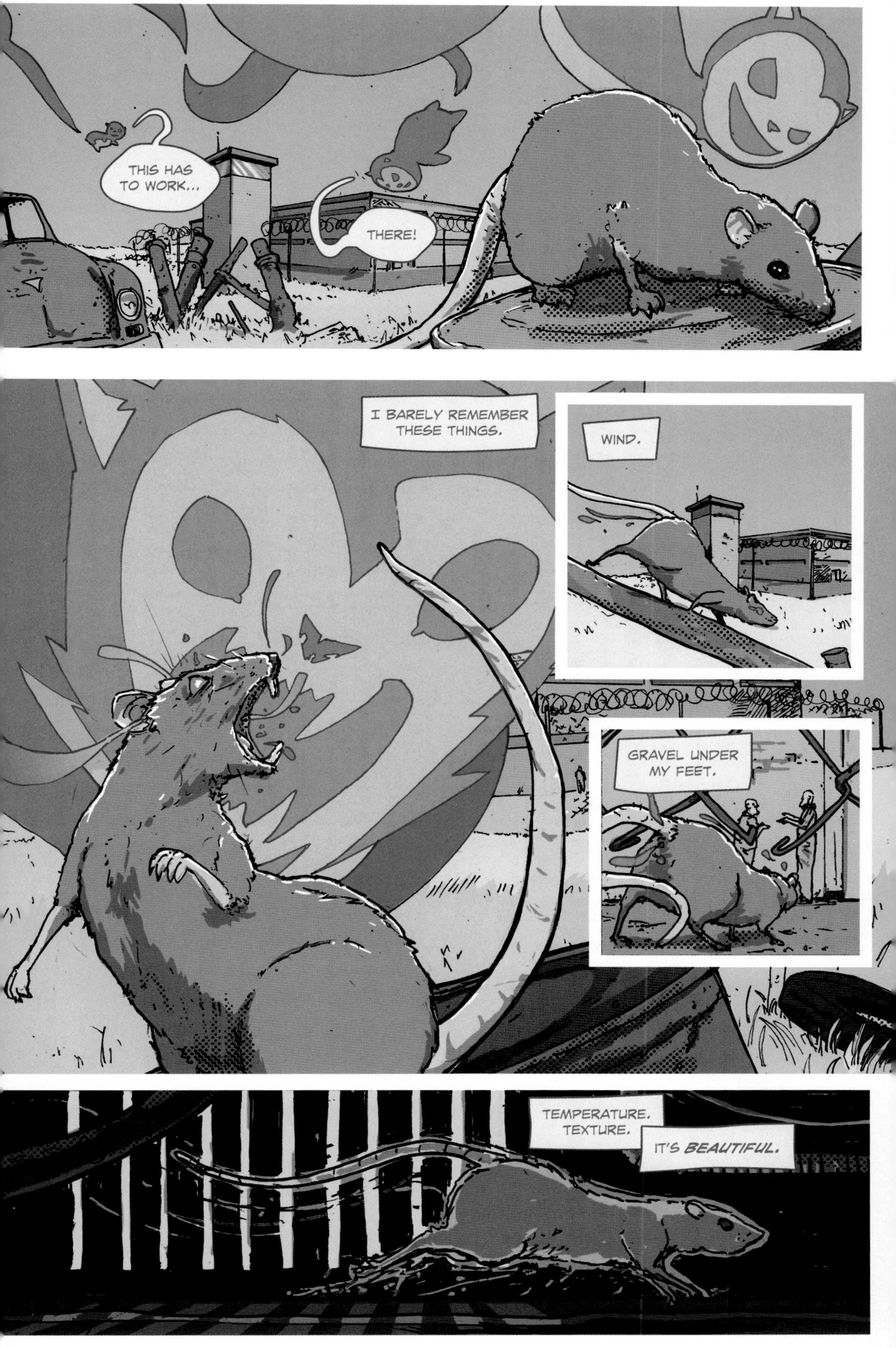
THIS HAS TO WORK...
THERE!
I BARELY REMEMBER THESE THINGS.
WIND.
GRAVEL UNDER MY FEET.
TEMPERATURE. TEXTURE.
IT'S *BEAUTIFUL.*

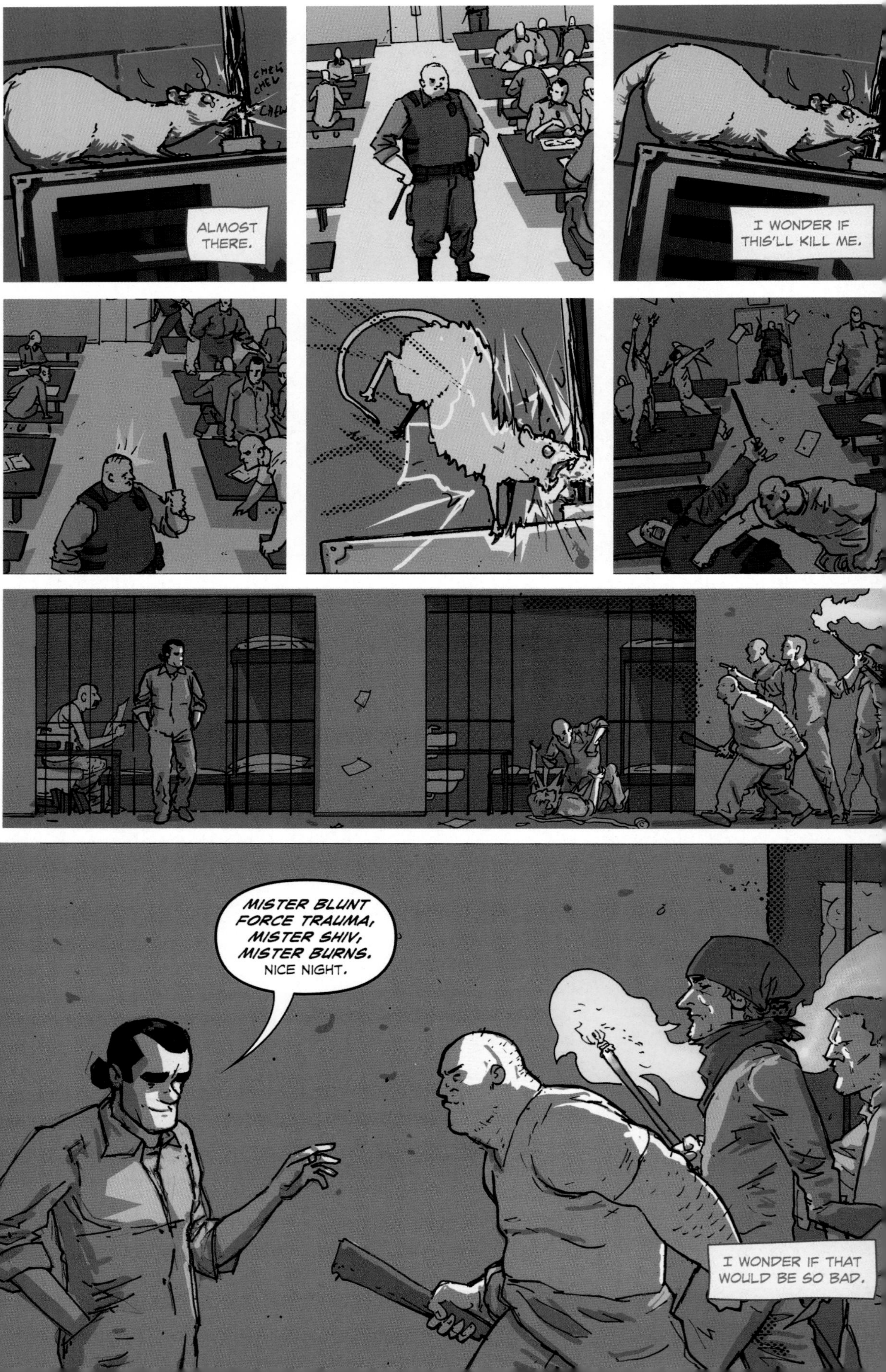
CHEW CHEW
CHEW
ALMOST THERE.
I WONDER IF THIS'LL KILL ME.
MISTER BLUNT FORCE TRAUMA, MISTER SHIV, MISTER BURNS. NICE NIGHT.
I WONDER IF THAT WOULD BE SO BAD.

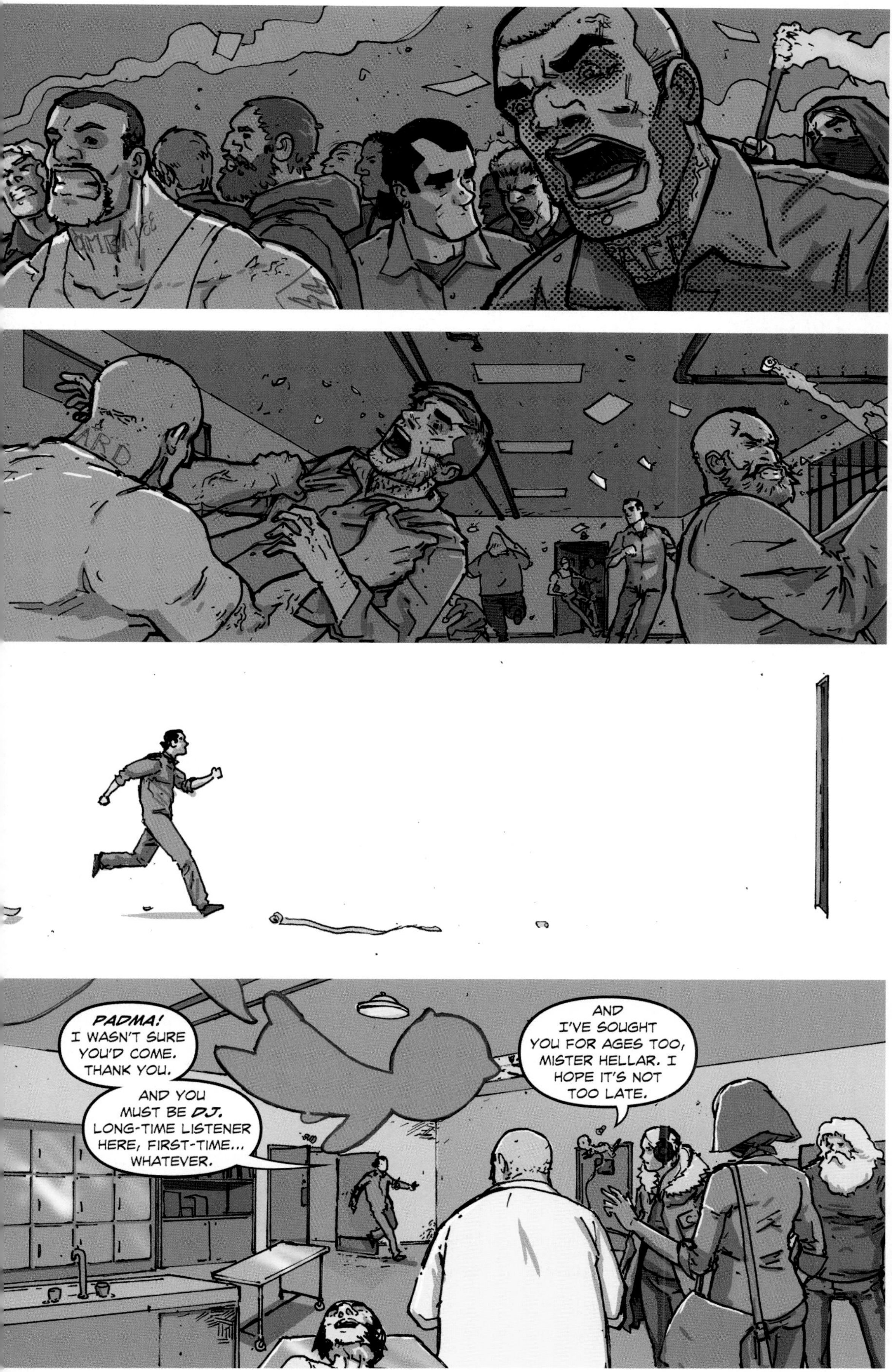
PADMA! I WASN'T SURE YOU'D COME. THANK YOU.
AND YOU MUST BE DJ. LONG-TIME LISTENER HERE, FIRST-TIME... WHATEVER.
AND I'VE SOUGHT YOU FOR AGES TOO, MISTER HELLAR. I HOPE IT'S NOT TOO LATE.

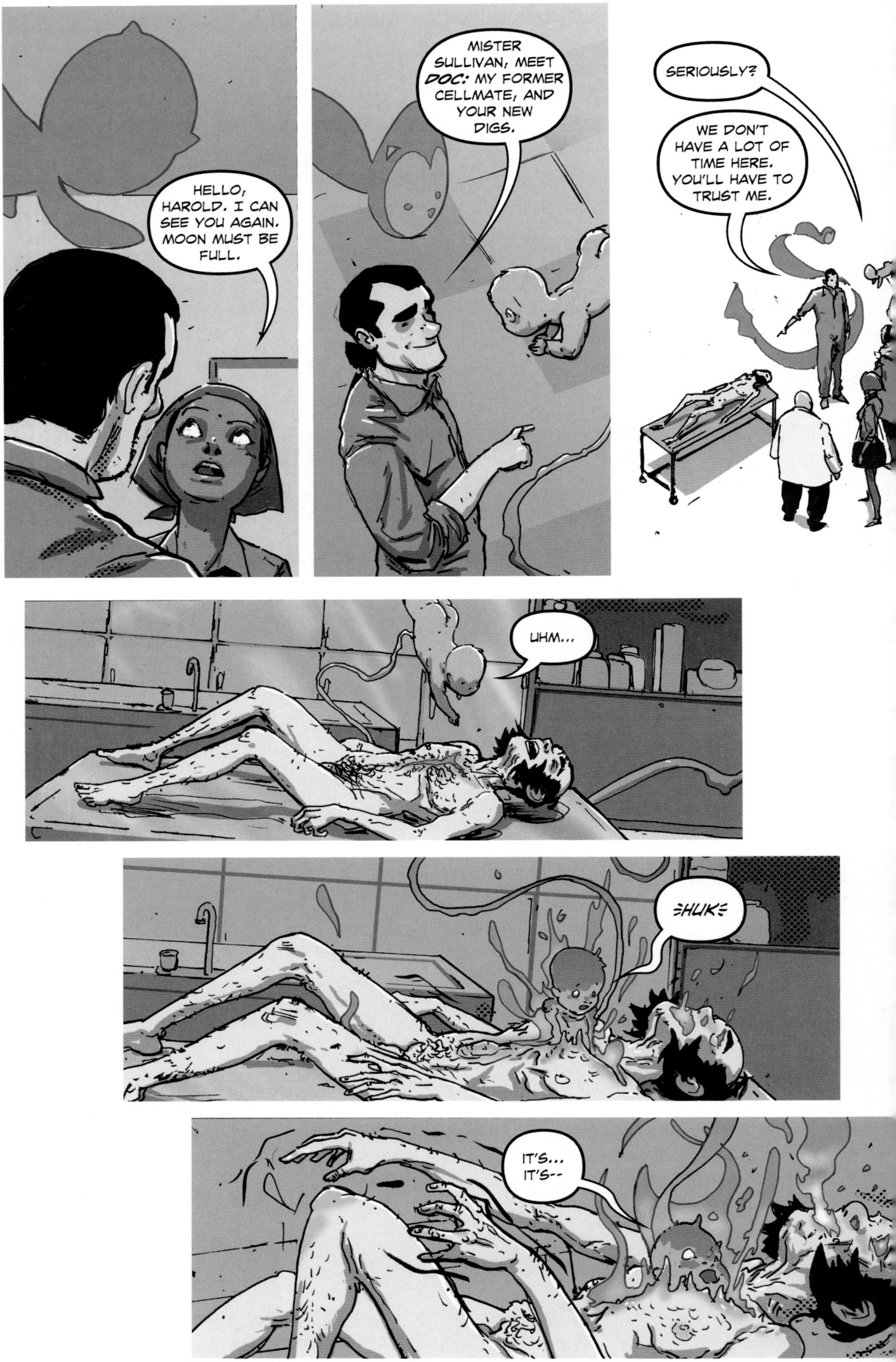
HELLO, HAROLD. I CAN SEE YOU AGAIN. MOON MUST BE FULL.
MISTER SULLIVAN, MEET DOC: MY FORMER CELLMATE, AND YOUR NEW DIGS.
SERIOUSLY?
WE DON'T HAVE A LOT OF TIME HERE. YOU'LL HAVE TO TRUST ME.
UHM...
HUK
IT'S... IT'S--

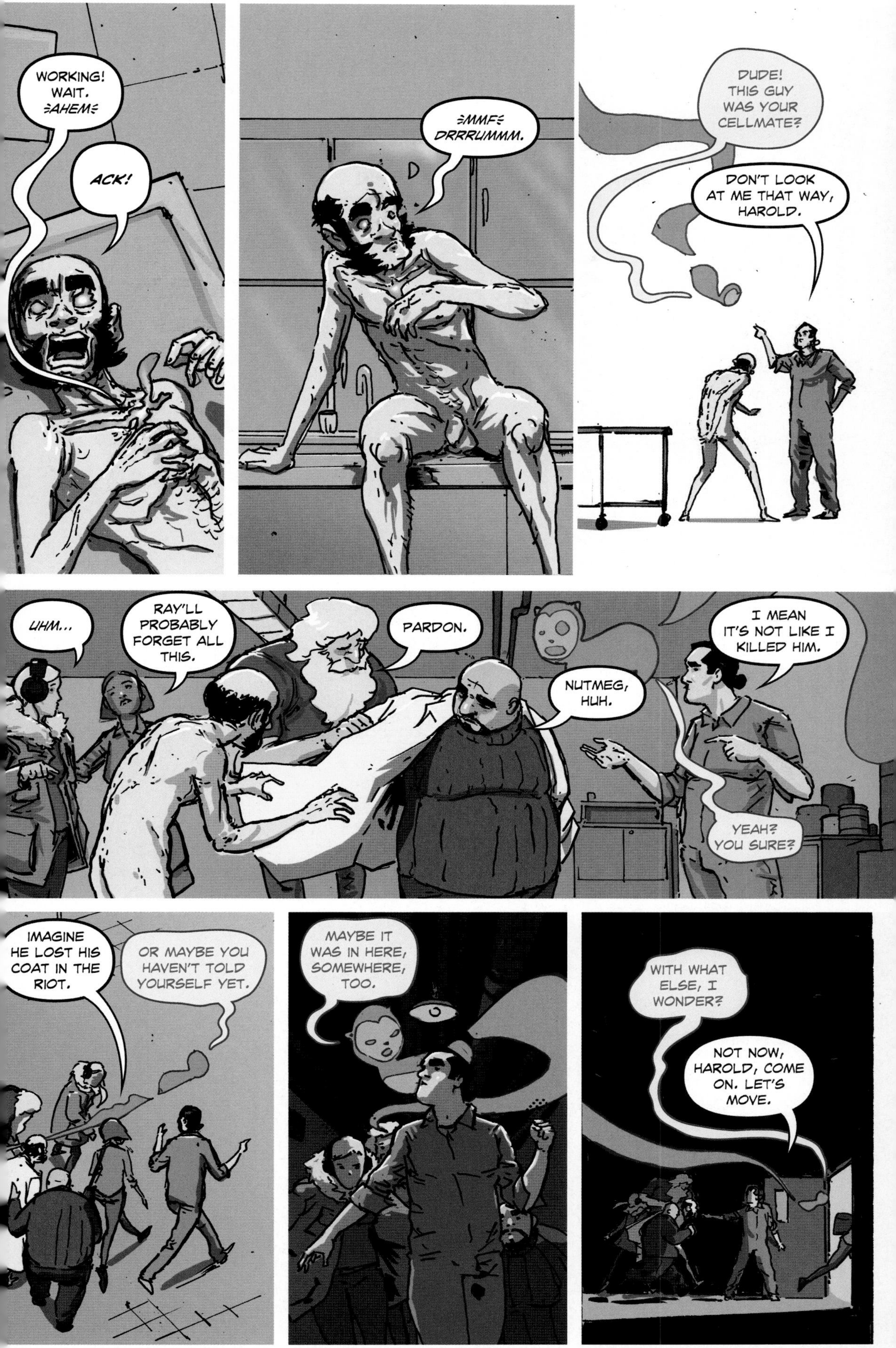
WORKING! WAIT. ≑AHEM≑
ACK!
≑MMF≑ DRRRUMMM.
DUDE! THIS GUY WAS YOUR CELLMATE?
DON'T LOOK AT ME THAT WAY, HAROLD.
UHM...
RAY'LL PROBABLY FORGET ALL THIS.
PARDON.
NUTMEG, HUH.
I MEAN IT'S NOT LIKE I KILLED HIM.
YEAH? YOU SURE?
IMAGINE HE LOST HIS COAT IN THE RIOT.
OR MAYBE YOU HAVEN'T TOLD YOURSELF YET.
MAYBE IT WAS IN HERE, SOMEWHERE, TOO.
WITH WHAT ELSE, I WONDER?
NOT NOW, HAROLD, COME ON. LET'S MOVE.

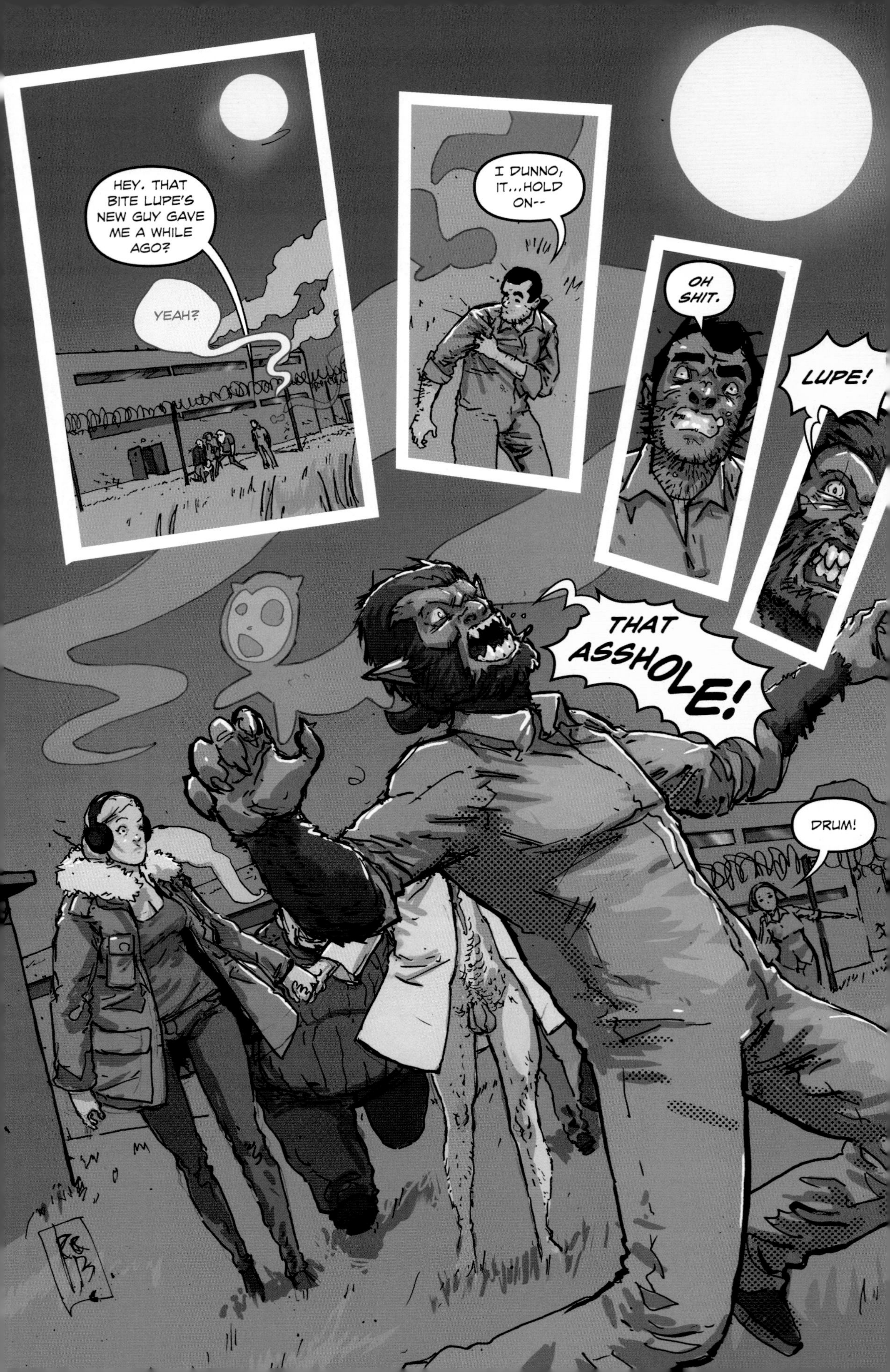
HEY. THAT BITE LUPE'S NEW GUY GAVE ME A WHILE AGO?
YEAH?
I DUNNO, IT...HOLD ON--
OH SHIT.
LUPE!
THAT ASSHOLE!
DRUM!

FIVE

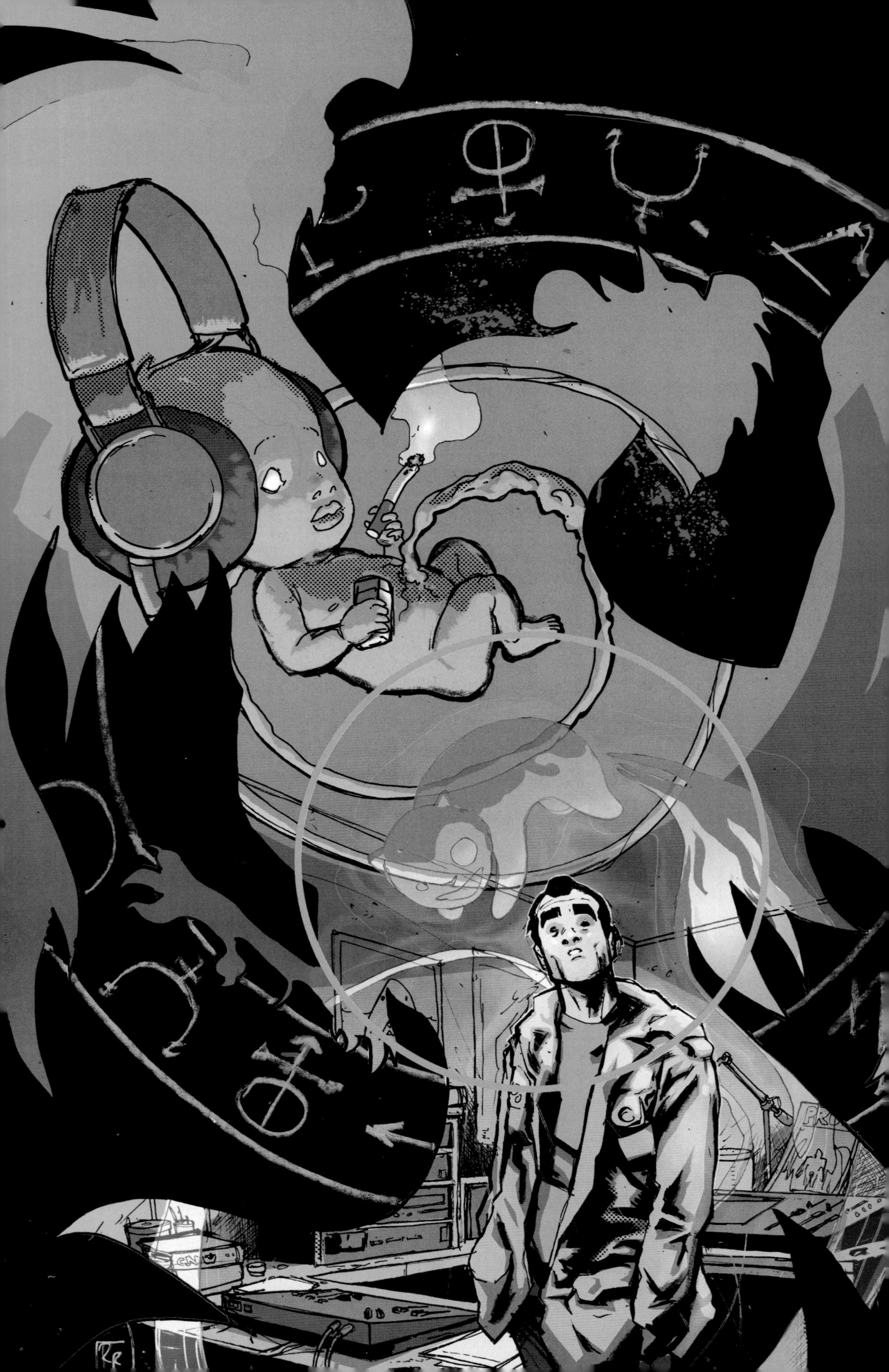

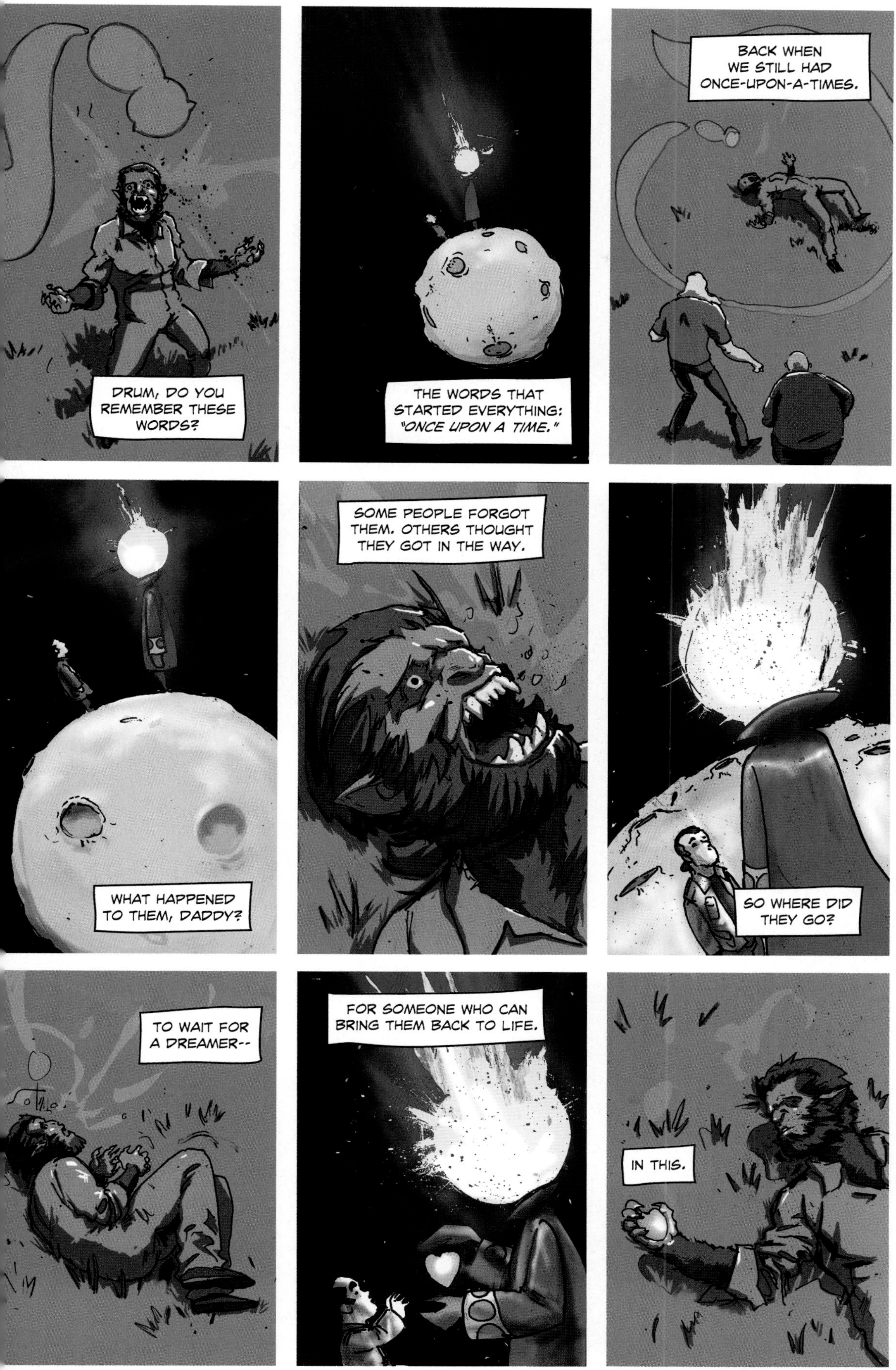
DRUM, DO YOU REMEMBER THESE WORDS?
THE WORDS THAT STARTED EVERYTHING: "ONCE UPON A TIME."
BACK WHEN WE STILL HAD ONCE-UPON-A-TIMES.
WHAT HAPPENED TO THEM, DADDY?
SOME PEOPLE FORGOT THEM. OTHERS THOUGHT THEY GOT IN THE WAY.
SO WHERE DID THEY GO?
TO WAIT FOR A DREAMER--
FOR SOMEONE WHO CAN BRING THEM BACK TO LIFE.
IN THIS.

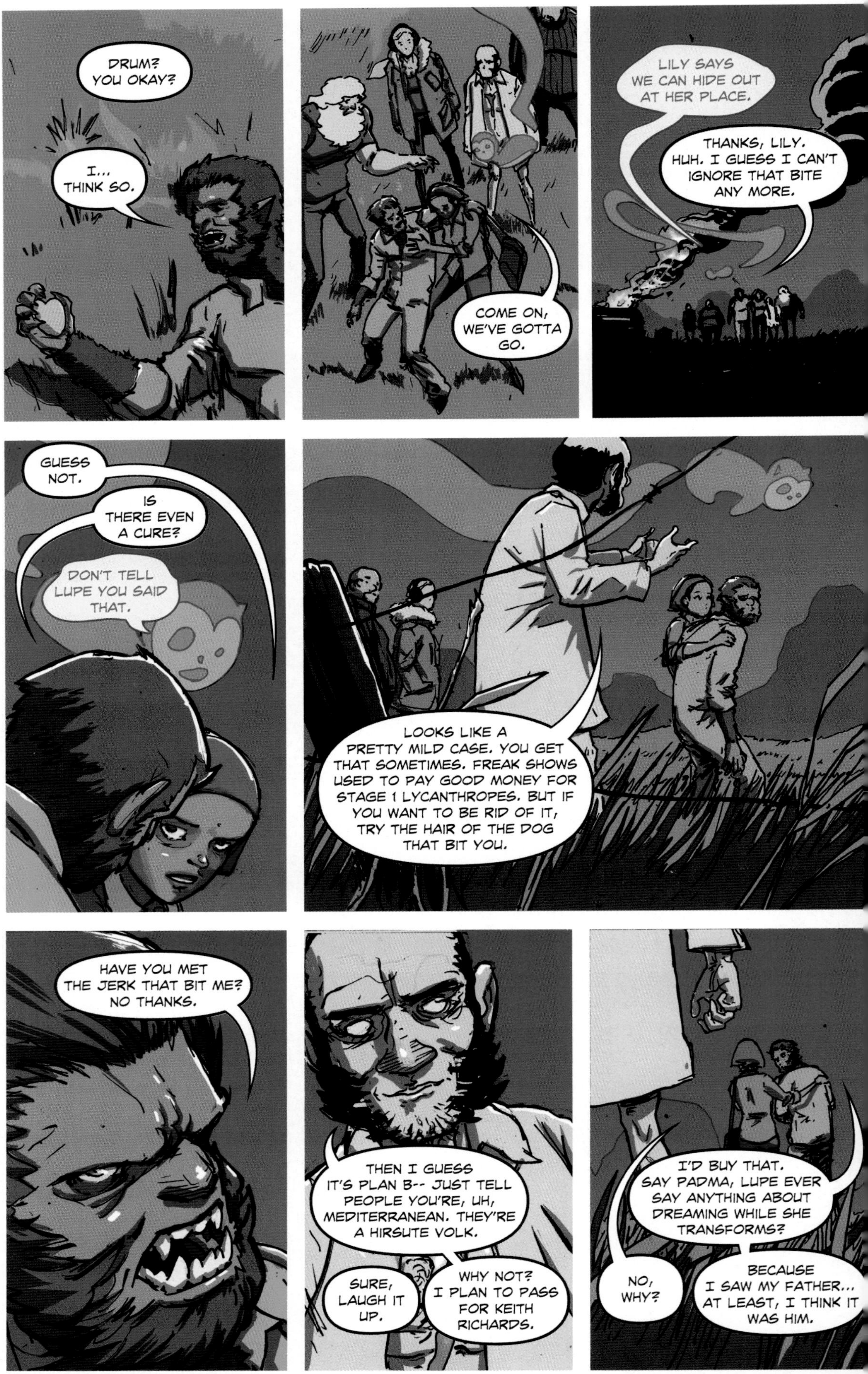
DRUM? YOU OKAY?
I... THINK SO.
COME ON, WE'VE GOTTA GO.
LILY SAYS WE CAN HIDE OUT AT HER PLACE.
THANKS, LILY. HUH. I GUESS I CAN'T IGNORE THAT BITE ANY MORE.
GUESS NOT.
IS THERE EVEN A CURE?
DON'T TELL LUPE YOU SAID THAT.
LOOKS LIKE A PRETTY MILD CASE. YOU GET THAT SOMETIMES. FREAK SHOWS USED TO PAY GOOD MONEY FOR STAGE 1 LYCANTHROPES. BUT IF YOU WANT TO BE RID OF IT, TRY THE HAIR OF THE DOG THAT BIT YOU.
HAVE YOU MET THE JERK THAT BIT ME? NO THANKS.
THEN I GUESS IT'S PLAN B-- JUST TELL PEOPLE YOU'RE, UH, MEDITERRANEAN. THEY'RE A HIRSUTE VOLK.
SURE, LAUGH IT UP.
WHY NOT? I PLAN TO PASS FOR KEITH RICHARDS.
I'D BUY THAT. SAY PADMA, LUPE EVER SAY ANYTHING ABOUT DREAMING WHILE SHE TRANSFORMS?
NO, WHY?
BECAUSE I SAW MY FATHER... AT LEAST, I THINK IT WAS HIM.

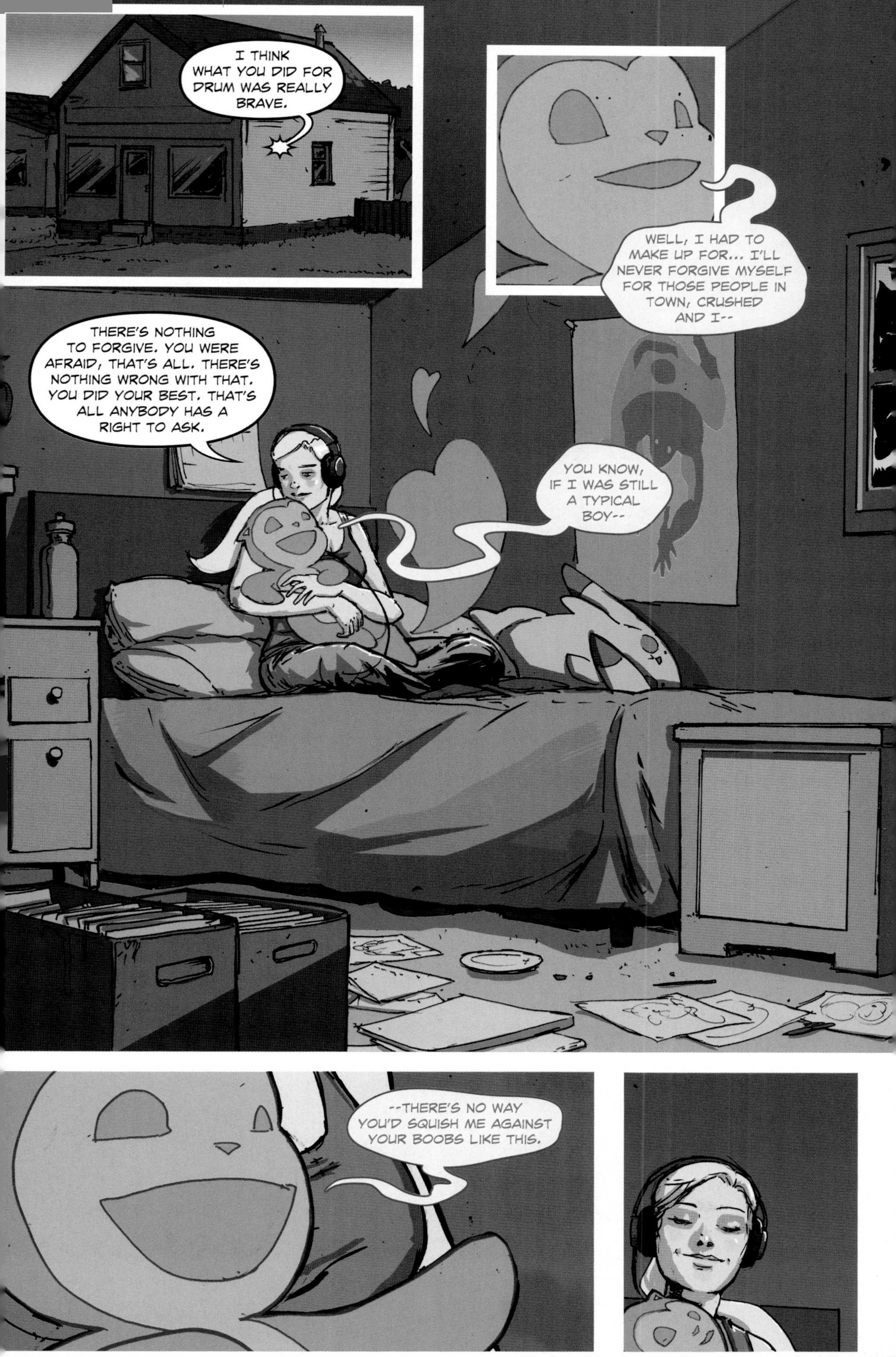
I THINK WHAT YOU DID FOR DRUM WAS REALLY BRAVE.
WELL, I HAD TO MAKE UP FOR... I'LL NEVER FORGIVE MYSELF FOR THOSE PEOPLE IN TOWN, CRUSHED AND I--
THERE'S NOTHING TO FORGIVE. YOU WERE AFRAID, THAT'S ALL. THERE'S NOTHING WRONG WITH THAT. YOU DID YOUR BEST. THAT'S ALL ANYBODY HAS A RIGHT TO ASK.
YOU KNOW, IF I WAS STILL A TYPICAL BOY--
--THERE'S NO WAY YOU'D SQUISH ME AGAINST YOUR BOOBS LIKE THIS.

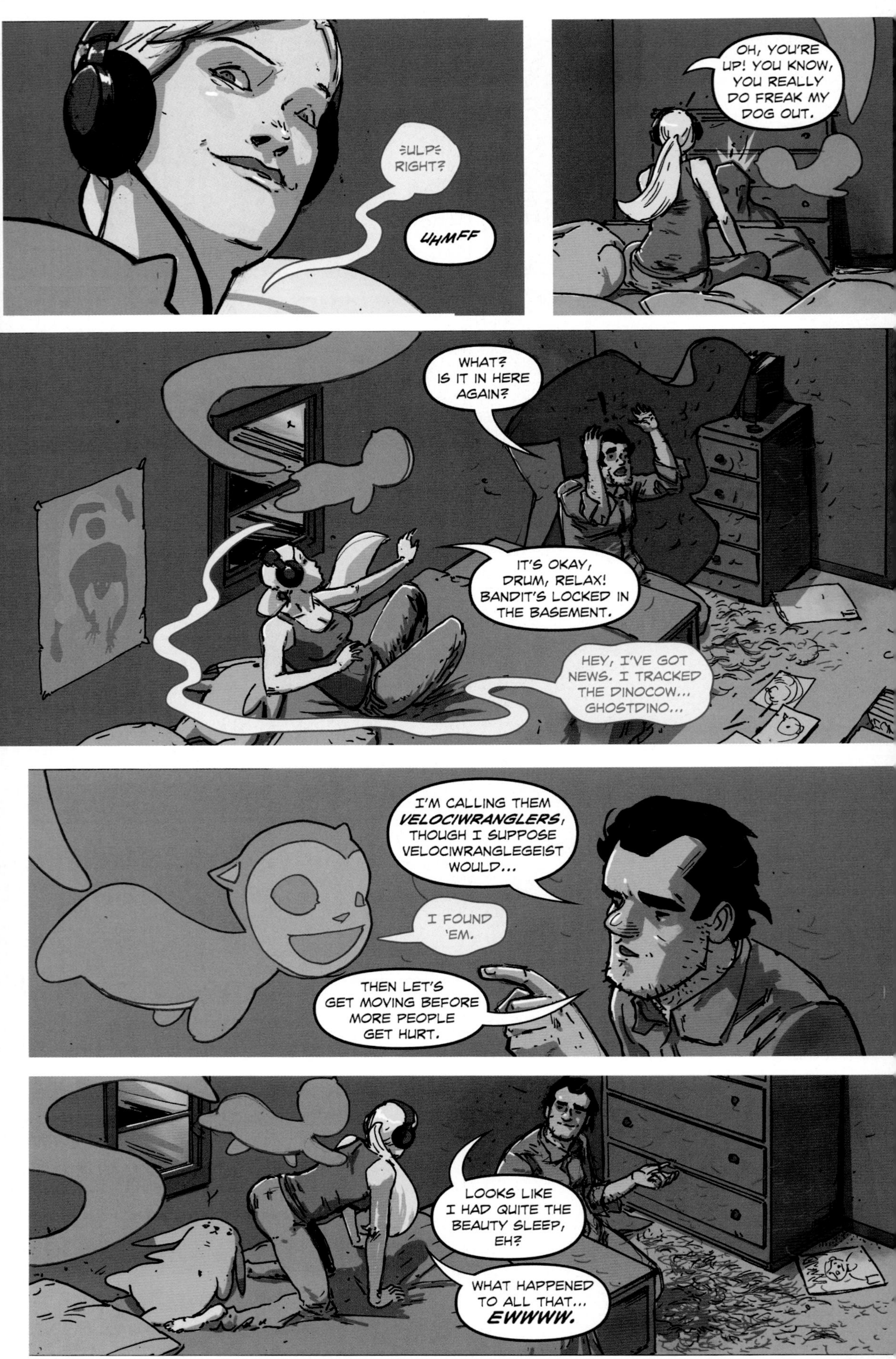

ƧULPƧ RIGHT?
UHMFF
OH, YOU'RE UP! YOU KNOW, YOU REALLY DO FREAK MY DOG OUT.
WHAT? IS IT IN HERE AGAIN?
IT'S OKAY, DRUM, RELAX! BANDIT'S LOCKED IN THE BASEMENT.
HEY, I'VE GOT NEWS. I TRACKED THE DINOCOW... GHOSTDINO...
I'M CALLING THEM VELOCIWRANGLERS, THOUGH I SUPPOSE VELOCIWRANGLEGEIST WOULD...
I FOUND 'EM.
THEN LET'S GET MOVING BEFORE MORE PEOPLE GET HURT.
LOOKS LIKE I HAD QUITE THE BEAUTY SLEEP, EH?
WHAT HAPPENED TO ALL THAT... EWWWW.

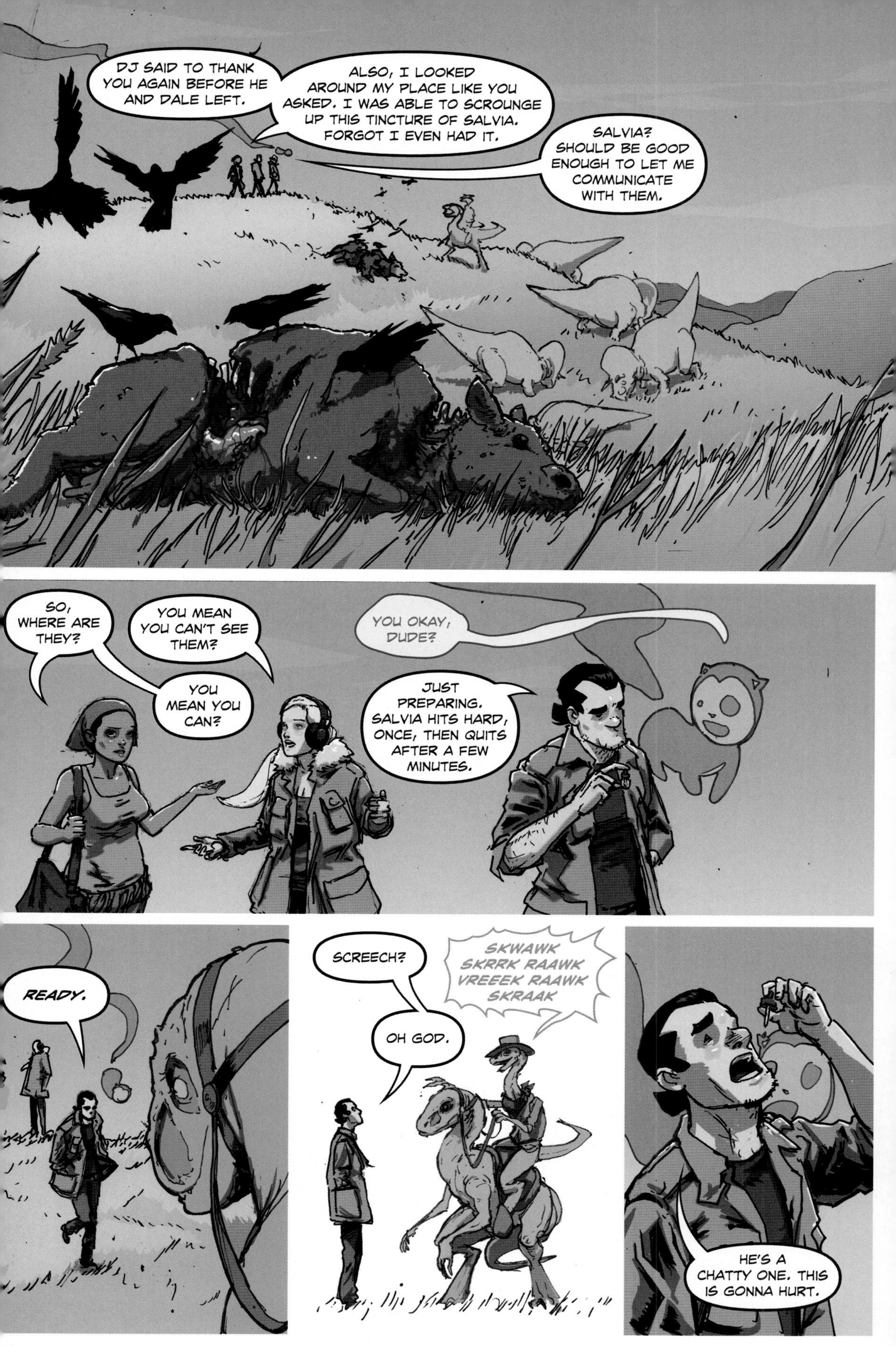
DJ SAID TO THANK YOU AGAIN BEFORE HE AND DALE LEFT.
ALSO, I LOOKED AROUND MY PLACE LIKE YOU ASKED. I WAS ABLE TO SCROUNGE UP THIS TINCTURE OF SALVIA. FORGOT I EVEN HAD IT.
SALVIA? SHOULD BE GOOD ENOUGH TO LET ME COMMUNICATE WITH THEM.
SO, WHERE ARE THEY?
YOU MEAN YOU CAN'T SEE THEM?
YOU MEAN YOU CAN?
YOU OKAY, DUDE?
JUST PREPARING. SALVIA HITS HARD, ONCE, THEN QUITS AFTER A FEW MINUTES.
HE'S A CHATTY ONE. THIS IS GONNA HURT.
READY.
SCREECH?
SKWAWK SKRRK RAAWK VREEEK RAAWK SKRAAK
OH GOD.

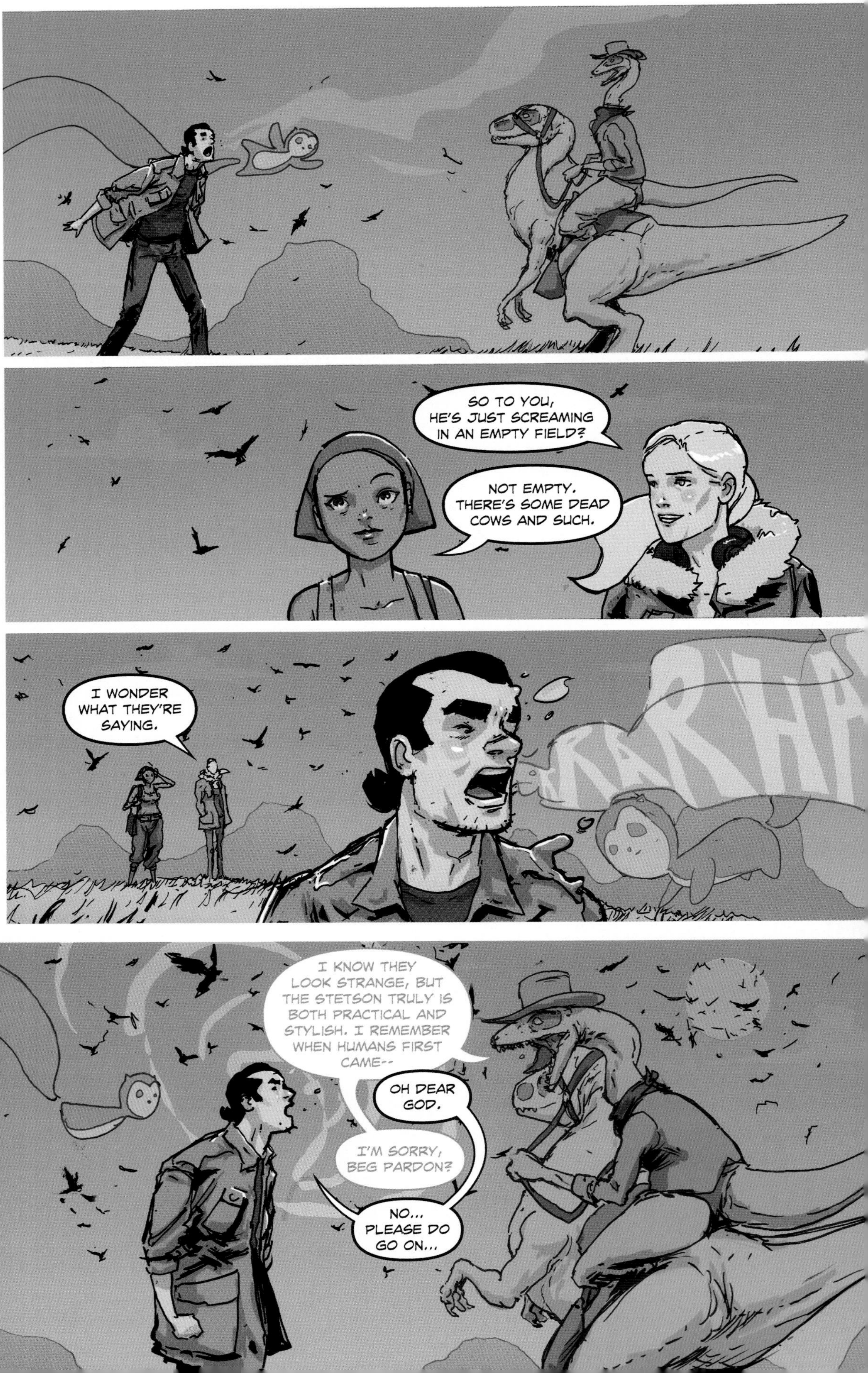
SO TO YOU, HE'S JUST SCREAMING IN AN EMPTY FIELD?
NOT EMPTY. THERE'S SOME DEAD COWS AND SUCH.
I WONDER WHAT THEY'RE SAYING.
RAR HA
I KNOW THEY LOOK STRANGE, BUT THE STETSON TRULY IS BOTH PRACTICAL AND STYLISH. I REMEMBER WHEN HUMANS FIRST CAME--
OH DEAR GOD.
I'M SORRY, BEG PARDON?
NO... PLEASE DO GO ON...

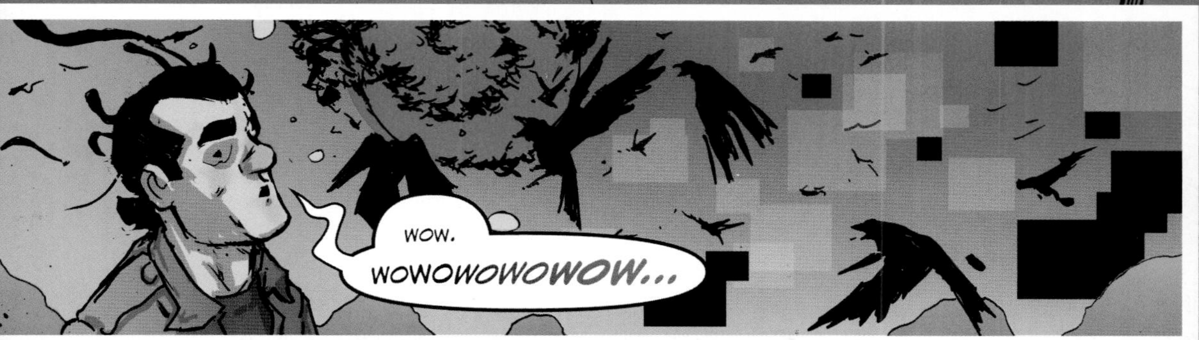
WOW.
WOWOWOWOWOWOW...

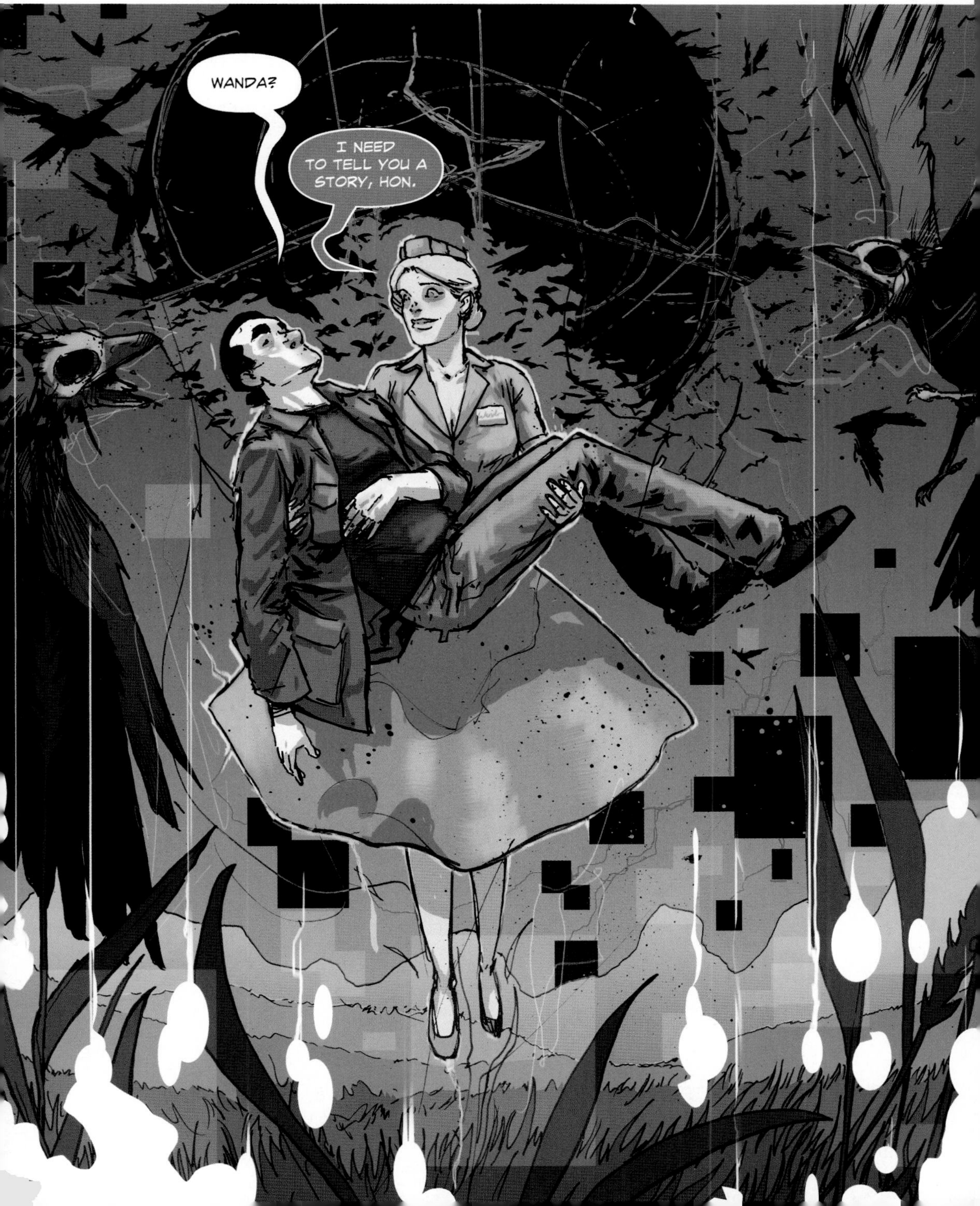
WANDA?
I NEED TO TELL YOU A STORY, HON.

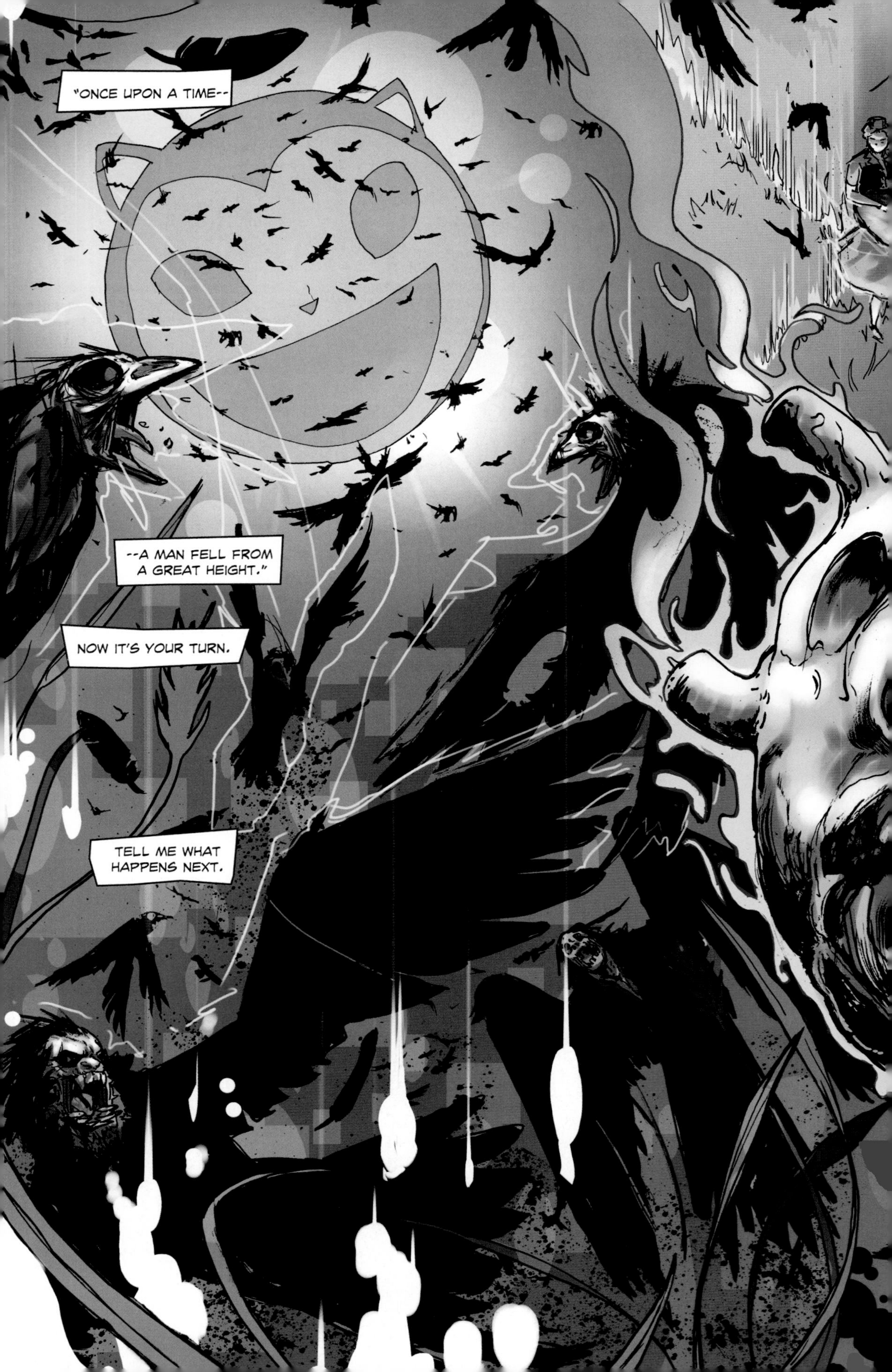
"ONCE UPON A TIME--
--A MAN FELL FROM A GREAT HEIGHT."
NOW IT'S YOUR TURN.
TELL ME WHAT HAPPENS NEXT.

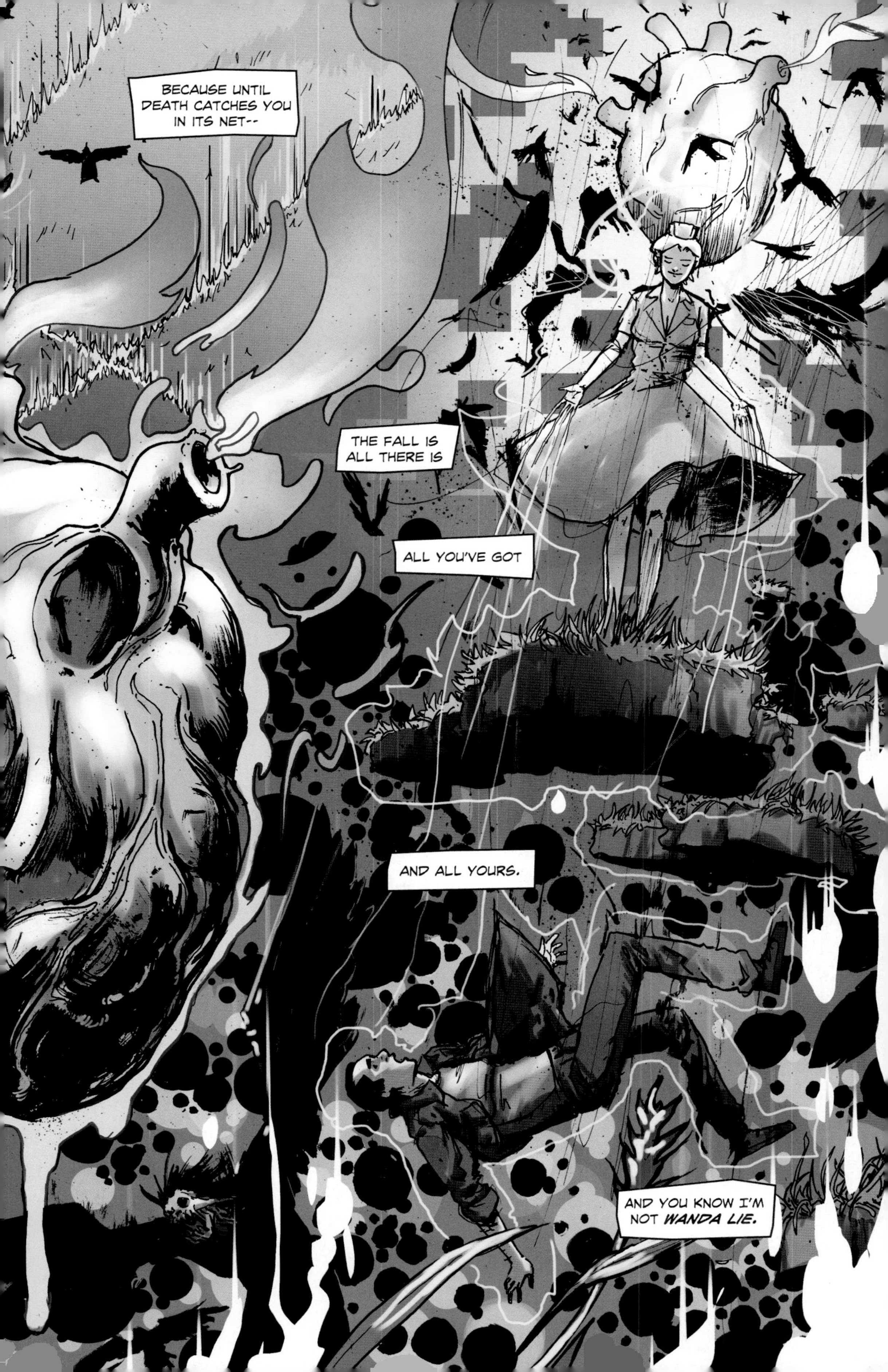
BECAUSE UNTIL DEATH CATCHES YOU IN ITS NET--
THE FALL IS ALL THERE IS
ALL YOU'VE GOT
AND ALL YOURS.
AND YOU KNOW I'M NOT *WANDA LIE.*

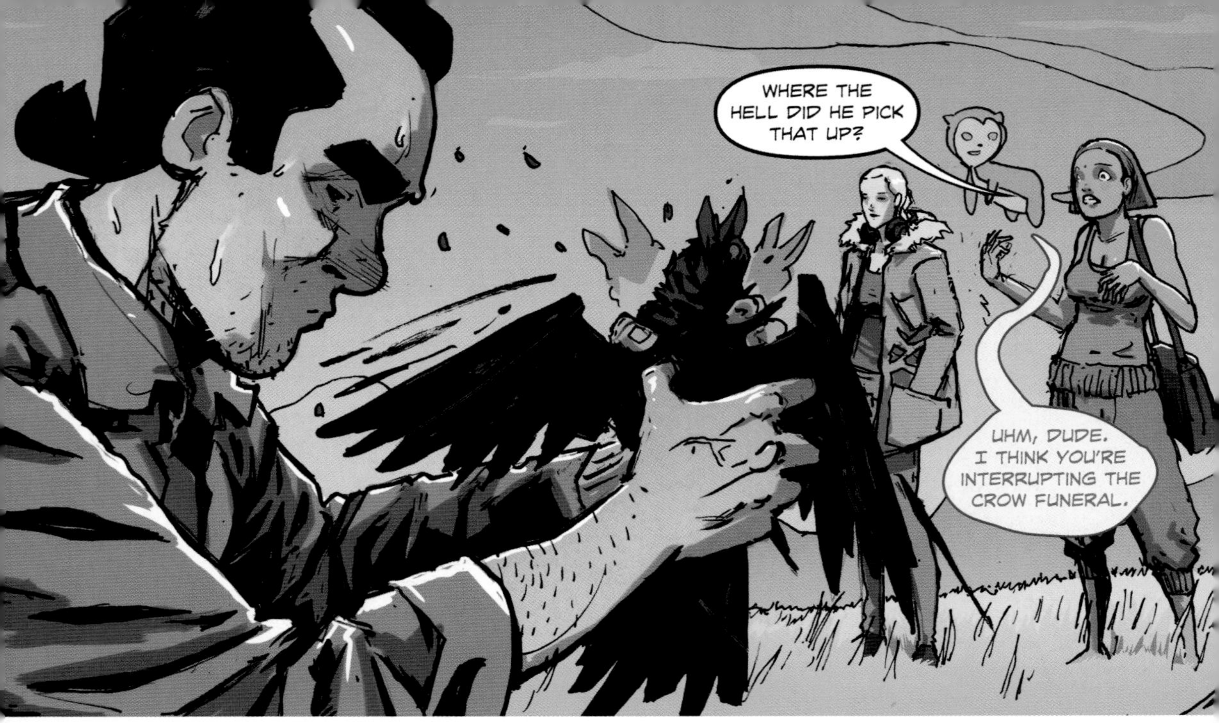
WHERE THE HELL DID HE PICK THAT UP?
UHM, DUDE. I THINK YOU'RE INTERRUPTING THE CROW FUNERAL.

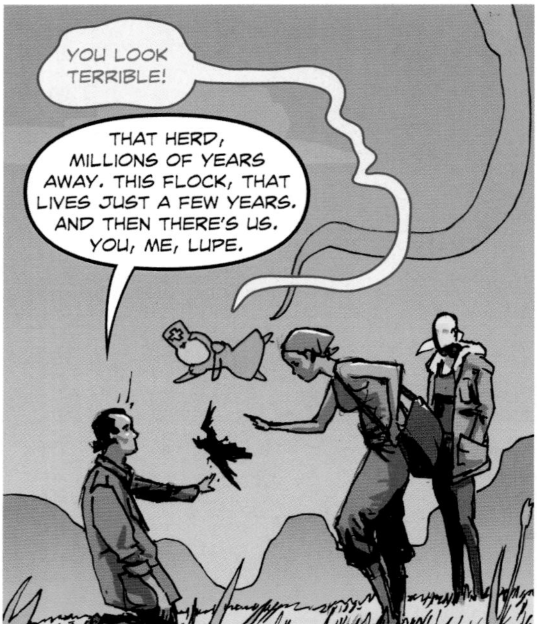
YOU LOOK TERRIBLE!
THAT HERD, MILLIONS OF YEARS AWAY. THIS FLOCK, THAT LIVES JUST A FEW YEARS. AND THEN THERE'S US. YOU, ME, LUPE.

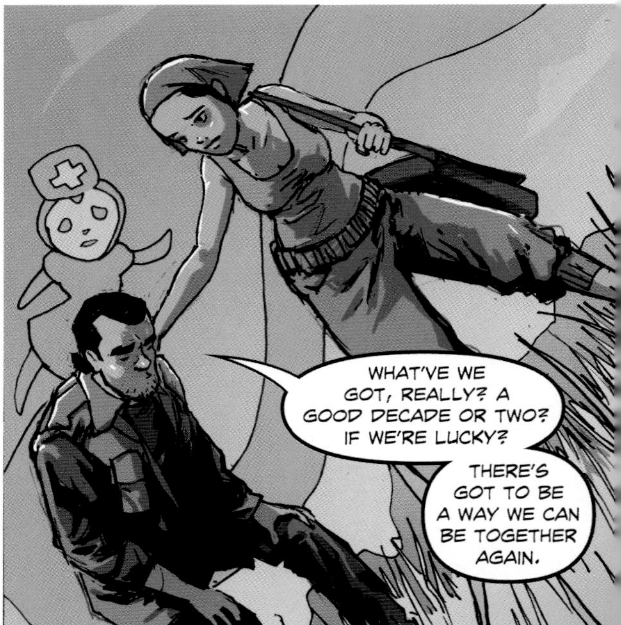
WHAT'VE WE GOT, REALLY? A GOOD DECADE OR TWO? IF WE'RE LUCKY?
THERE'S GOT TO BE A WAY WE CAN BE TOGETHER AGAIN.

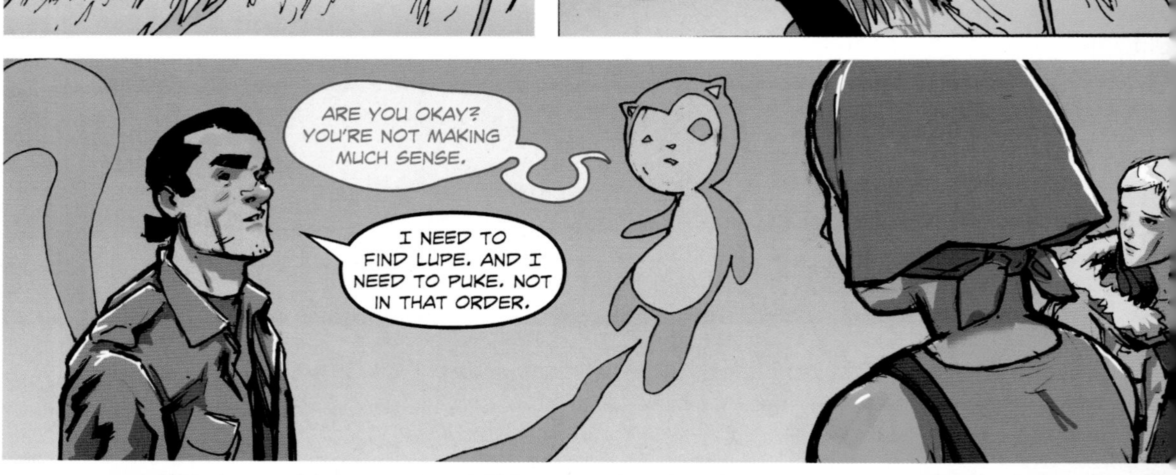
ARE YOU OKAY? YOU'RE NOT MAKING MUCH SENSE.
I NEED TO FIND LUPE. AND I NEED TO PUKE. NOT IN THAT ORDER.

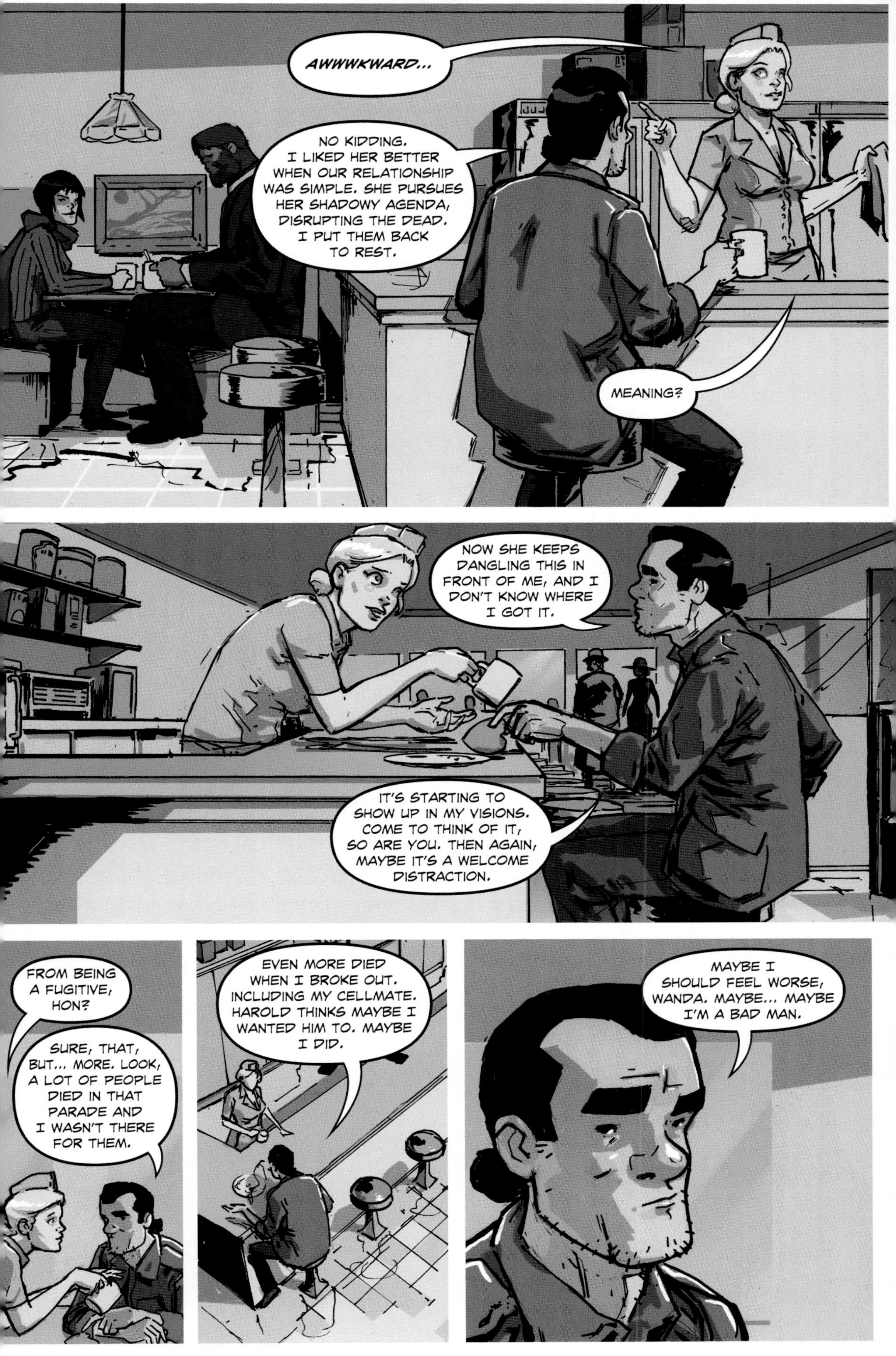
AWWWKWARD...
NO KIDDING. I LIKED HER BETTER WHEN OUR RELATIONSHIP WAS SIMPLE. SHE PURSUES HER SHADOWY AGENDA, DISRUPTING THE DEAD. I PUT THEM BACK TO REST.
MEANING?
NOW SHE KEEPS DANGLING THIS IN FRONT OF ME, AND I DON'T KNOW WHERE I GOT IT.
IT'S STARTING TO SHOW UP IN MY VISIONS. COME TO THINK OF IT, SO ARE YOU. THEN AGAIN, MAYBE IT'S A WELCOME DISTRACTION.
FROM BEING A FUGITIVE, HON?
SURE, THAT, BUT... MORE. LOOK, A LOT OF PEOPLE DIED IN THAT PARADE AND I WASN'T THERE FOR THEM.
EVEN MORE DIED WHEN I BROKE OUT. INCLUDING MY CELLMATE. HAROLD THINKS MAYBE I WANTED HIM TO. MAYBE I DID.
MAYBE I SHOULD FEEL WORSE, WANDA. MAYBE... MAYBE I'M A BAD MAN.

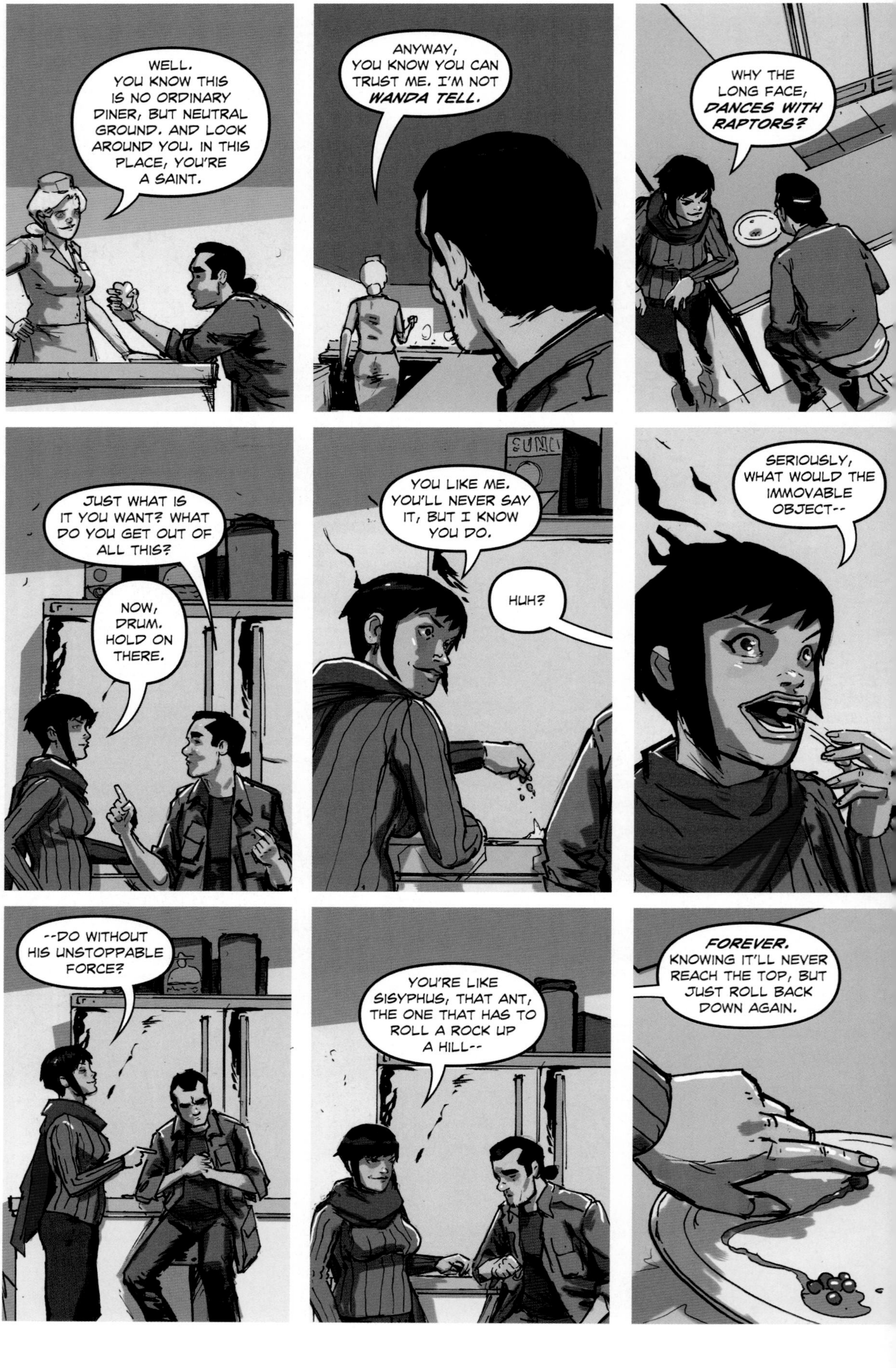
WELL. YOU KNOW THIS IS NO ORDINARY DINER, BUT NEUTRAL GROUND. AND LOOK AROUND YOU. IN THIS PLACE, YOU'RE A SAINT.
ANYWAY, YOU KNOW YOU CAN TRUST ME. I'M NOT *WANDA TELL.*
WHY THE LONG FACE, *DANCES WITH RAPTORS?*
JUST WHAT IS IT YOU WANT? WHAT DO YOU GET OUT OF ALL THIS?
NOW, DRUM. HOLD ON THERE.
YOU LIKE ME. YOU'LL NEVER SAY IT, BUT I KNOW YOU DO.
HUH?
SERIOUSLY, WHAT WOULD THE IMMOVABLE OBJECT--
--DO WITHOUT HIS UNSTOPPABLE FORCE?
YOU'RE LIKE SISYPHUS, THAT ANT, THE ONE THAT HAS TO ROLL A ROCK UP A HILL--
FOREVER. KNOWING IT'LL NEVER REACH THE TOP, BUT JUST ROLL BACK DOWN AGAIN.

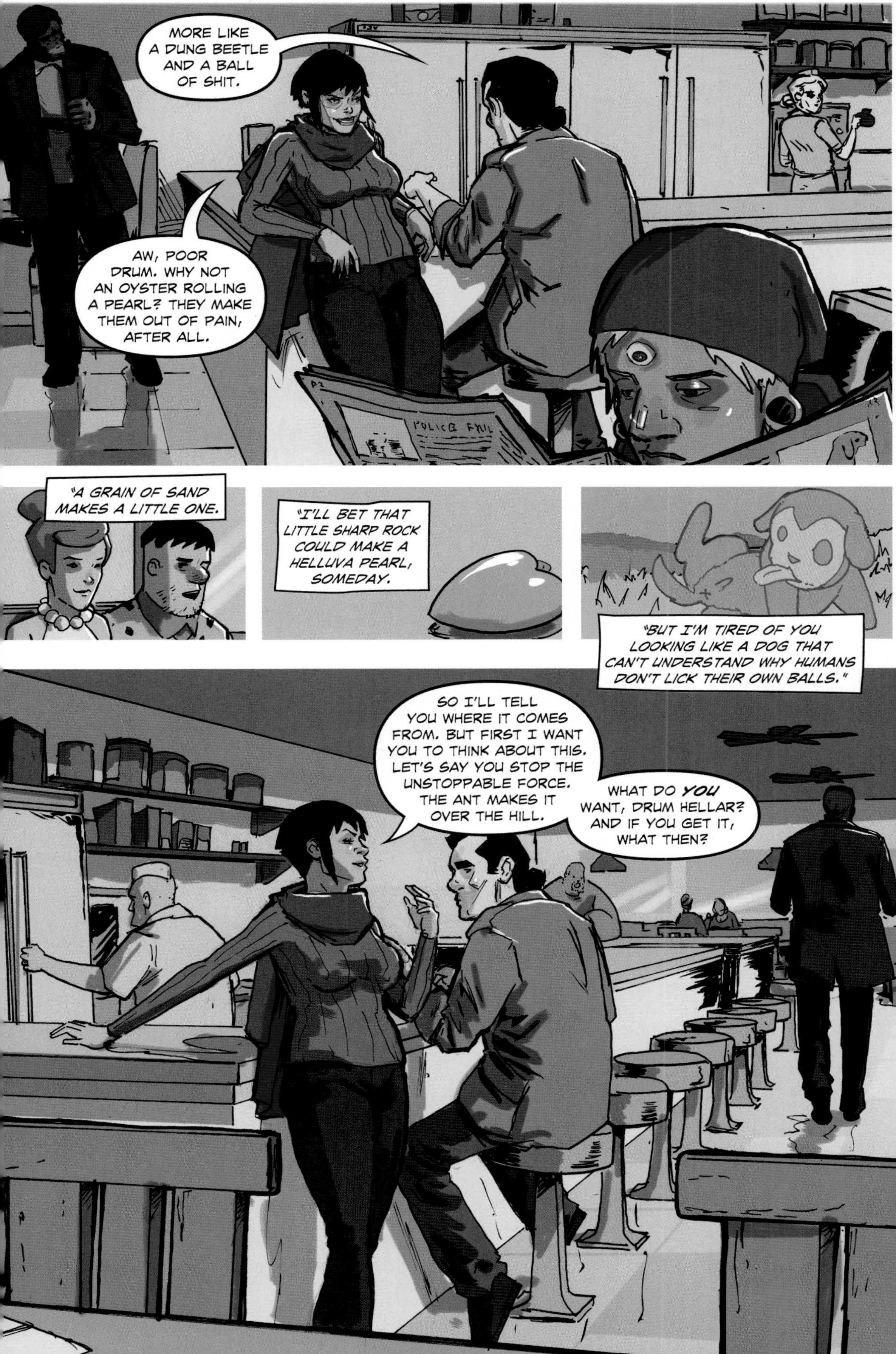

MORE LIKE A DUNG BEETLE AND A BALL OF SHIT.
AW, POOR DRUM. WHY NOT AN OYSTER ROLLING A PEARL? THEY MAKE THEM OUT OF PAIN, AFTER ALL.
POLICE FYI
"A GRAIN OF SAND MAKES A LITTLE ONE.
"I'LL BET THAT LITTLE SHARP ROCK COULD MAKE A HELLUVA PEARL, SOMEDAY.
"BUT I'M TIRED OF YOU LOOKING LIKE A DOG THAT CAN'T UNDERSTAND WHY HUMANS DON'T LICK THEIR OWN BALLS."
SO I'LL TELL YOU WHERE IT COMES FROM. BUT FIRST I WANT YOU TO THINK ABOUT THIS. LET'S SAY YOU STOP THE UNSTOPPABLE FORCE. THE ANT MAKES IT OVER THE HILL.
WHAT DO *YOU* WANT, DRUM HELLAR? AND IF YOU GET IT, WHAT THEN?

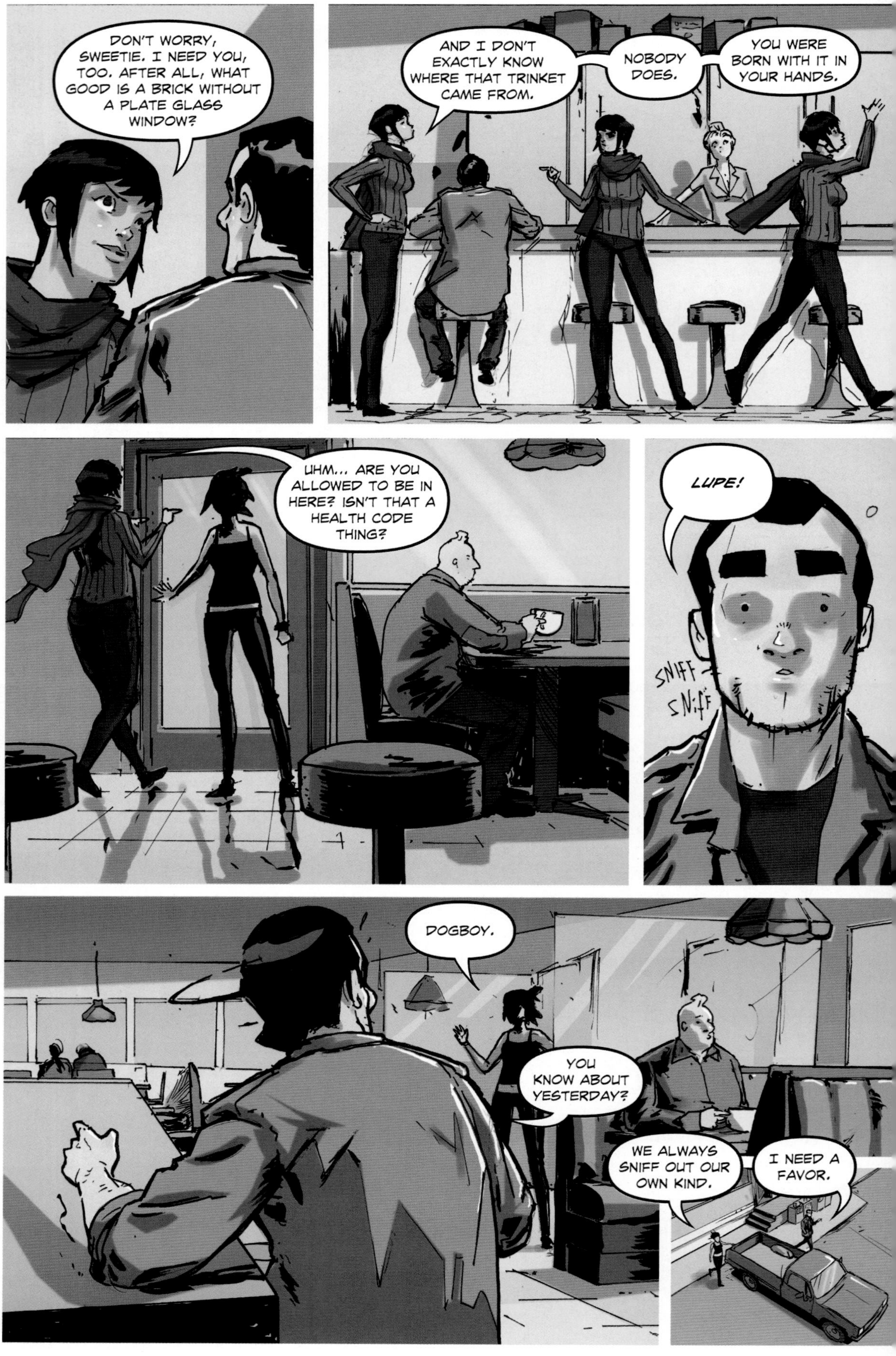
DON'T WORRY, SWEETIE. I NEED YOU, TOO. AFTER ALL, WHAT GOOD IS A BRICK WITHOUT A PLATE GLASS WINDOW?
AND I DON'T EXACTLY KNOW WHERE THAT TRINKET CAME FROM.
NOBODY DOES.
YOU WERE BORN WITH IT IN YOUR HANDS.
UHM... ARE YOU ALLOWED TO BE IN HERE? ISN'T THAT A HEALTH CODE THING?
LUPE!
SNIFF
SNIFF
DOGBOY.
YOU KNOW ABOUT YESTERDAY?
WE ALWAYS SNIFF OUT OUR OWN KIND.
I NEED A FAVOR.

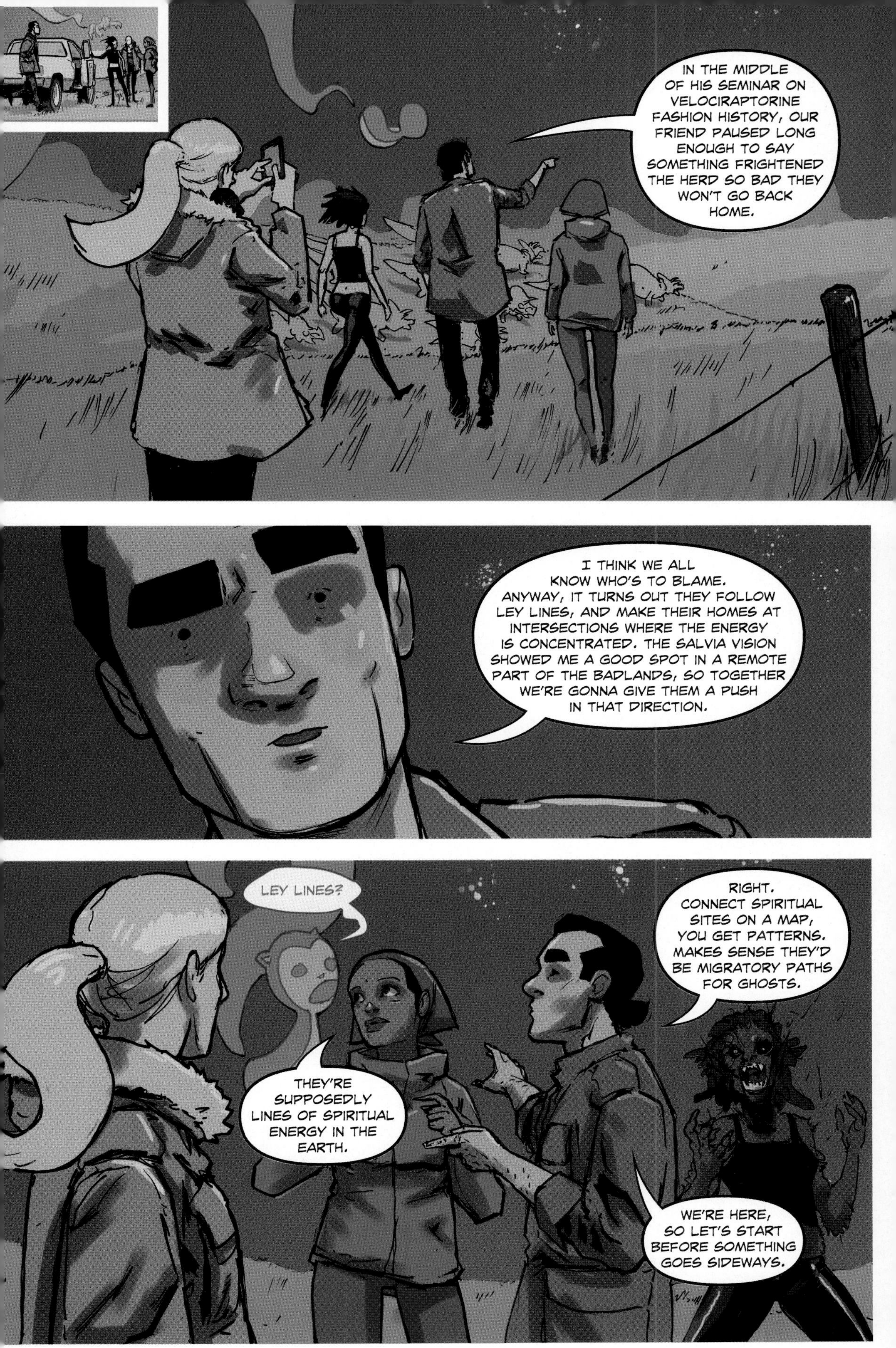
IN THE MIDDLE OF HIS SEMINAR ON VELOCIRAPTORINE FASHION HISTORY, OUR FRIEND PAUSED LONG ENOUGH TO SAY SOMETHING FRIGHTENED THE HERD SO BAD THEY WON'T GO BACK HOME.
I THINK WE ALL KNOW WHO'S TO BLAME. ANYWAY, IT TURNS OUT THEY FOLLOW LEY LINES, AND MAKE THEIR HOMES AT INTERSECTIONS WHERE THE ENERGY IS CONCENTRATED. THE SALVIA VISION SHOWED ME A GOOD SPOT IN A REMOTE PART OF THE BADLANDS, SO TOGETHER WE'RE GONNA GIVE THEM A PUSH IN THAT DIRECTION.
LEY LINES?
THEY'RE SUPPOSEDLY LINES OF SPIRITUAL ENERGY IN THE EARTH.
RIGHT. CONNECT SPIRITUAL SITES ON A MAP, YOU GET PATTERNS. MAKES SENSE THEY'D BE MIGRATORY PATHS FOR GHOSTS.
WE'RE HERE, SO LET'S START BEFORE SOMETHING GOES SIDEWAYS.

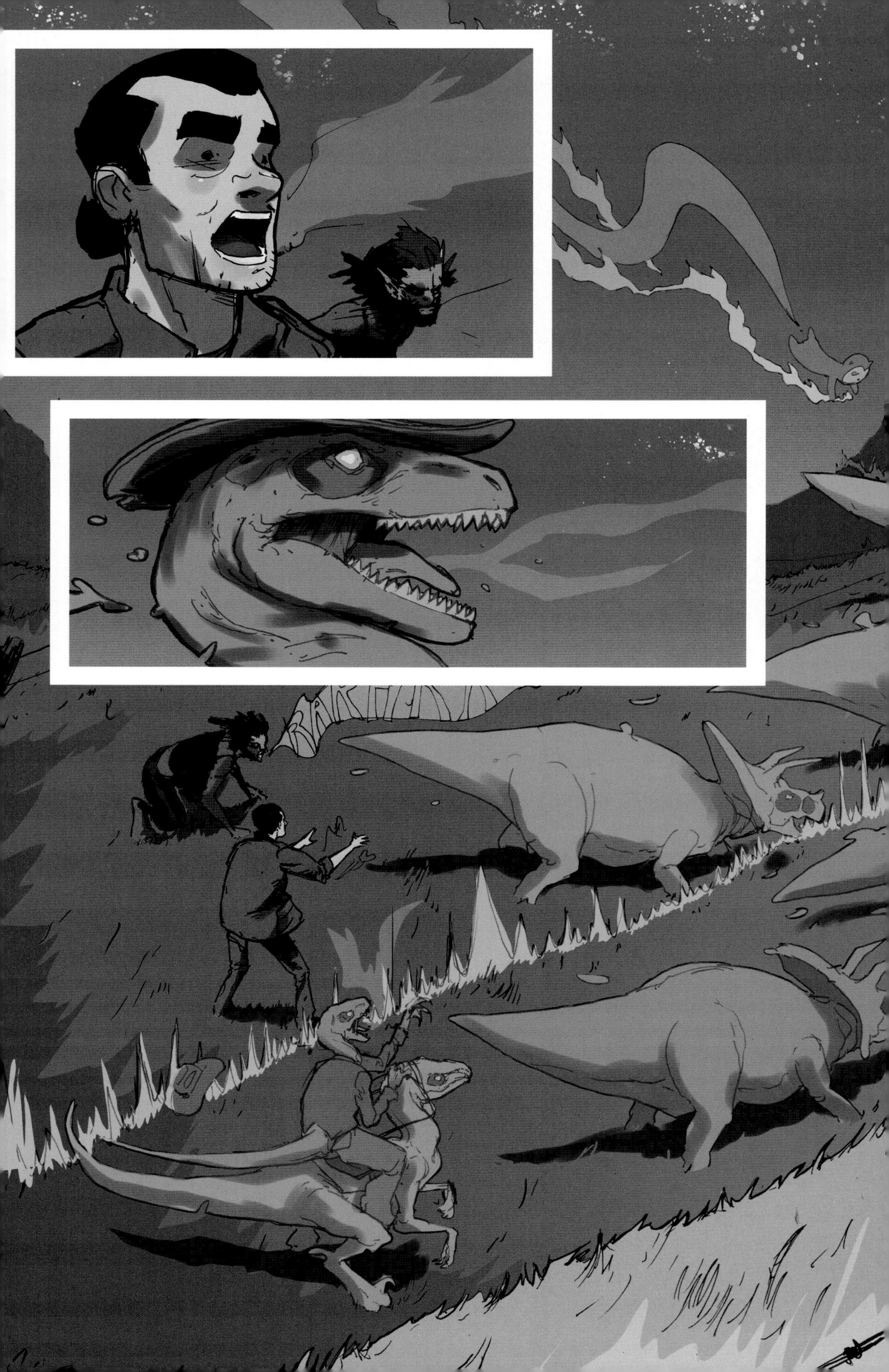

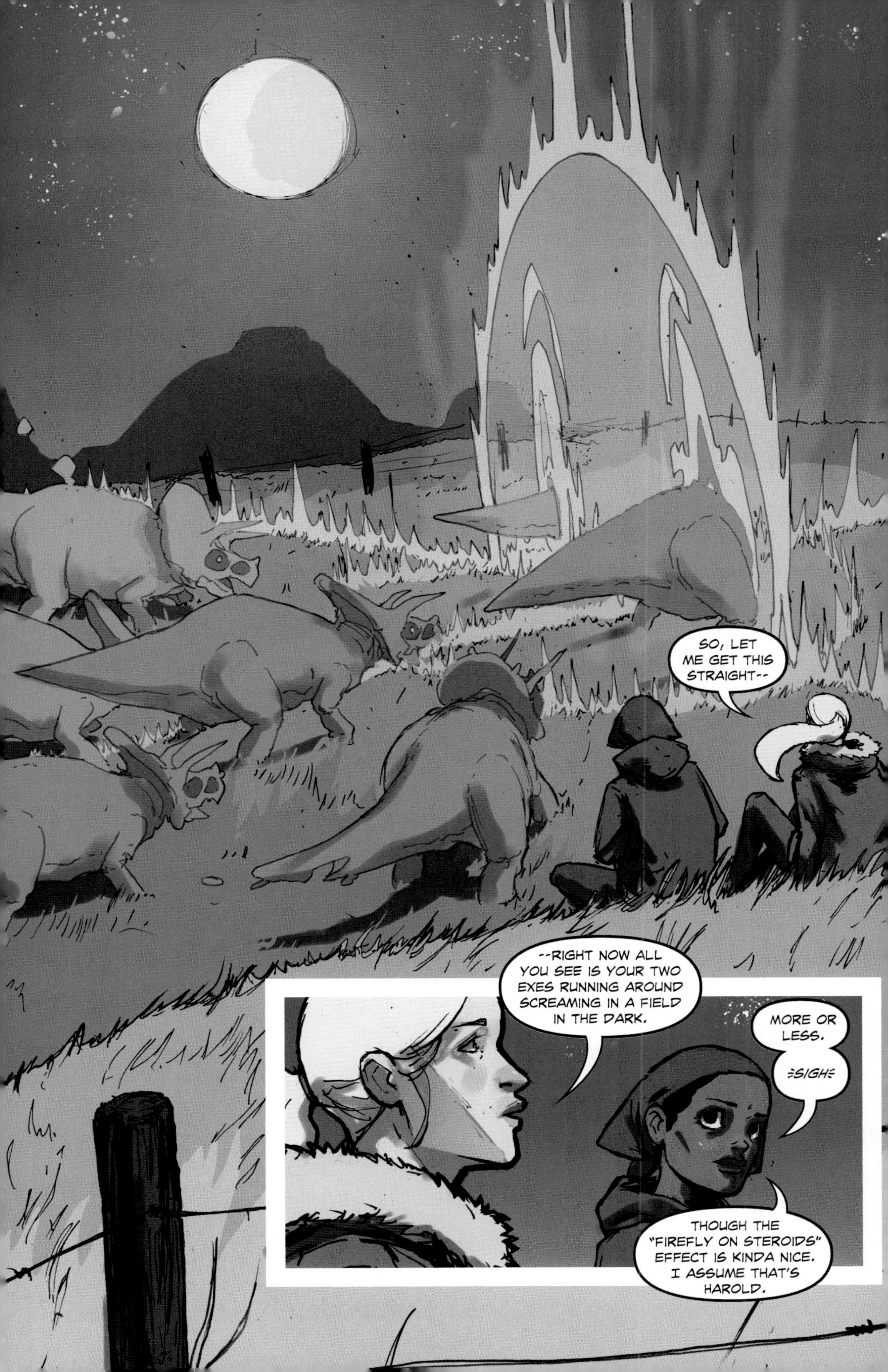
SO, LET ME GET THIS STRAIGHT--
--RIGHT NOW ALL YOU SEE IS YOUR TWO EXES RUNNING AROUND SCREAMING IN A FIELD IN THE DARK.
MORE OR LESS.
SIGH
THOUGH THE "FIREFLY ON STEROIDS" EFFECT IS KINDA NICE. I ASSUME THAT'S HAROLD.

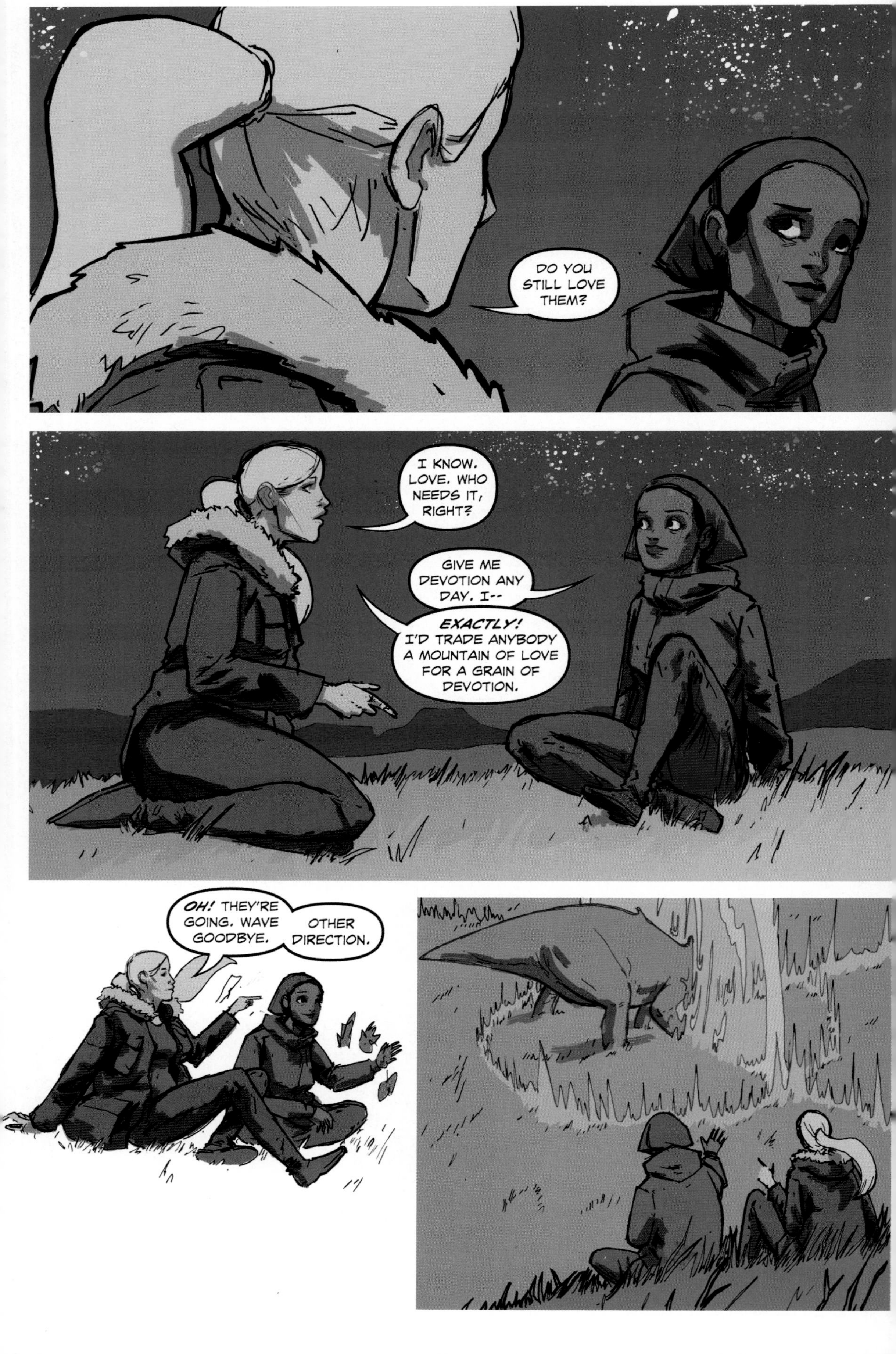
DO YOU STILL LOVE THEM?
I KNOW. LOVE. WHO NEEDS IT, RIGHT?
GIVE ME DEVOTION ANY DAY. I--
EXACTLY! I'D TRADE ANYBODY A MOUNTAIN OF LOVE FOR A GRAIN OF DEVOTION.
OH! THEY'RE GOING. WAVE GOODBYE.
OTHER DIRECTION.

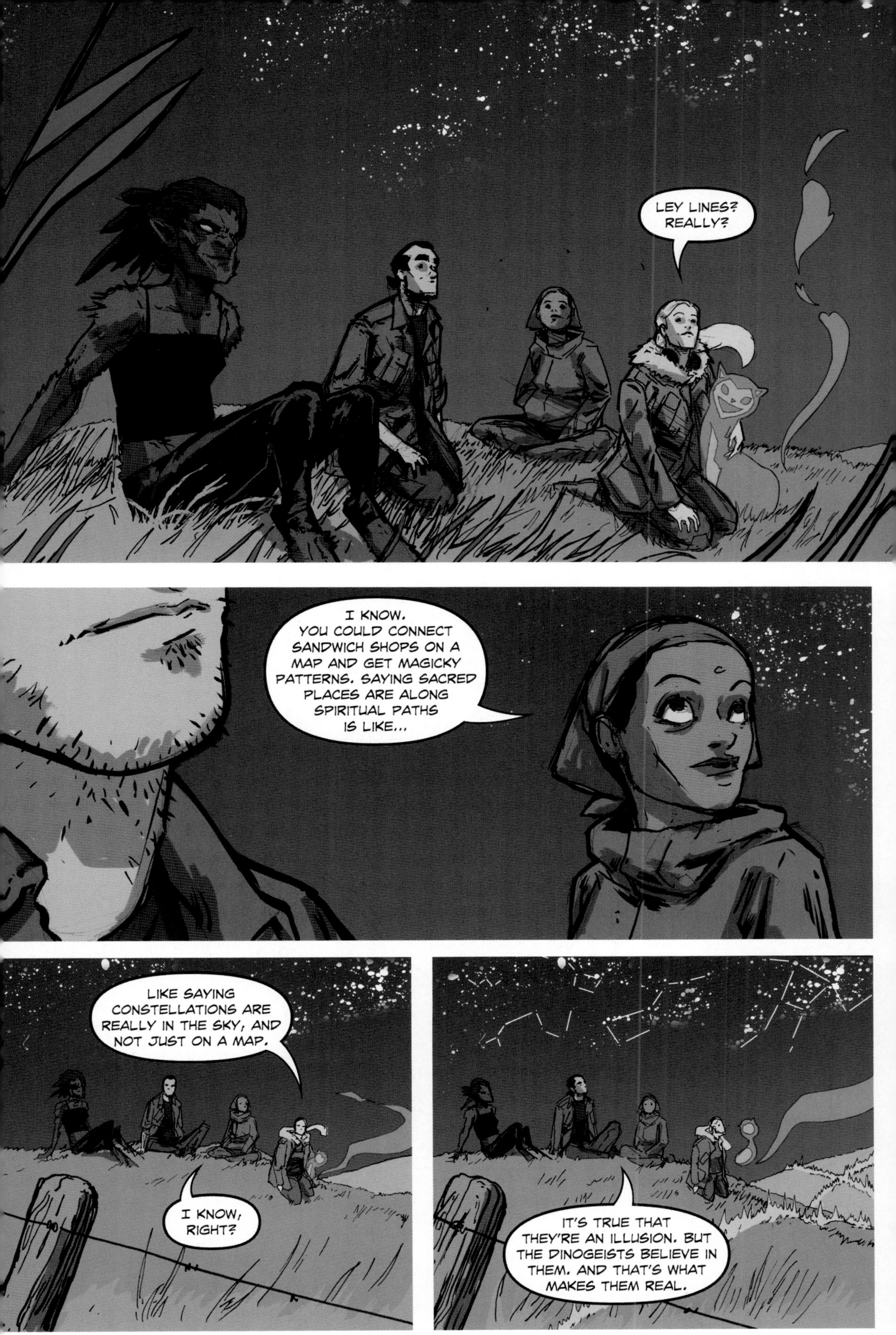
LEY LINES? REALLY?
I KNOW. YOU COULD CONNECT SANDWICH SHOPS ON A MAP AND GET MAGICKY PATTERNS. SAYING SACRED PLACES ARE ALONG SPIRITUAL PATHS IS LIKE...
LIKE SAYING CONSTELLATIONS ARE REALLY IN THE SKY, AND NOT JUST ON A MAP.
I KNOW, RIGHT?
IT'S TRUE THAT THEY'RE AN ILLUSION. BUT THE DINOGEISTS BELIEVE IN THEM. AND THAT'S WHAT MAKES THEM REAL.

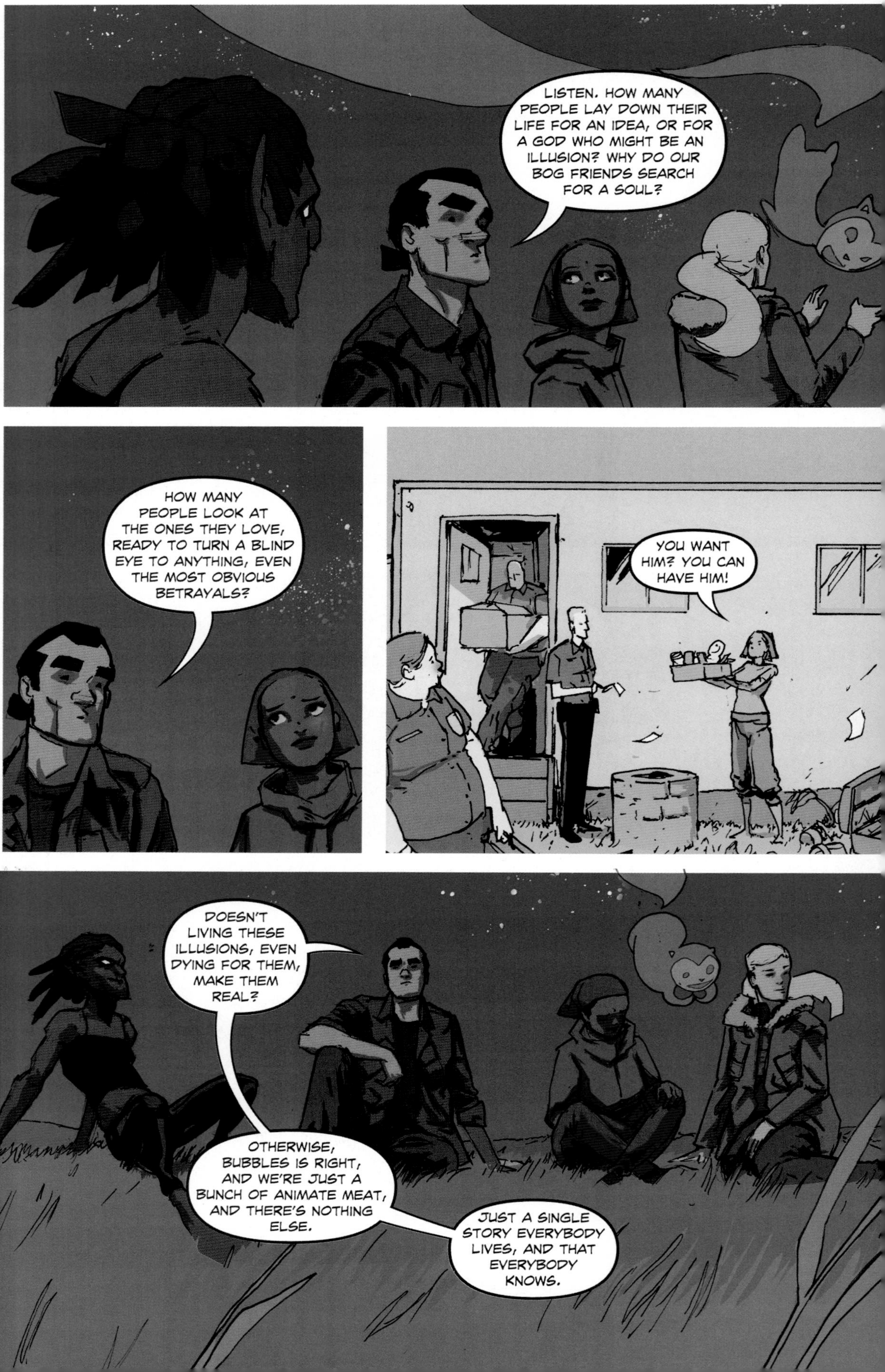
LISTEN. HOW MANY PEOPLE LAY DOWN THEIR LIFE FOR AN IDEA, OR FOR A GOD WHO MIGHT BE AN ILLUSION? WHY DO OUR BOG FRIENDS SEARCH FOR A SOUL?
HOW MANY PEOPLE LOOK AT THE ONES THEY LOVE, READY TO TURN A BLIND EYE TO ANYTHING, EVEN THE MOST OBVIOUS BETRAYALS?
YOU WANT HIM? YOU CAN HAVE HIM!
DOESN'T LIVING THESE ILLUSIONS, EVEN DYING FOR THEM, MAKE THEM REAL?
OTHERWISE, BUBBLES IS RIGHT, AND WE'RE JUST A BUNCH OF ANIMATE MEAT, AND THERE'S NOTHING ELSE.
JUST A SINGLE STORY EVERYBODY LIVES, AND THAT EVERYBODY KNOWS.

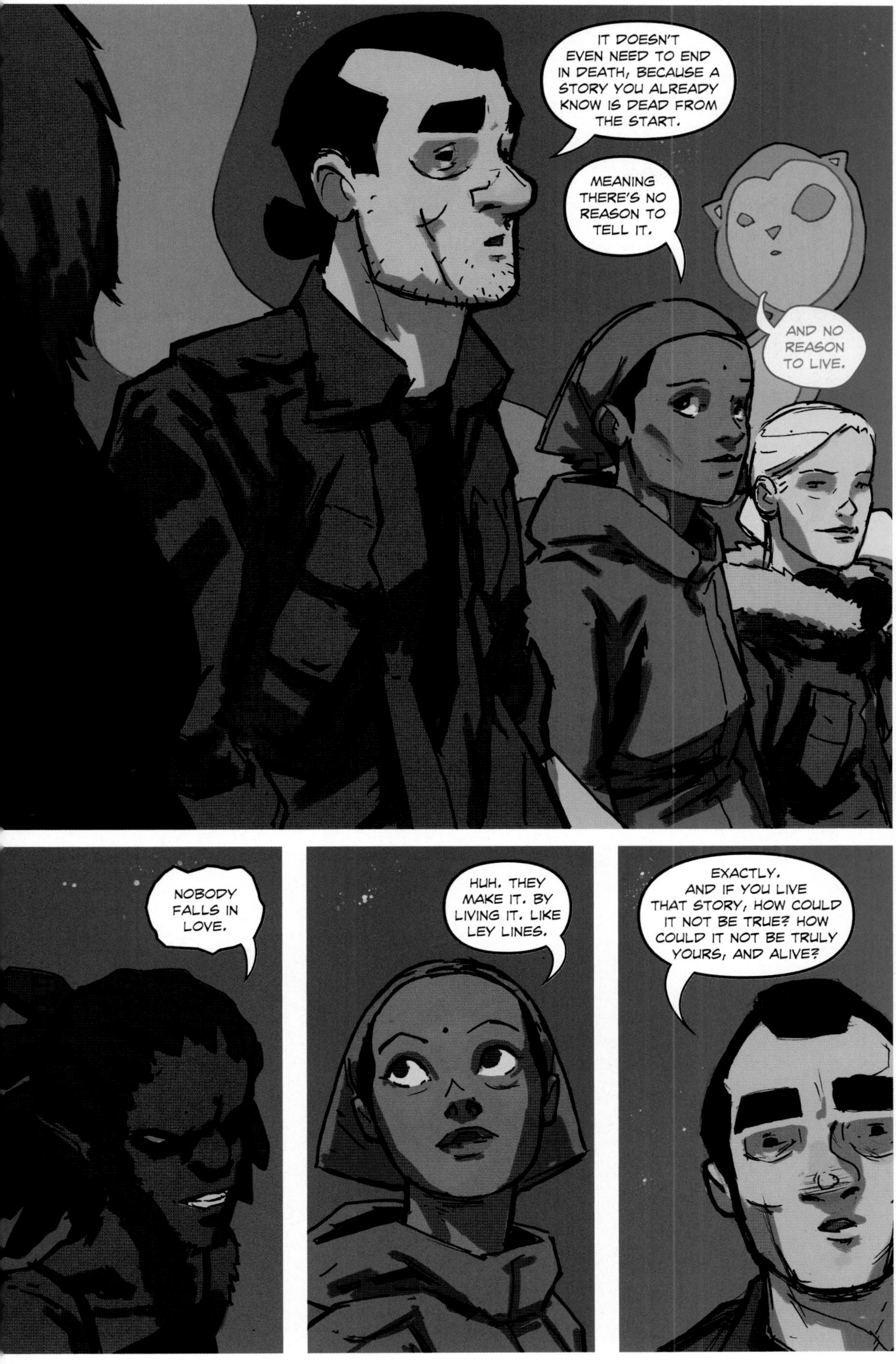
IT DOESN'T EVEN NEED TO END IN DEATH, BECAUSE A STORY YOU ALREADY KNOW IS DEAD FROM THE START.
MEANING THERE'S NO REASON TO TELL IT.
AND NO REASON TO LIVE.
NOBODY FALLS IN LOVE.
HUH. THEY MAKE IT. BY LIVING IT. LIKE LEY LINES.
EXACTLY. AND IF YOU LIVE THAT STORY, HOW COULD IT NOT BE TRUE? HOW COULD IT NOT BE TRULY YOURS, AND ALIVE?

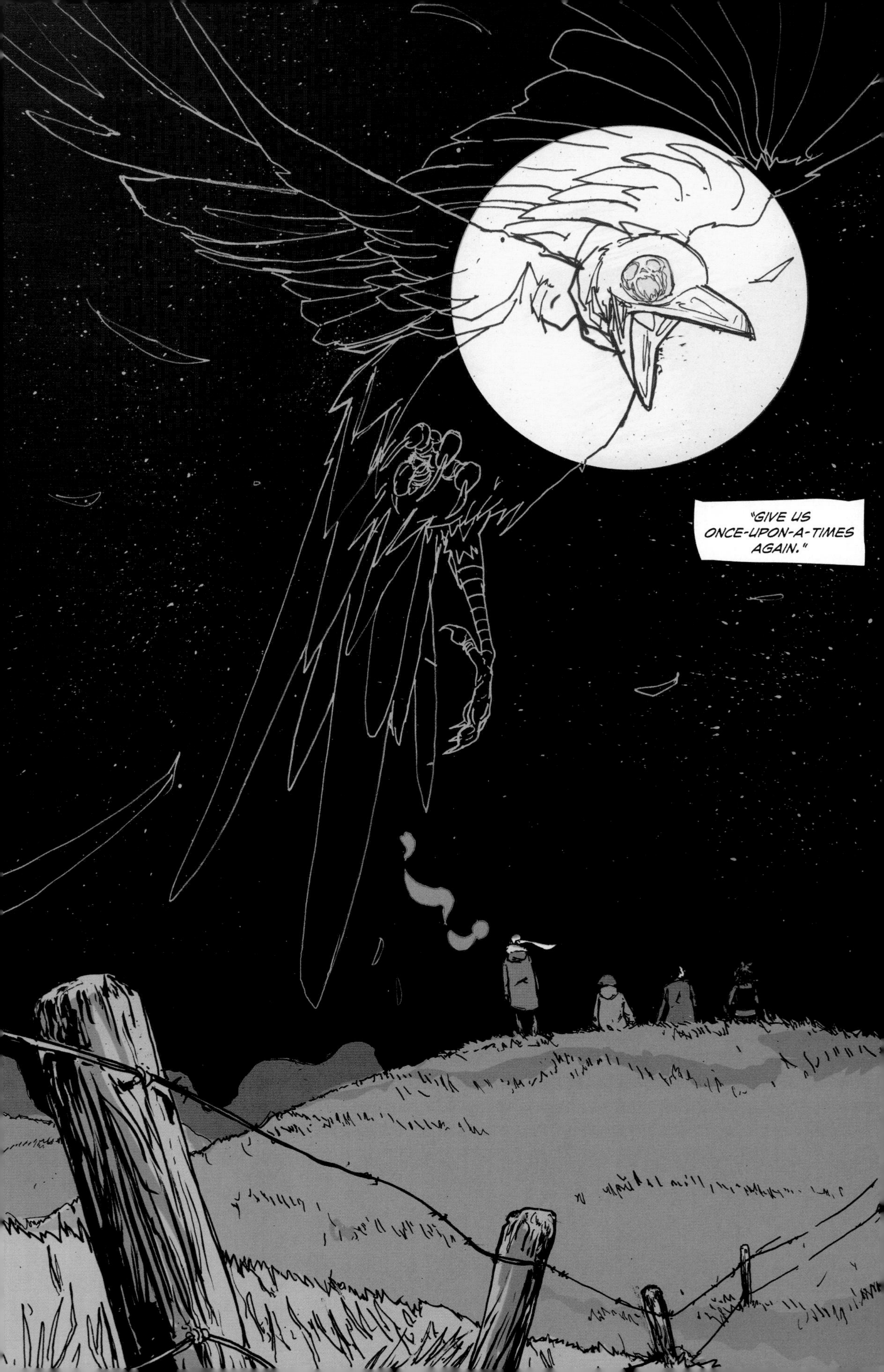
"GIVE US ONCE-UPON-A-TIMES AGAIN."

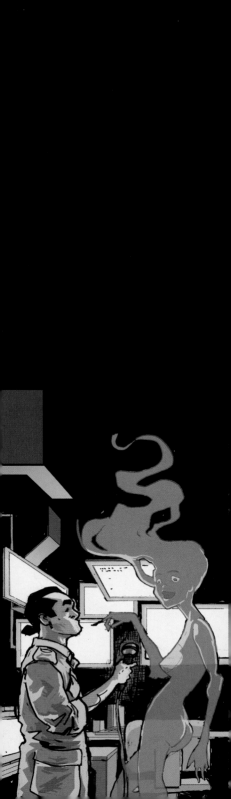

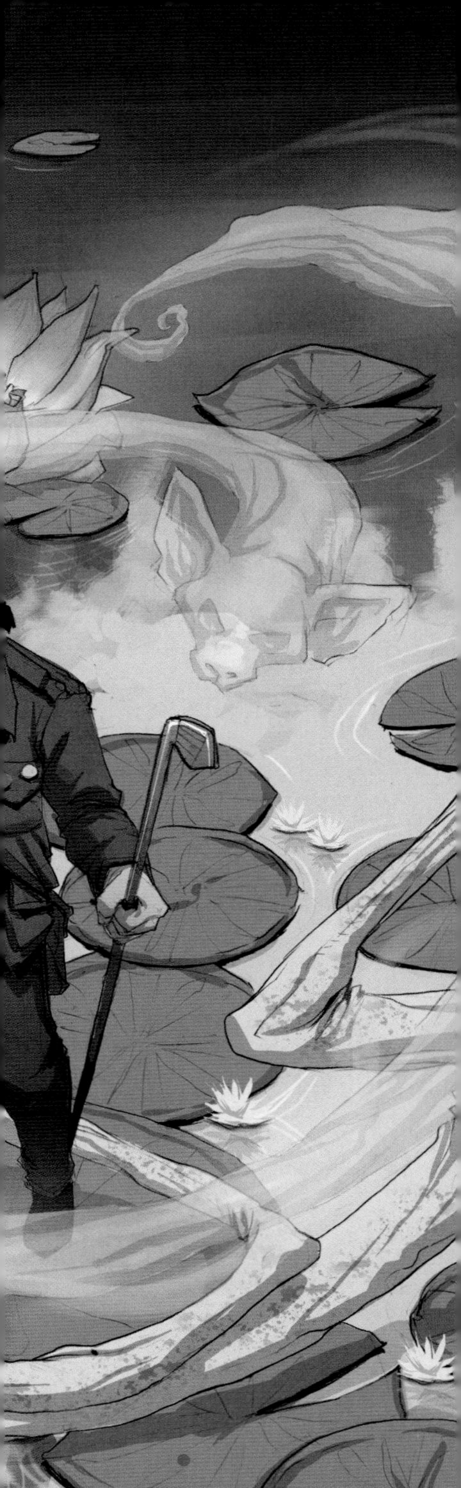

by ROC UPCHURC

ISSUE ONE ALTERNATE COVER C

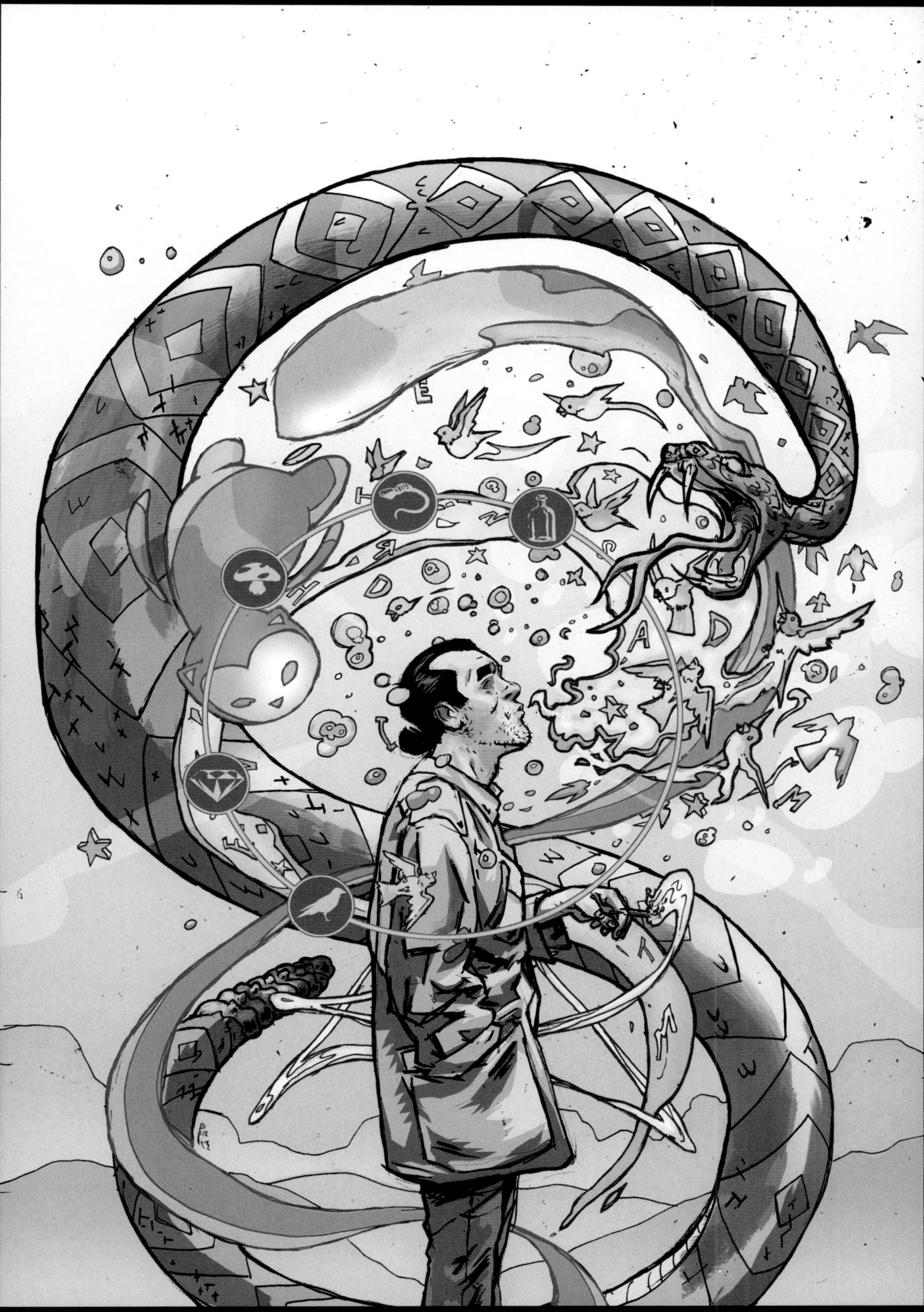

by RILEY ROSSMO

ISSUE ONE ALTERNATE COVER D

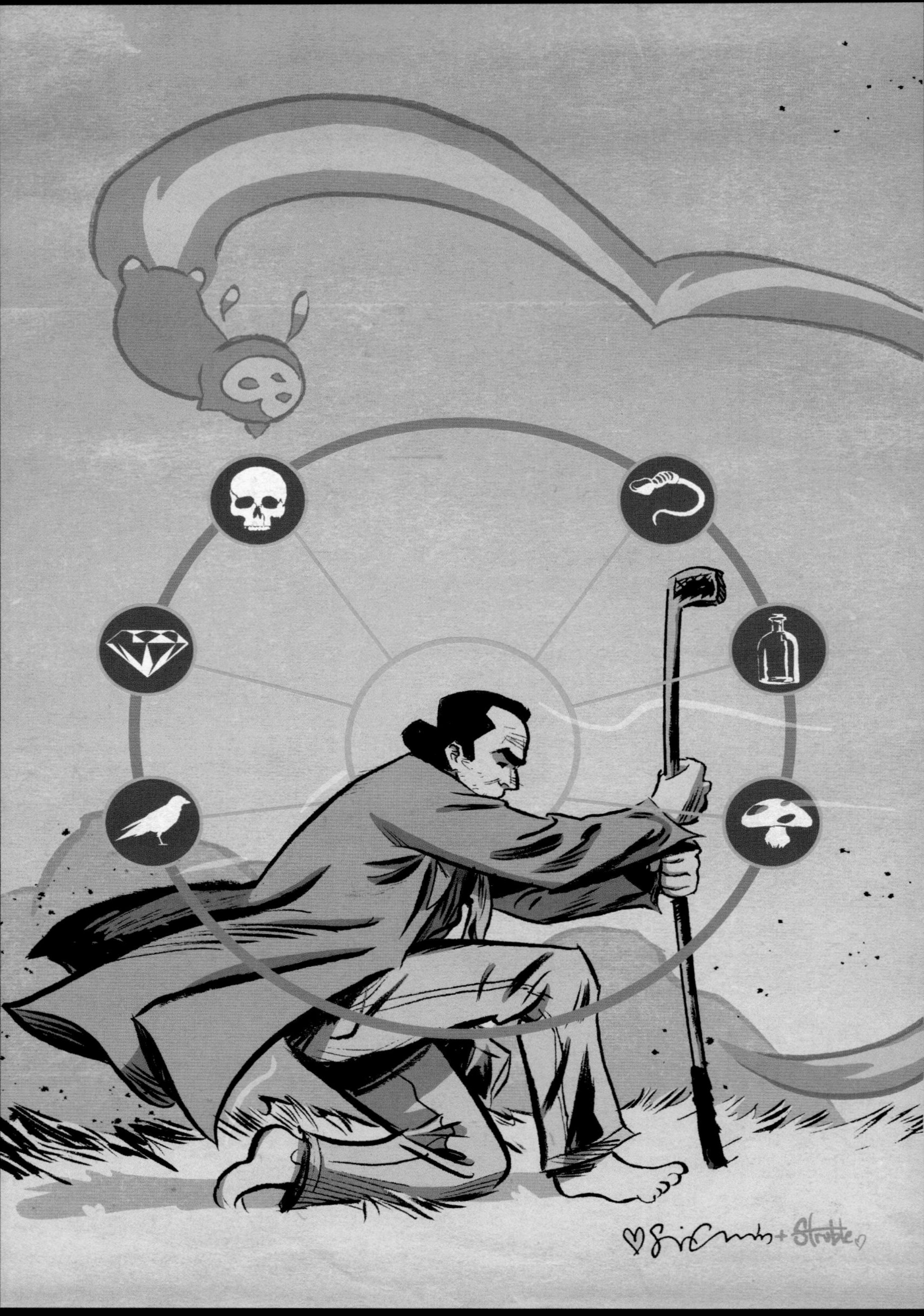

by SINA GRACE and SHAUN STEVEN STRUBLE

ONE SE

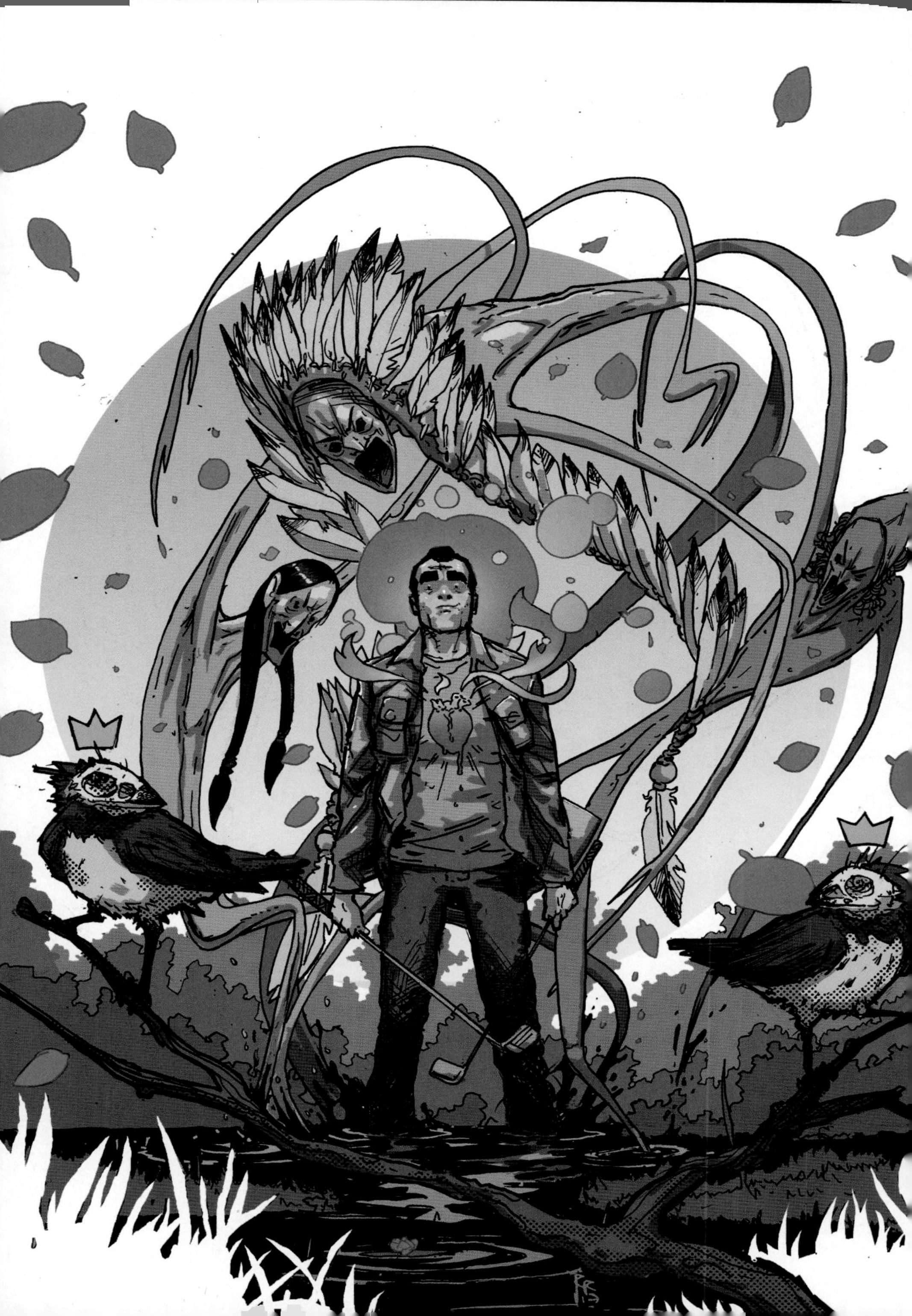

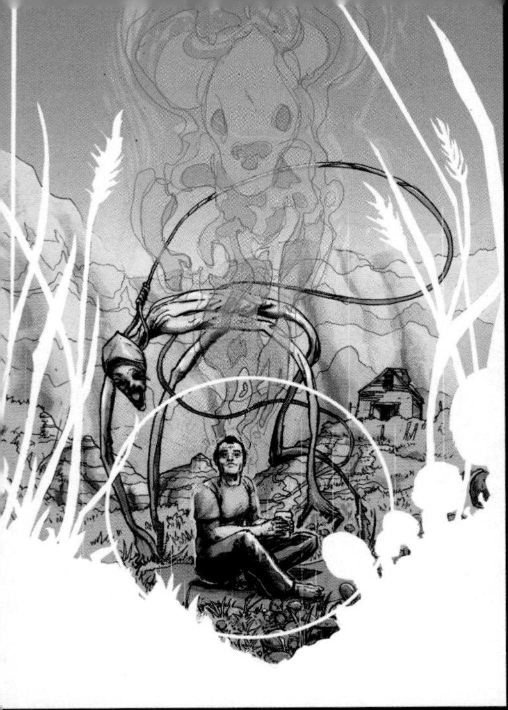
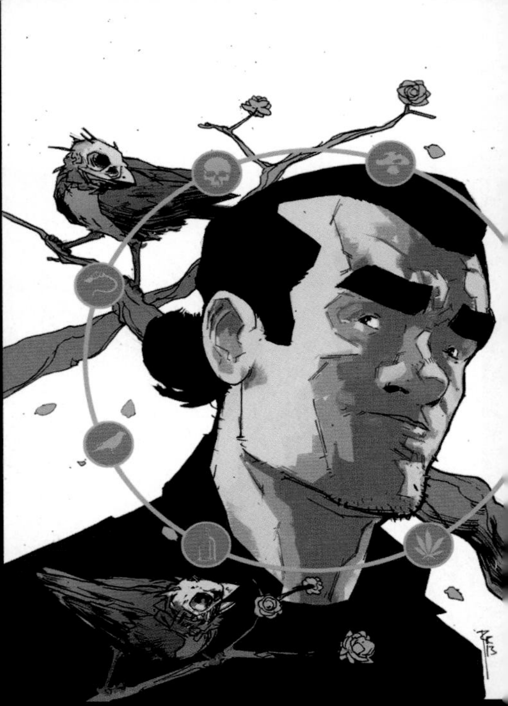
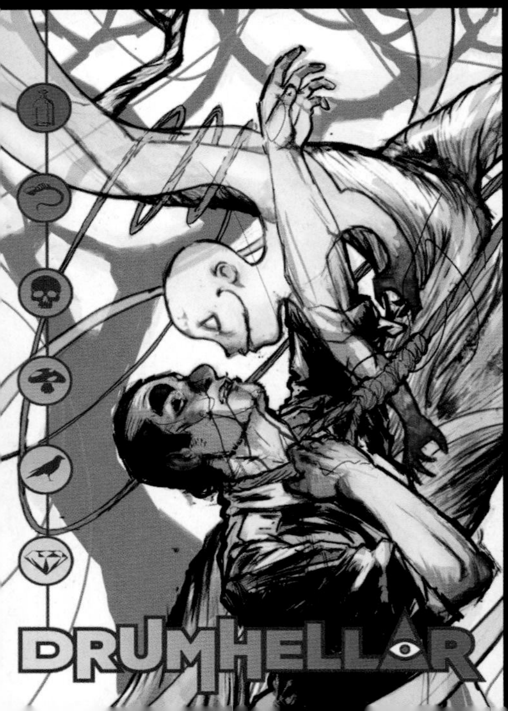
DRUMHELLAR
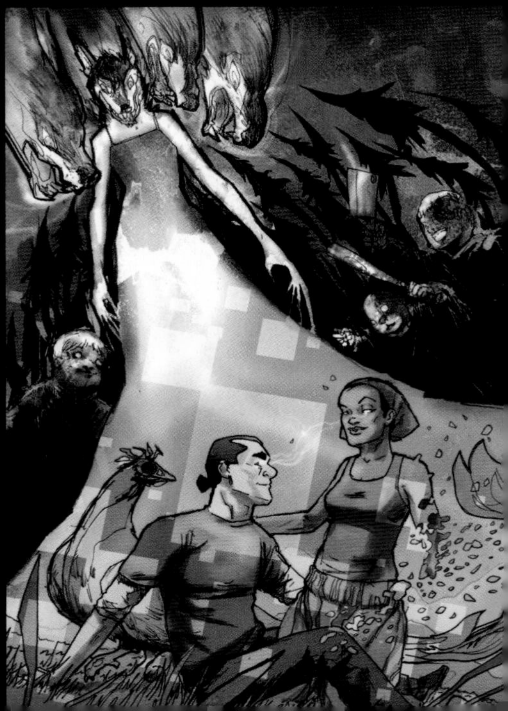

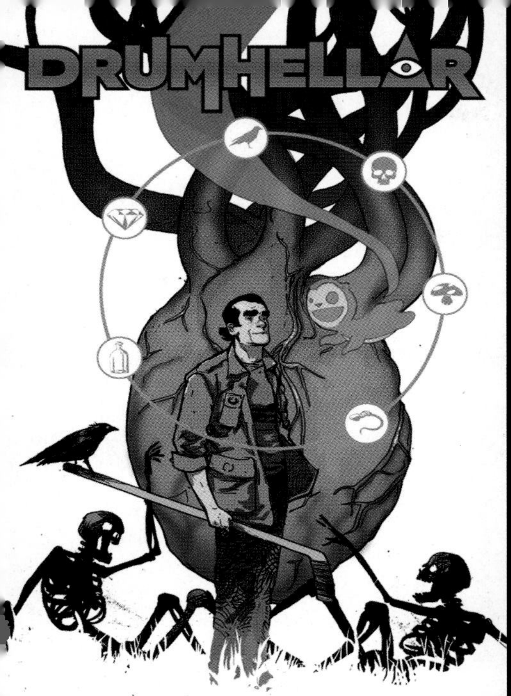
DRUMHELLAR

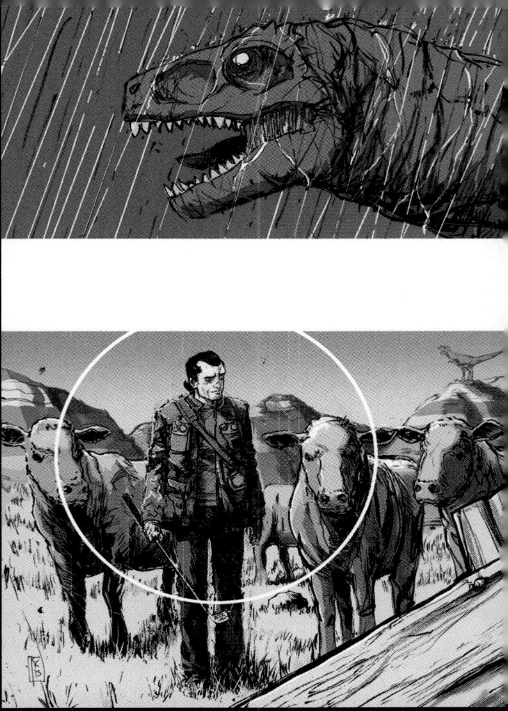

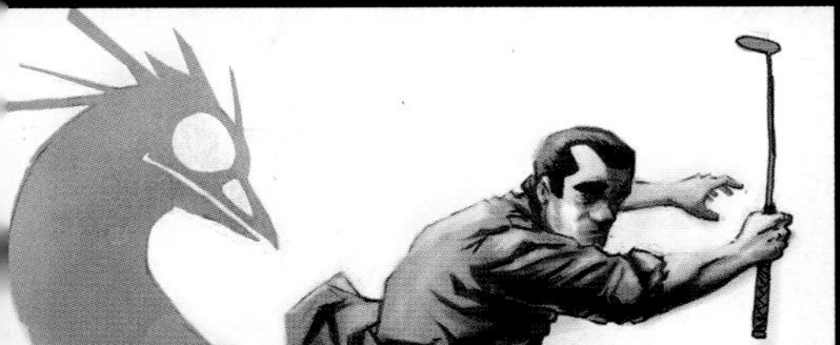

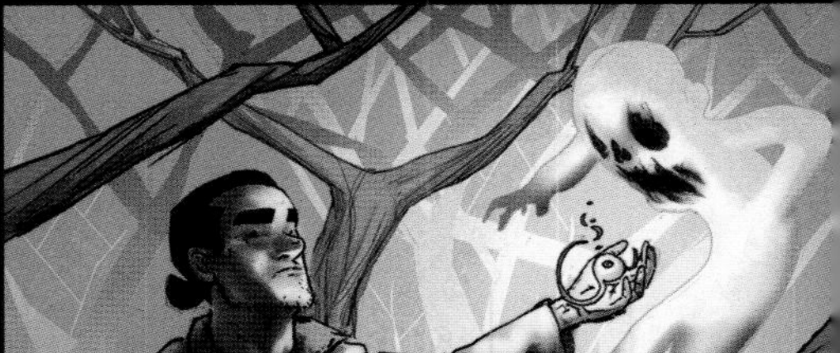

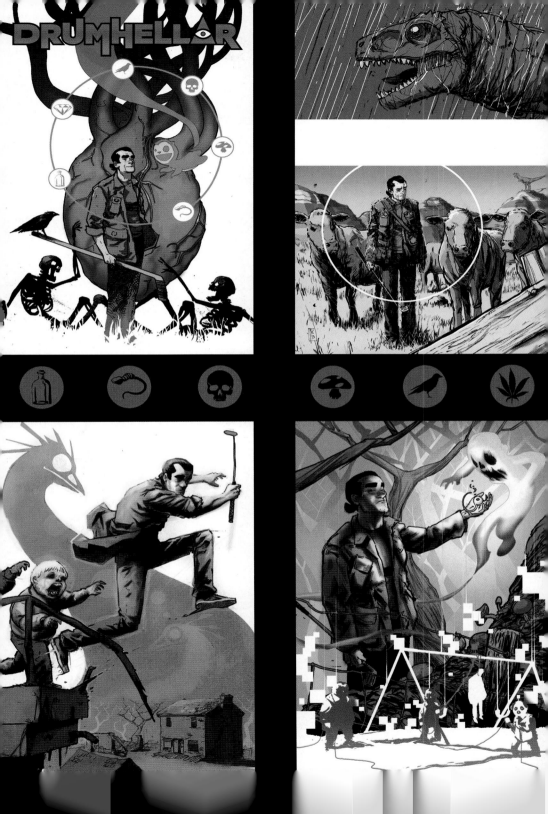

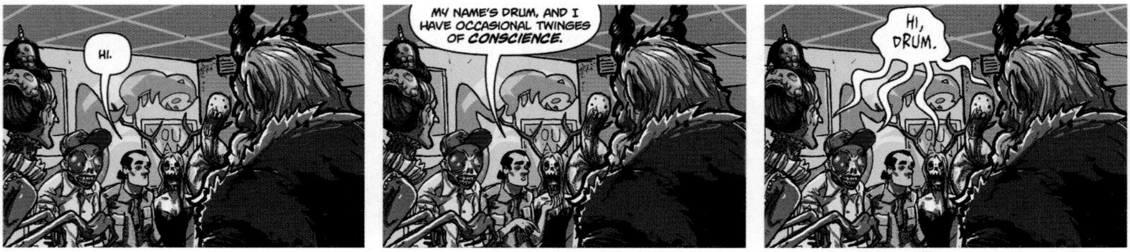
HI.
MY NAME'S DRUM, AND I HAVE OCCASIONAL TWINGES OF *CONSCIENCE.*
HI, DRUM.

NOVEMBER, 2013 **ROSSMO/LINK** *image* Shadowline™ DRUMHELLAR

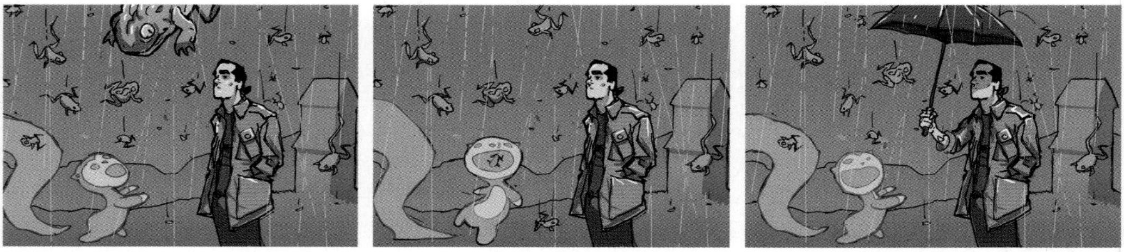

NOVEMBER, 2013 **ROSSMO/LINK** *image* Shadowline™ DRUMHELLAR

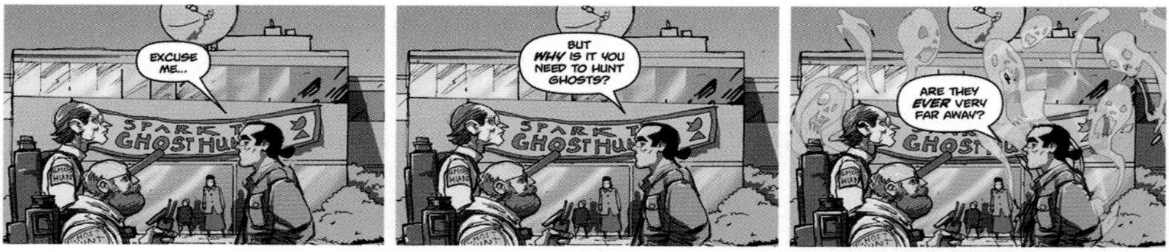
EXCUSE ME...
SPARK T GHOST HU
BUT *WHY* IS IT YOU NEED TO HUNT GHOSTS?
ARE THEY *EVER* VERY FAR AWAY?

NOVEMBER, 2013 **ROSSMO LINK** *image* Shadowline™ DRUMHELLAR

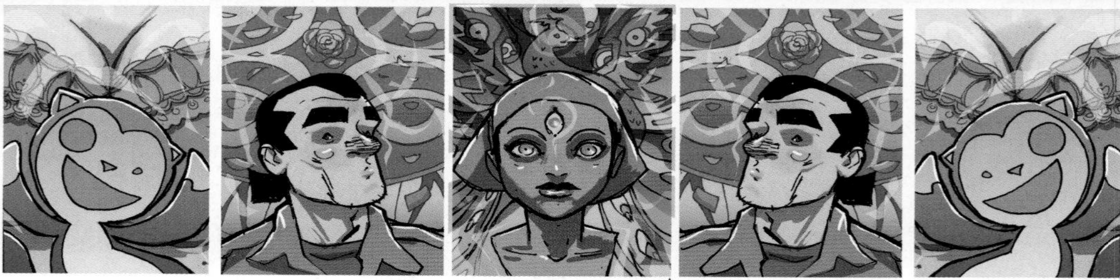

NOVEMBER, 2013 **ROSSMO** DRUMHELLAR **LINK** *image* Shadowline™

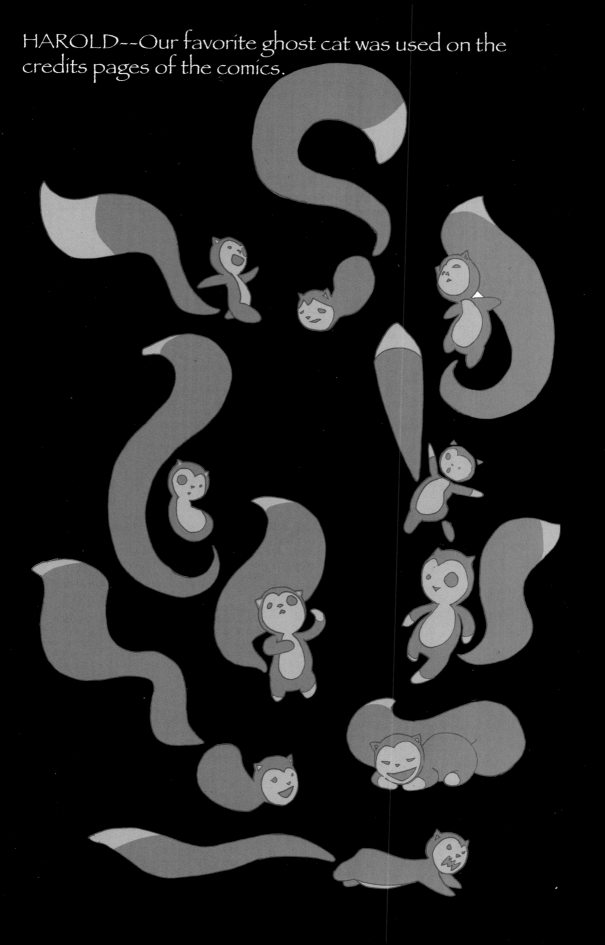

HAROLD--Our favorite ghost cat was used on the credits pages of the comics.

We think this beautiful sketch of PADMA by Riley is suitable for framing.

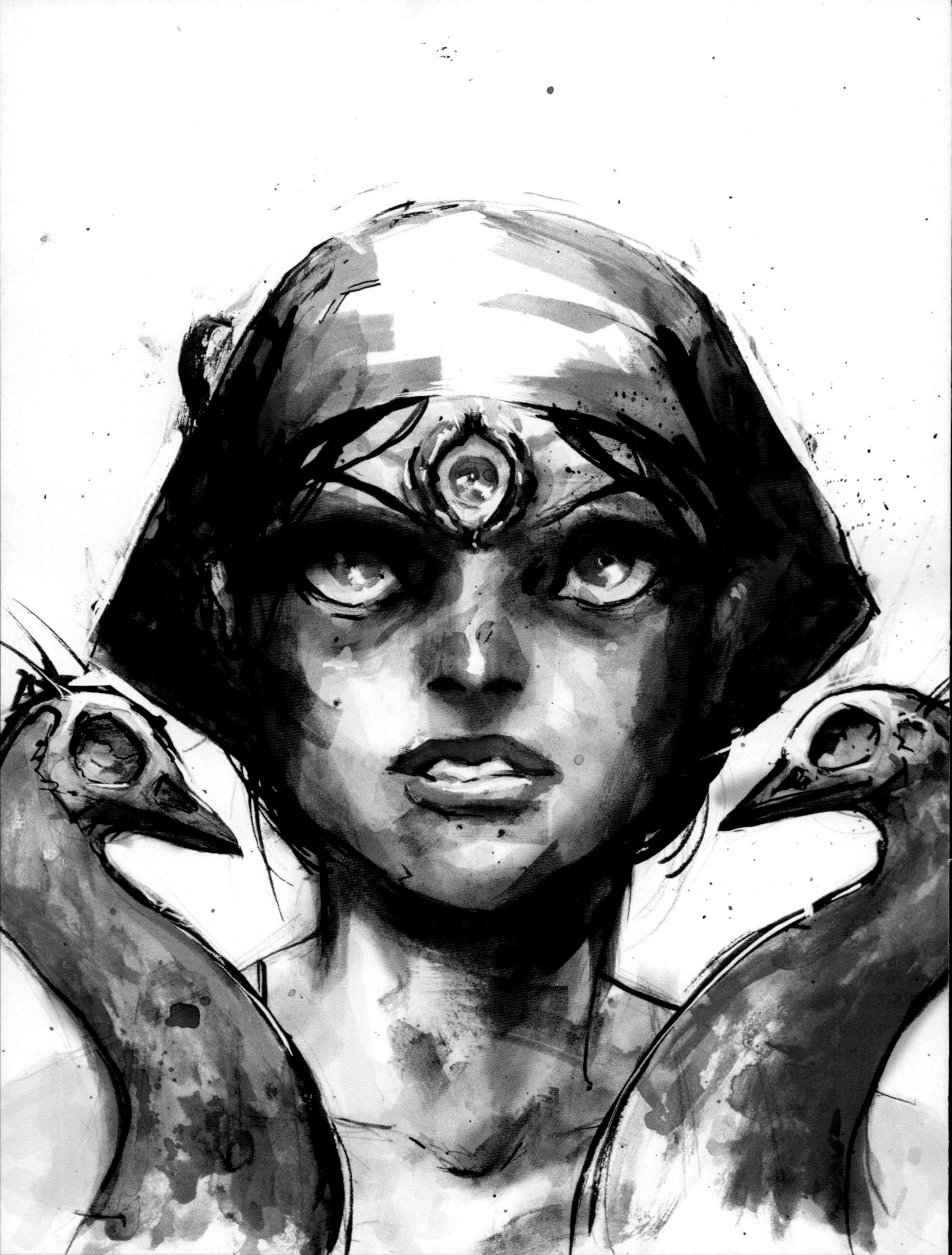

Books by Riley Rossmo you're bound to enjoy...

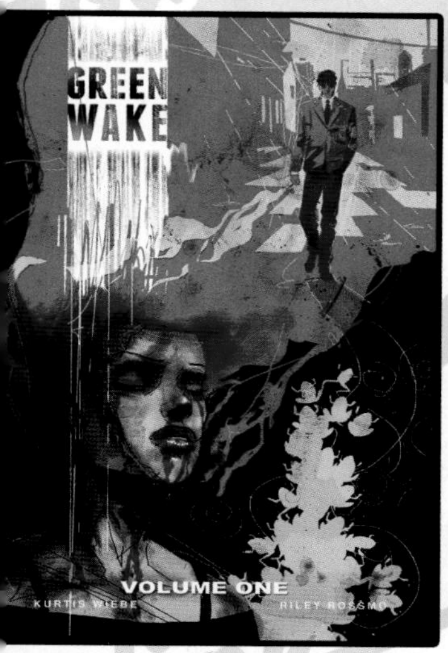

GREEN WAKE
VOLUME ONE
KURTIS WIEBE
RILEY ROSSMO

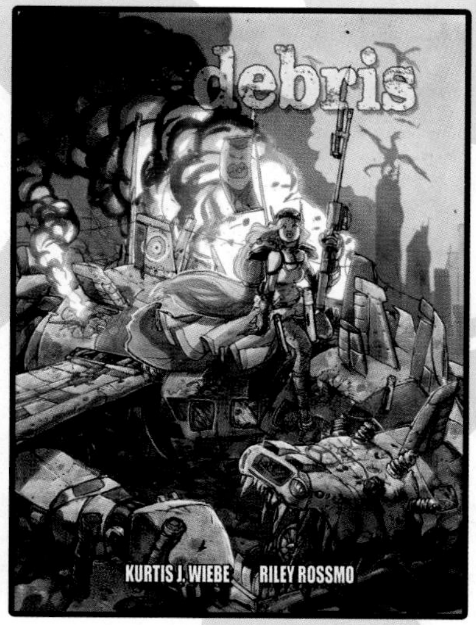

debris
KURTIS J. WIEBE
RILEY ROSSMO

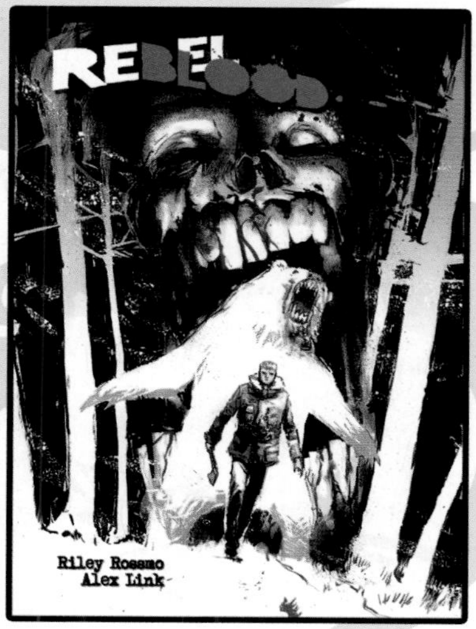

Riley Rossmo
Alex Link

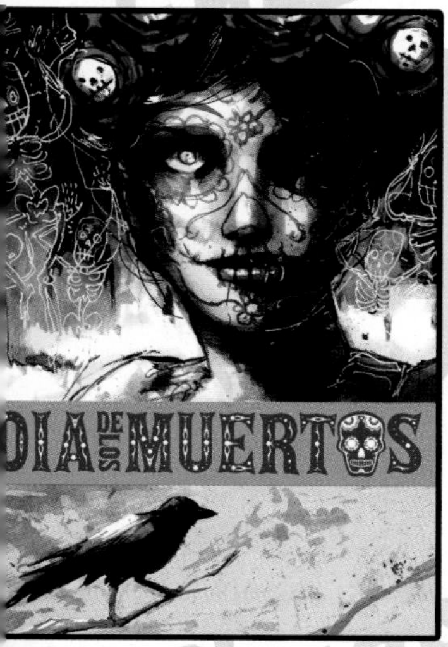

DIA DE LOS MUERTOS

With KURTIS WIEBE
GREEN WAKE
VOLUME ONE
ISBN: 978-1-60706-261-5
VOLUME TWO: LOST CHILDREN
ISBN: 978-1-60706-525-8
DEBRIS
ISBN: 978-1-60706-720-7

With VARIOUS
DIA DE LOS MUERTOS

With ALEX LINK
REBEL BLOOD
ISBN: 978-1-60706-591-3

With A.J. LIEBERMAN
COWBOY NINJA VIKING
VOLUME ONE
ISBN: 978-1-60706-261-5
VOLUME TWO
ISBN: 978-1-60706-344-5

With ALEXANDER GRECIAN
PROOF
BOOK ONE: GOATSUCKER
ISBN: 978-1-58240-944-3
BOOK TWO: THE COMPANY OF MEN
ISBN: 978-1-60706-017-8
BOOK THREE: THUNDERBIRDS
ARE GO!
ISBN: 978-1-60706-134-2
BOOK FOUR: JULIA
ISBN: 978-1-60706-285-1
BOOK FIVE: BLUE FAIRIES
ISBN: 978-1-60706-348-3
BOOK SIX: ENDANGERED
ISBN: 978-1-60706-391-9

With NICK SPENCER
BEDLAM

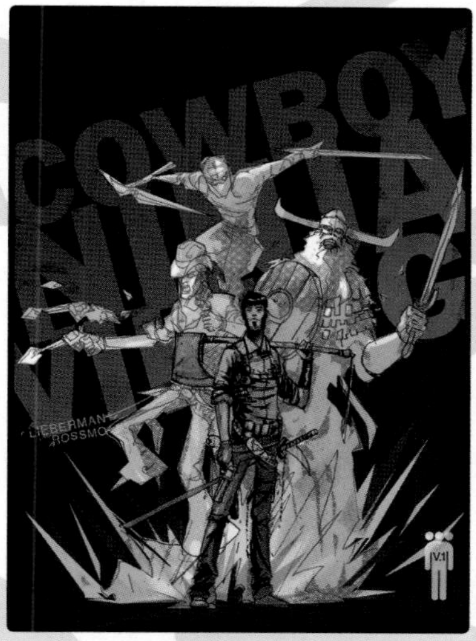

LIEBERMAN
ROSSMO

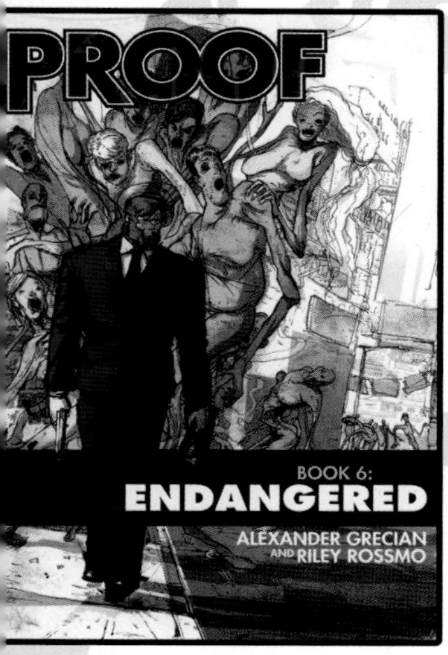

PROOF
BOOK 6:
ENDANGERED
ALEXANDER GRECIAN
AND RILEY ROSSMO

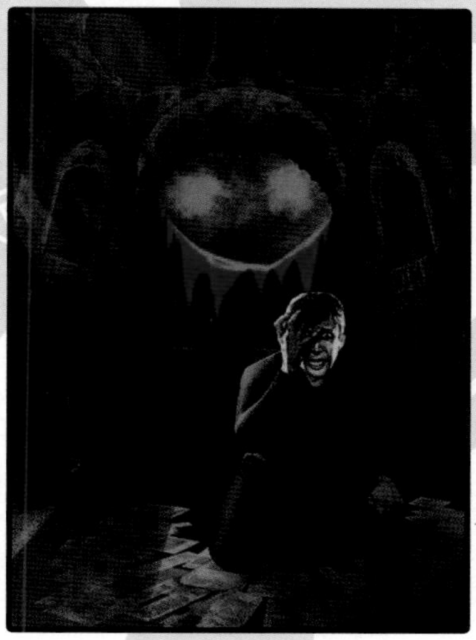

THIS *is diversity! Graphic Novels For the Discriminating Reade*

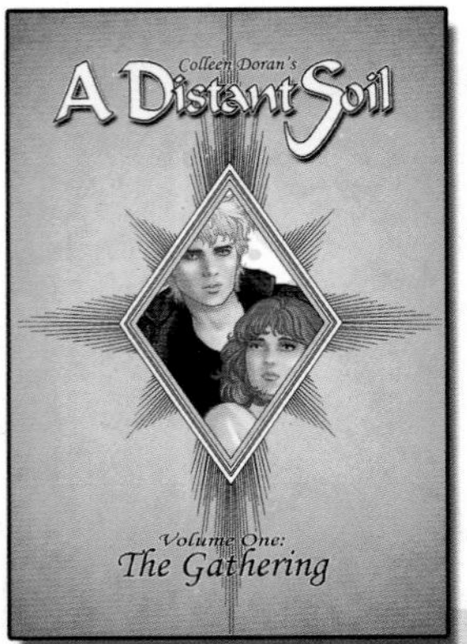

Colleen Doran's
A Distant Soil
Volume One:
The Gathering

A DISTANT SOIL

Colleen Doran's legendary magnum opus completely remastered and re-edited with beautiful new die-cut covers. Five volumes.

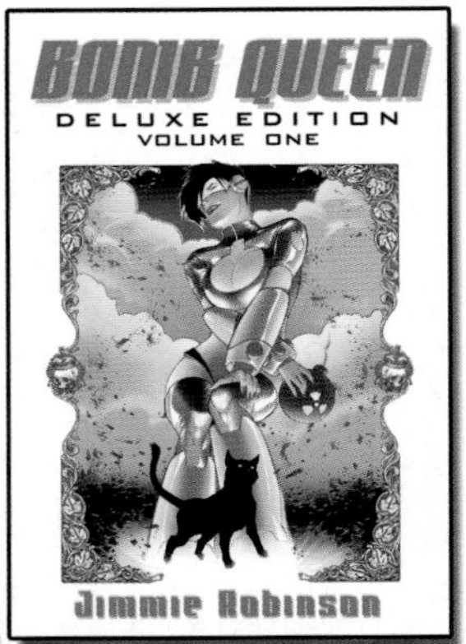

BOMB QUEEN
DELUXE EDITION
VOLUME ONE
Jimmie Robinson

BOMB QUEEN DELUXE

Jimmie Robinson's adults only satire of politics, sex and social mores. Not for the easily offended! Four Over-size hardcover volumes.

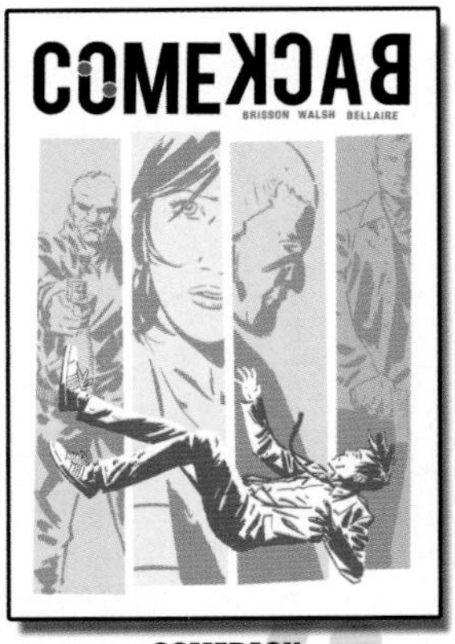

COMEBACK
BRISSON WALSH BELLAIRE

COMEBACK

Comeback is more than a company--we will bring your loved ones back moments before their untimely deaths...for a price.

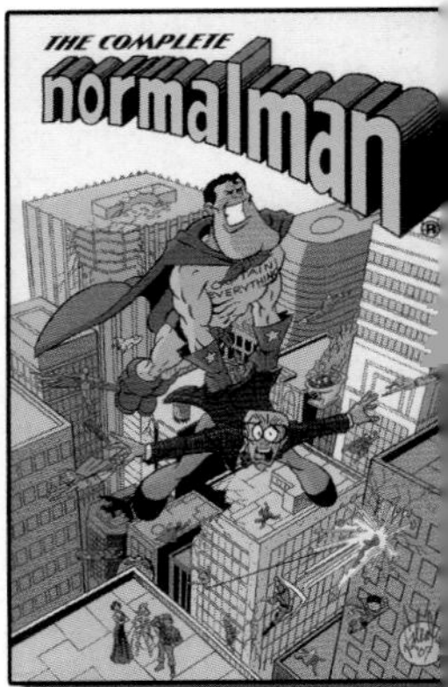

THE COMPLETE
normalman

COMPLETE normalman

The legendary classic paro series collected in o gigantic volume for the fi time!

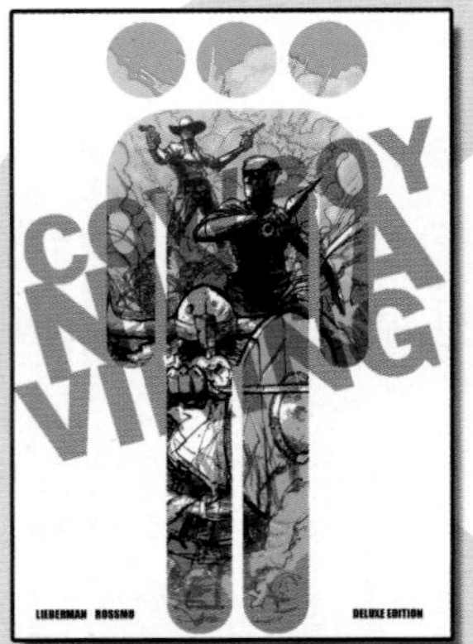

COWBOY
NINJA
VIKING
LIEBERMAN ROSSMO
DELUXE EDITION

COWBOY NINJA VIKING

Now in a Deluxe Oversize hardcover edition! Duncan has three distinct personalities...of course he's a government agent.

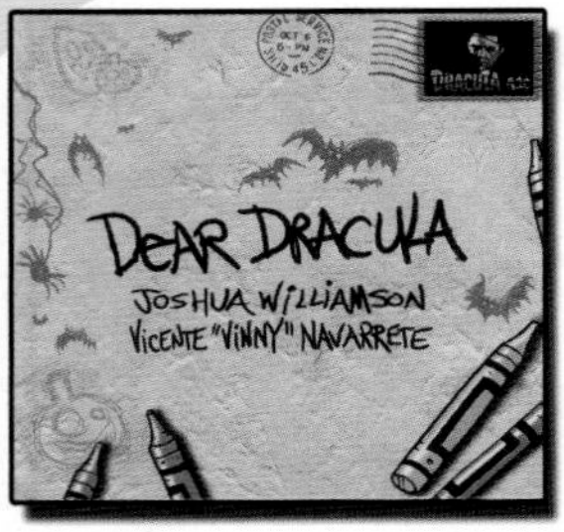

DEAR DRACULA
JOSHUA WILLIAMSON
VICENTE "VINNY" NAVARRETE

DEAR DRACULA

All Sam wants this Halloween is to become a real vampire! So he writes a letter to his hero, Count Dracula...who pays him a visit!

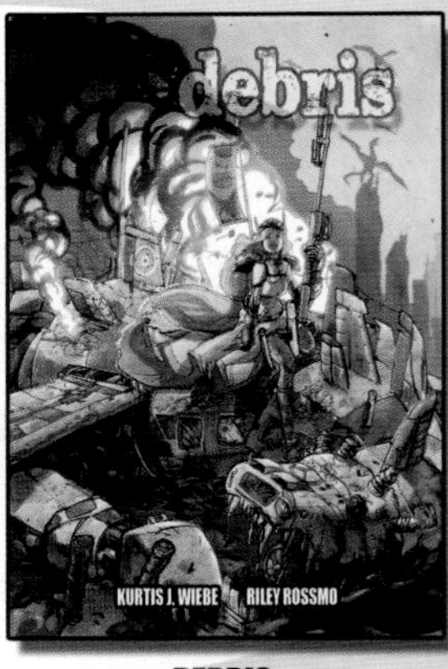

debris
KURTIS J. WIEBE
RILEY ROSSMO

DEBRIS

Maya must find a source of pure water to save the world before the garbage monsters bring it all to an end.

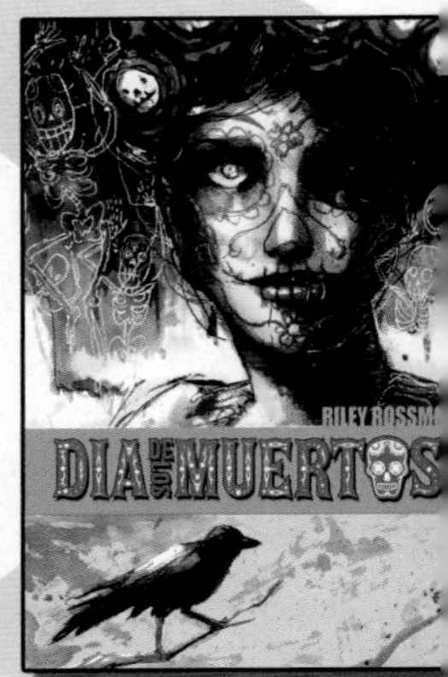

DIA DE LOS MUERTOS

DIA DE LOS MUERTOS

Nine acclaimed writers a one amazing artist, Ri Rossmo, tell tales from t Mexican Day of the Dead.

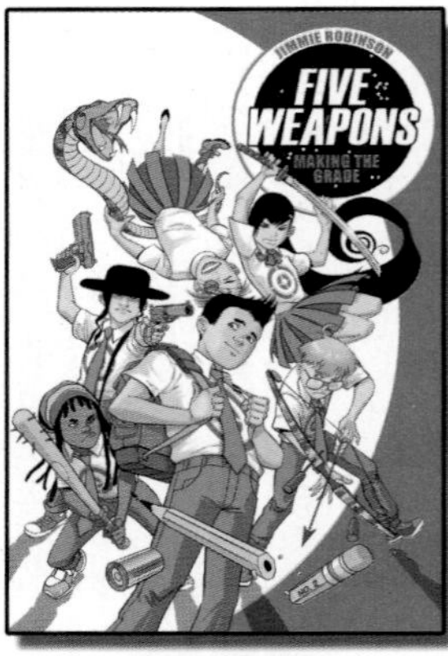

JIMMIE ROBINSON
FIVE WEAPONS
MAKING THE GRADE

FIVE WEAPONS

In a school for assassins, Tyler has the greatest of them all going for him...his mind! Jimmie Robinson's latest epic makes the grade.

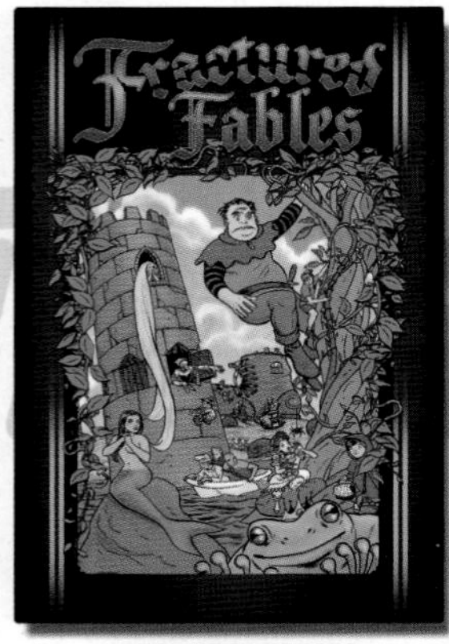

Fractured Fables

FRACTURED FABLES

Award winning cartoonists put a wicked but hilarious spin on well worn Fairy tales in this not-to-be-missed anthology.

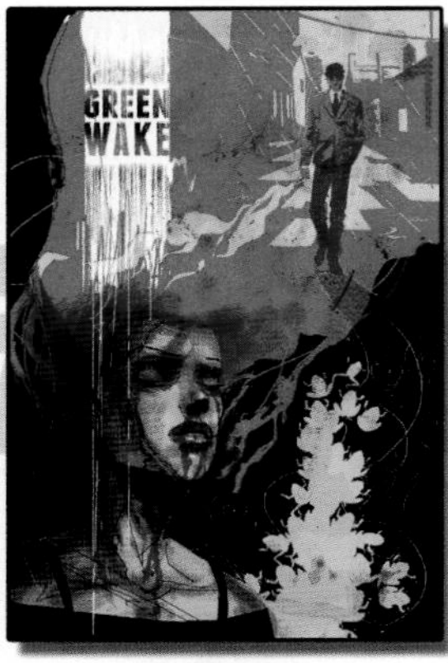

GREEN WAKE

GREEN WAKE

A riveting tale of loss and horror that blends mystery and otherworldly eccentricity in two unforgettable, critically acclaimed volumes.

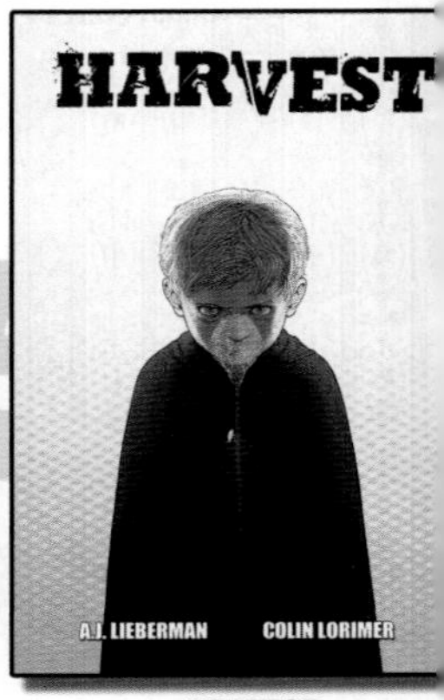

HARVEST
A.J. LIEBERMAN
COLIN LORIMER

HARVEST

Welcome to Dr. Benjan Dane's nightmare. His o way out is to bring down t man who set him harvesting organs.